THE HANDY GUIDE TO SCOTS

The Handy Guide
to Scots

WILLIAM GRAHAM

THE RAMSAY HEAD PRESS
EDINBURGH

First published in 1986 by
The Ramsay Head Press
15 Gloucester Place
Edinburgh EH3 6EE

ISBN 0 902859 92 7

Reprinted in 1991

Printed in Scotland
by W. M. Bett Ltd., Tillicoultry.

Contents

INTRODUCTION

Perhaps you are a visitor to Scotland, or have recently settled here, or are even a native-born Scot with only a very average knowledge of your country, and a very sub-average knowledge of the guid Scots tongue.

Probably, then, such expressions as **bottomless breeks,** a **curly-heidit chisel,** a **pee-the-bed,** and a **dreepin roast** will be out-and-out Greek to you. If so, turn to **How It's Said in Scots,** pages 10 to 16, to find out the meaning of these and a fair number of other like phrases.

At least, whatever you do, don't just start wading through the Scots-English vocabulary section if you want to get a genuine feel for the language and the temper of the people – for whom it is the native tongue.

Next, turn if you wish to **The Flowers of Edinburgh and Other Strange Matters,** or to the pages dealing with **Scottish Place Names;** then to the vocabulary, and finally to the not-quite-so-serious **Mixtie-Maxtie Quiz** at the end of the book. Pronunciation is bracketed after awkward words, but it may help, too, to give a general guide here and now.

A in the Scots pronunciation of such words as **want, warm, wash, water** retains the more usual **a** sound as in **arm.**

Ai = English **a** as in **fate** – **brainch, cairt, mair, sair.**

Ei, ie = English **e** in **me** – **dreip, seik, steir, scrieve.**

Eu, as in **sheuch,** is pronounced **yoo** in the Lothians and other districts, and **yu** (shyuch) elsewhere. Other examples are **deuk, neuk, heuk, eneuch.**

Ey, y = English **i** as in **mine** – **gey, Mey, stey, syne.**

I in the Scots version of some English words of two or more syllables is pronouned **ee** as in **sweet,** and some writers indicate this in their spelling – **adverteesment, feenish, parteeclar, exhibeetion, peety, rideeclous, speerit.**

Ou = English **oo** in **moon** – **broun, flouer, hou, nou.**

Ow, owe = English **ow** in **down.** Unlike English, Scots never uses **ou** for this sound – **bowel, growe, lowe, sowl, thow.**

Ui and **u**-consonant-e = English **i** in **bin** in areas south of the Forth and Clyde. In other areas it is more like the **u** in the French word **plume** – **fuil, guid, ruit, stuid, mune, spune.** However, in such words as **muir, puir** where the **ui** precedes the consonant **r,** it is pronounced like English **a** in **fate.**

Ch and **gh** have a **kh** sound quite lost to English – **loch, fricht, licht, nicht, micht, richt, brugh.** On the other hand, the English **ch** sound as in **chin** is retained at the beginning and end of words such as **chaumer, chaunt, chairge, fleich, streitch.**

Ng is pronounced as in English **singer,** with the **g** sound completely suppressed. This is an important distinction, especially in the pronunciation of words common to both English and Scots – **anger, finger, hunger, single.**

R has a much more prominent sound in Scots than in English, the Scots 'rolled **r**' being well enough known not to require further mention.

Pronunciation, as already suggested, varies in various parts of the country. The main dialect divisions are, very broadly and each with numerous modifications in pronunciation, intonation and vocabulary, as follows:

1. Southern Scots in Roxburgh, Selkirk and the larger (eastern) part of Dumfries;

2. Mid Scots in the huge area enclosed within a line from Bute to West Angus in the north, and from Wigtown, Kirkcudbright and West Dumfries to Berwick in the south;

3. North-East and Northern Scots from East Angus to Elgin to Caithness;

4. Insular Scots in the Islands of Orkney and Shetland.

As has already been indicated, Scots has such a wealth of dialects that it would be impossible to give here anything like a detailed description of each. For instance, in North-East Scots certain characteristics that are immediately noticeable are: the substitution of **f** for **wh** – **fat/fit** for **what,** and **fa** for **who;** the substitution of **ee** for **oo** or **o** – **peel** for **pool, steen** for **stone;** and of an **ah**

8

sound for Mid Scots **aw** – **ba** for **baw;** of **dd** for **th** – **badder** for **bother, fadder** for **father;** and in certain areas of **vr** for **wr** – **vrang** for **wrong.**

No mention has so far been made of the Gaelic tongue in Scotland – for the simple reason that the subject of Gaelic is quite without the scope of this book. However, if evidence of the importance of that great language to Scotland were required, you need only turn to the section, Scottish Place Names, to discover that the overwhelming majority of these have their source in Scottish Gaelic.

Lastly, the author wishes to acknowledge his use, in the section on place names, of information gained from W. J. Watson's **The History of the Celtic Place-Names of Scotland,** from David Dorward's **Scotland's Place-Names,** and from J. Kevan McDowall's **Carrick Gallovidian;** also his indebtedness to **The Scottish National Dictionary** which, as in **The Scots Word Book** (1977) he has consulted as the ultimate authority in all matters concerning the Scots language.

HOW IT'S SAID IN SCOTS

In the introduction to this book you were confronted with several Scots expressions, chosen at random to show that Scots is not simply a somewhat 'dreich' catalogue of words and their meanings. Here is a fairly representative sample of these down-to-earth, no-nonsense, yet quite often vivid and amusing ways of saying things which put life – everyday life – into the language, and character into the people who have used it down through the years and the generations.

The various items are arranged in the alphabetical order of key words. Meanings and, where necessary, pronunciations are provided in brackets.

Aa/aw (all)	A Johnnie-aa-thing	A small general merchant
	An aabody's body	A universal yes-man
Able	No able for	Having no appetite for
Aglee (awry)	Gang aglee	Go awry, of human affairs
Ail	What ails ye at . . .?	What do you dislike about . . .?
At	The wife's aye at me	My wife's always scolding me
Auld (old)	Auld i the horn	Wise; astute
Back	Come back on	Repeat, of food
	The back o three	Shortly after three o'clock
Bash (a blow)	Go on the bash	Go on a heavy drinking bout
Baurley (respite)	Hae a bit baurley	Have a short breather
Bed	A pee-the-bed	A dandelion. Another word for the dandelion is **clock,** because by blowing off all the seeded 'umbrellas' children 'could tell the time'
Ben (inside)	But and ben	Front and back of a house
	Faur (far) ben wi somebody	Deep in someone's favour
Better	Mak a better o	Improve upon
Birse (bristle)	Get your birse up	Make you angry
Bit (small)	Juist (Jist) a bit laddie	Just a little lad
Black (exceedingly)	I feel black affrontit	I feel deeply ashamed

10

Blin (blind)	A blin tam	A bundle of rags made up to pass as a child and carried by beggar women to excite pity
Blink	In a blink	In an instant
Bonny (large, of sum of money)	It'll cost a bonny penny	It'll cost a great deal of money
Brae (steep road)	Gang doun (doon) the brae	Deteriorate in health or circumstances
Braw (comely)	Sunday braws	Best clothes. **Braw** can also be used in the sense of **bonny** above
Breeks (trousers)	Bottomless breeks	The kilt
Bucket	Tak a guid bucket	Be a heavy drinker
By (past, as preposition and adverb)	I wadna pit (put) it by ye	I believe you're quite capable of
	It's aa by nou (noo)	It's all over and done with
Byle (boil)	On the byle	At boiling point, of kettle
Causey (street)	A causey (cawzy or cawssy) saint and a hous (hooss) deil (deel)	A person who acts irreproachably to outsiders, and quite shamefully at home
Caa (order)	Caa a dram	Order a drink
Caw (proceed; drive)	Caw canny	Proceed carefully
	Caw a bike	Propel a bike with its pedals
Cheep	Gie (Gee) never a cheep	Say not a word
Chisel	A curly-heidit (heedit) chisel	A chisel with the handle-end frayed with hammering
Chitterin (shivering)	A chitterin bite	A little food eaten after bathing
Claes (clothes)	Shiftin claes	Clothes into which one changes out of working attire
Claw (scratch)	Claw somebody's back	Flatter someone
Coals	Take ower the coals	Call to account
Cock	Cock the wee finger	To drink; tipple
Collie	He never as much as said collie will ye lick	He never offered a single scrap of food
Come	Come tae	Recover from a faint
	Come the peter owre	Dictate to
Cowp (overturn)	Cowp somebody's hurly (barrow)	Upset someone's plans
Crack (talk)	Get on the crack wi	Start a conversation with
	Caw (get going) the crack	Chat
Crap (stomach)	To hae (have) a crap for aa corns	To have an appetite for any kind of food that might be presented

Craw (crow)	Crouse (crooss – confident) i the craw	Confident in speech
Cried	To be cried in church	To have marriage banns read in church
Creepin	The days are creepin in	The days – or rather the daylight – are shortening
Cry	Cry in on a neibour (nee-)	Pay a neighbour a call
Day	Day and day about (aboot)	On alternate days
Dee (die)	Dee a guid strae (straw) daith	Die a natural death (in one's bed)
Deil (Devil)	The Deil's pictur books	Playing cards
	Deil a haet	Not a whit
Doo (dove)	A paddle-doo	A frog that used to be kept in a cream jug to help with paddling movement to make butter
Dourles (sulks)	Tak the dourles (doorls)	Go into a huff
Dowp (buttocks)	A wee egg-dowpit body	A little person with a pear-shaped figure
Drap (drop)	A drap o the auld kirk	A dram of whisky
	A bit and a drap	A little to eat and drink
	A drappie in the ee (eye)	Enough drink to make slightly inebriated
Dree (endure)	Dree yin's (one's) weird	Endure one's fate
Dreep (drip)	A sammy-dreep	A spiritless person
	To dreep a waw (wall)	To let oneself down from a wall with arms fully stretched before dropping
	A dreepin roast	A good source of income
Droun/droon (drown)	Droun the miller	Put too much water in whisky
Ee (eye)	Pit (put) somebody's ee out (oot)	Supplant someone
Eeran (errand)	Gang yince (once) eeran	Go for one special purpose
Efter (after)	Five efter ten	Five minutes past ten
Egg	A peeled egg	A piece of good luck
Fair (exceedingly)	To be fair taen (taken) on wi	To be exceedingly interested in
Faut (lack)	For faut o	For want of
Faw (fall)	To faw ower	To go to sleep
Feet	To chynge (change) yin's feet	To put on clean stockings
Fettle	In grand fettle	In excellent condition

12

Fiddler	A fiddler's biddin	A last-minute invitation
Fine	Fine ham an haddies!	A likely story!
	Fine I ken	Well I know
Fore (front)	Still to the fore	Still surviving
Fou (full)	Miraculous fou (foo)	Very drunk
Fyle (befoul)	Fyle the stamack	Put the stomach out of order
Gang (go)	Gang your dinger	Go about a pursuit very vigorously
	Gang through the mill	Undergo an ordeal
Gate (road)	Tak the gate	Depart
	Gang your ain gate	Take your own way
Gee (stir)	Gee (jee) yin's ginger	Bother oneself
Gemm (game)	The roarin gemm	Curling
Get	Get on to somebody	Upbraid someone
Gless (glass)	To rin the gless	To use up one's allotted time
Grauvat (cravat, scarf)	A Scotch grauvat	An embrace
Greek	Short o the Greek	Stuck for words
Greitin (weeping)	A greitin cheese	A cheese with the oil oozing out
Grue (shiver from aversion)	Tak the grue	Be disgusted
Guddle (muddle)	In a fair guddle	In a complete mess
Guid (good)	Come guid (gid) for	Be surety for
Haud (hold)	Haud up	Keep fair, of weather
	Haud hame	Make for home
	Haud in wi	Curry favour with
Haun (hand)	A haun's turn	A stroke of work
	Tak yin's haun aff (off)	Strike with one's hand
Hech-howe (high-low)	Back to the auld hech-howe	Back to the old routine
Heid (head)	Aa ower the heid o	All because of
	On the heid o	Pre-occupied with
High	High i the bend	Haughty
Hou (how)	Hou's (hoo's) aa wi ye?	How are you getting on?
Hover (pause)	Hover (o as in roll) a blink	Pause a moment
Humph (back)	Come up yin's humph	Occur to one, come into one's mind
Ill (badly)	Tak something ill out	Be upset about something
In (conscious)	No in	Not 'with it'
Joug (jug)	A left-haundit joug (joog)	A chamberpot
Juist (just)	Juist (jist) that	Quite so

13

Kail (broth)	Cauld (cold) kail het (heated) again	A speech, sermon or story gone stale with telling
Keek (peep)	A keekin-gless	A mirror
Keevee (qui vive)	Be on the keevee	Be on the alert
Kintra (country)	Cauf (calf) kintra	One's native district
Kirk (church)	Mak a kirk or a mill o't	Make or mar it
Kist (chest)	A kist o whussles	A church organ (and an organist was a whussle-grinder!)
Kizzen (cousin)	A Scotch kizzen	A distant relative
Laich (low)	Flee laich (ch as in loch)	Be unambitious
Laldie	Get laldie	Get a beating
Leatherin (flogging)	A skelpit leatherin or simply a skelpin (slapping)	A thrashing
Lick	A cat's lick	A hasty wash
Louse	Skin a louse for its tallow	Do the meanest job for gain
	A skin-a-louse	A skinflint
Lowp (jump)	A lowpin-on stane (stone)	A block placed outside churches, hostelries etc. to help riders to mount their horses
	A lowpen-steik (stitch)	A dropped stitch
Lowsin (loosening)	Lowsin (z) time	Time to finish the day's work
Lug (ear)	Get the wrang sou (soo, a pig) by the lug	Get the wrong impression
	To warm somebody's lugs	To box someone's ears
Luif/loof (palm of hand)	Creish the luif (lif)	Bribe
	A lick-ma-luif	A toady
Mairriage	Mairriage lines	Marriage certificate
	A mairriage lintel	A lintel stone over door of house bearing the initials of the newly-married occupants, and date of marriage
Maut (mault)	When the maut wins (gets) abune (above) the meal	When the drinker becomes drunk
Meat (food)	To be like yin's meat	To be well-fed looking
Middlin (moderate)	Fair to middlin	Quite well
Morn (tomorrow)	The morn's mornin	Tomorrow morning

14

Mou (mouth)	Doun (doon) i the mou (moo)	Dejected
	Mealy-moud	Afraid to speak frankly
Munelicht (moonlight)	A munelicht (licht as in loch) flittin	A clandestine house removal by night
Notion	Tak a notion o	Take a liking for
Pairts (talents)	A lad o pairts	A talented youth
Parritch (porridge)	Save your braith to cool your parritch	'Pipe down'
Pease-brose (pease-meal in boiling water)	Pease-brose and pianaes	State of genteel poverty
Pigs (broken pieces of earthenware)	Gaen aa to pigs and whussles	Gone all 'to pot'
Poke-shakins (shakings of the bag)	The poke-shakins o the faimily	The youngest of the family
	To trail the poke	To beg
Puir (poor)	Pit (put) on a puir (pare) mouth (mooth)	Pretend to be in poor circumstances
Preen (pin)	No worth a preen	Of very little value
Quattin (quitting)	Quattin time	Time to finish the day's work
Reamin (foaming)	Reamin fou (foo)	Filled to overflowing
Redd (clear)	To redd the thrapple	To clear the throat
Rickmatick (group)	The hale rickmatic	The whole lot
Rise	An early rise	A getting out of bed early in the morning
	Take a rise out o	Make fun of
Road	Never look the road o	Show no sign of recognition
Room	The guid (good) room	The sitting-room
Rue (repentance)	Tak the rue	Regret
Scant (scarcity)	Scant and want	Poverty
Scot	Scot free	Tax free (from the Old Norse word, **skat,** for tax)
Scotch	A Scotch canary	A yellow-hammer
Screw-driver	A Glesca screw-driver	A hammer (mis)used to drive in screw nails
Sensible (aware)	Sensible drunk	Drunk, but still in command of one's senses
Sin	Sin your mercies	Show ingratitude for heaven's favours
Shave (slice)	A shave o breid	A slice of bread

Sheep-shank (leg of sheep)	Think yoursel nae sheep-shank	Consider yourself of no little importance
Skail (disperse)	Skailin time	Time to break up, of a meeting
Sleep	A sleepie-mannie	A mote in the eye
Slock (slake)	Slock yin's drouth (drooth)	Slake one's thirst
Sma (small)	Think yoursel nae sma drink	Consider yourself of no little importance
Smirr (drizzle)	A smirr o rain	A drizzle of rain
Smit (infection)	Get the smit	Be infected with
Souch (voice, way of speaking)	Keep a calm souch (soo – ch as in loch)	Stay unperturbed
Souk (suck)	Souk (sook) in wi	Ingratiate oneself with
Sour (soor)	Sour dook	Sour milk
Speak	Speak pan loaf	Talk with an affected accent
Swatch (a copy)	Tak a swatch aff (off)	Follow the example of
Syne (since)	Auld langsyne	Bygone times
Table	Sit in to the table	Draw your chair up to the table
Through	Through wi a job	Finished with a job
Til (to)	Tak til ye	Help yourself (at table)
Tinker	Tinker's tea	Tea brewed in a pan over a fire
Trummlin (trembling)	Trummlin Tam	Table jelly; potted meat
Turn	On the turn	Beginning to curdle, of milk
Tyne (lose)	Tyne the gate o	Lose the knack of
Unco (exceedingly)	The unco guid	The very self-righteous people
Want (as in 'man')	To hae a want	To be mentally defective
Waur (worse)	The waur o the weir (weer)	The worse for the wear
Weel (well)	To be weel at yoursel	To be plump and healthy
Whussle (whistle)	To wat/weet the whussle	To have a drink
Wulk (whelk)	As fou's (foo's) a wulk	Very drunk
Yokit (yoked)	Get yokit tae	Get started on

THE FLOWERS OF EDINBURGH
AND OTHER STRANGE MATTERS

Perhaps you already know who or what were the Flowers of Edinburgh – and the Flowers o the Forest – and the Heart of Midlothian – and a Nor Loch trout ...? But in case you don't, here are their meanings, and the meanings of other similar expressions:

The Flowers of Edinburgh referred to two very dissimilar aspects of Edinburgh. They were either the belles of Edinburgh society, or the smells of Edinburgh garbage, got rid of by the dwellers in the high buildings by throwing it into the narrow streets below. ('Gardiloo!')

The Curse of Scotland was the nine of diamonds because, according to one version, the Duke of Cumberland wrote 'No quarter' on the back of this playing card after Culloden; or because the nine of diamonds bore a likeness to the arms of the Earl of Stair who played a part in the tragedy of the massacre of Glencoe.

A left-haundit joug (jug) was one of the names given to the old Scots po – or rather, chamberpot!

The jougs, on the other hand, was an instrument of punishment consisting of a hinged collar chained to a wall and locked round the wrongdoer's neck.

A Scotch Convoy was the accompanying of a friend back to his home, or only halfway back, or to his home and part of the way back again, according to the part of the country, or the state of sobriety, you happened to be in.

Bundling was an old Scottish custom arising out of the lack of accommodation in most houses, and the shortage of heating fuel. It consisted of the practice by young couples of going to bed in the family bedroom, fully clothed, to do their courting.

The Heart of Midlothian was the ancient Tolbooth Prison erected in 1561. A heart shaped out in granite to mark the site of the prison doorway can still be seen on the 'causey' outside St Giles.

The Flowers o the Forest were the seventy Selkirk men who died at the battle of Flodden and whose memory is preserved in the two versions of the song of that name by Jean Eliot and Alison Rutherford.

The Land o the Leal (the land of the loyal people) in the song of that name was Heaven. It was written by Lady Nairne.

A black house in the West Highlands and Hebrides was a drystane (no mortar used) and turf house with thatched roof and a fire in the centre of the earth floor.

Paddy's Market was the name of a street market in Glasgow frequented by the Irish section of the population. In time it was commonly applied to any back-street shop that sold all sorts of wares.

Paddy's Milestone, on the other hand, is a popular name for Ailsa Craig, the massive 1114-foot high island-rock standing in the middle of the Firth of Clyde over nine miles out of Girvan. It received its name as being the main landmark for Irish immigrants to the south-west of Scotland.

The Black Watch got its name when, in 1724, a company of soldiers was formed to deal with the many free-booters who levied 'black mail' from farmers and land-owners in return for a guarantee that their crops and cattle would not be stolen.

The Honours of Scotland are the regalia of the King-dom of Scotland, and consist of the Crown, the Sceptre, and the Sword of State.

Handfasting in earlier times in Scotland was a sort of trial marriage to ensure compatibility. Couples cohabited quite commonly, and if the relationship proved not to the liking of either party after a year and a day, they could separate without any stigma being attached to the woman. Any child born of the relationship was put in the father's care.

The Riding of the Marches is an annual festival in a number of Border towns to commemorate the old yearly inspection of the 'mairches' or burgh boundaries.

A **Nor Loch trout** was not a trout at all, but a leg of mutton from the slaughterhouse that was situated alongside what used to be the Nor Loch in Edinburgh, but was drained to become Princes Street Gardens.

A **Nigger** was the name given to a fireclay brick placed in a fire to reduce the amount of coal used. The name came from the adjective, niggard.

Christie Cleek was a bogyman figure used to put the fear of death into children in the nursery. The name came from that of a Perth butcher called Andrew Christie who took to living in a cave as a cannibal, dragging wayfaring horesemen from the saddle with a 'cleek' or hooked pole.

The Deil's mark, found on the body of a woman at her trial as a witch, was taken as a clear indication that she was in league with the Devil. Further, and quite indisputable, evidence was forthcoming if a needle was driven into the mark and the woman showed no reaction whatsoever.

Arse-verse was a spell written on the side or back of a house to ward off fire. The word came from the Latin verb ardere (participle arsum) to burn.

The Paisley shawl wasn't originally made in Paisley at all, but in Edinburgh, in the late eighteenth century. The famous pattern didn't really originate in Paisley either, being based on an ancient Hindu design.

The tangle o the isles referred to in the well-known song is a rough sort of seaweed growing along the coast of northern Scottish islands.

A **slip-coffin** was one used over and over again for the burial of people who couldn't afford to pay for a coffin of their own. It had hinges on the bottom so that the body could be let into the grave and the coffin retrieved for further use.

SCOTS AND GAELIC
PLACE-NAMES

As will be seen from the following selection, most Scottish place-names have a Celtic, and more especially a Scottish Gaelic, source. The remainder are largely of Teutonic origin, having been introduced by the Anglian settlers who invaded south-east Scotland from Northumbria in the early part of the seventh century.

A list of common place-name elements follows the main list, to enable readers to do a little exploring on their own.

Abbreviations: Br. Celtic – British (Pictish) Celtic; G. – Scottish Gaelic; Irish – Irish Gaelic; O. Norse – Old Norse; W. – Welsh.

Aberdeen – Br. Celtic **aber,** river mouth: mouth of the river Don.

Aberdour – Br. Celtic **aber,** joining of waters, **dobhar,** a streamlet: mouth of a streamlet.

Aberfoyle – G. **obar-phuill,** mouth of the slow stream.

Ailsa Craig – G. **eile,** the other, **sa** (emphatic), **creag,** rock. (?)

Airdrie – G. **ardruigh,** high incline.

Alloway – G. **aill,** steep river bank, **uaigh,** a tomb with a cairn: or, G. **allmhagh,** rock-plain.

Arbroath – G. **ar** a contraction for **aber** – **aberbrothach,** mouth of the erupting stream.

Ardentinny – G. **aird,** height, **an-teine,** of the fire.

Ardgour – G. **aird gobhar,** goat's height/point.

Ardmore – G. **aird,** height. **mor,** big.

Ardnamurchan – **aird na murchu,** promontory of the sea otter.

Ardrishaig – G. **aird driseag,** thorny promontory.

Ardrossan – G. **aird rossan** promontory of the little wood.

Argyll – G. **oirer Ghaidheal,** coastland of the Gael.

Arthur's Seat – G. **suidhe,** seat.
Atholl – G. **ath Fodhla,** the new Ireland.
Auchinleck – G. **achadh** (field) **nan leac,** stony field.
Awe, Loch – G. **loch,** loch, Obha, from **abha,** river.
Ayr – G. **a-reidh,** smooth water: or, O. Norse **eyrr,**
    beach.
Ballachulish – G. **baile,** homestead, **caolas,** by the strait.
Ballantrae – G. **baile nan traigh,** village on the shore.
Ballater – G. **bealach,** a pass, **tir,** land.
Balloch – G. **bealach,** a pass.
Barr – G. **barr,** hilltop.
Benmore – G. **beinn,** mountain, **mor,** big.
Berwick – Anglo-Saxon **bere,** barley, **wic,** farm.
Bute, Kyles of – G. **Boid,** of Bute, **caol,** narrow.
Cairngorm – G. **carn,** a stony hill, **gorm,** blue.
Cairnryan – G. **carragh,** standing (memorial) stone,
    righ, a chief, **aon,** illustrious.
Cambusdoon – G. **camas,** bend: bend on the river
    Doon.
Cambuslang – G. **camas,** bend, creek, **long,** ship.
Carnwath – W. **carn,** cairn, gwydd, wood.
Carrick – G. **carraig,** rock.
Carstairs – W. **caer,** fortress, **Tarris** (person's name).
Clyde – G. Cluaide (?).
Craigellachie – G. **creag,** rock, **eilach,** water channel.
Crail – G. **carr,** crag, **all,** rock.
Cramond – W. **caer,** fort, **Almond,** the river.
Cree, River – G. **crioch,** boundary.
Crieff – G. **craoibh,** branch, tree.
Culzean – G. **cuilean,** caves.
Dailly – G. **dail,** field, **ath,** ford.
Dalbeattie – G. **dail beithigh,** field of the birch.
Dalkeith – W. **dol coed,** wooded dale.
Doon, Loch – G. **loch duin,** loch of the fort.
Douglas – G. **dubh,** black, **glas,** stream.
Drummore – G. **drum,** ridge, **mor,** big.
Dumbarton – G. **dun,** fort, **Breatainn,** fort of the
    Britons.
Dumfries – G. **dun phreas,** fort of corpses: or, fort of
    the Friesians.
Dunbar – G. **dun,** fort, **barr,** summit.

Dundee – G. **dun Deagh,** fort of Daigh (person's name).

Dunkeld – G. **dun Chaillean,** fort of the Caledonians.

Dunoon – G. **dun obhainn,** fort of the river.

Duntocher – G. **dun,** fort, **tochar,** wall.

Dunure – G. **dun,** fort, **ur,** new.

Ecclefechan – G. **eaglais,** church (of St. Fechan).

Edinburgh – G. **aodainn,** brow, hillface, **brugh,** fortress. **Not** Edwin's burgh.

Elgin – G. Eilgin, **Elg,** Ireland, – **in** (diminutive) – Little Ireland.

Esk, River – Irish **esc,** water.

Falkirk – Scots **faw,** greyish-brown, **kirk,** church.

Fauldhouse – Scots **fauld,** enclosed piece of cultivated ground – house in a 'fauld'.

Fiddich, Glen – G. **gleann,** glen, Fiddich (person's name).

Findhorn – G. **fionn Eire,** white Ireland.

Fintry – G. **fionn,** white: (or) W. **ffin,** boundary, Br. Celtic **tref,** homestead.

Fort William – called after William of Orange.

Galloway, Mull of – G. **maol,** headland, **Gall ghaidhil,** stranger Gaels.

Gareloch – G. **gearr,** short.

Glasgow – G. **glas,** green, W. **cau,** hollow.

Glen App – G. **gleann,** glen, **ap,** water/loch.

Glencoe – G. **gleann,** glen, **comhann,** narrow.

Gleneagles – G. **gleann,** glen, **eaglais,** church.

Glenfinnan – G. **gleann Fhionghuin,** Fingon's glen.

Glengarry – G. **gleann,** glen, **garadh,** copse.

Glenrothes – G. **gleann,** glen, **rath,** fort.

Greenock – G. **grianaig** (dative case of **grianag**), at a sunny hill.

Inveresk – G. **inbhir,** river mouth, **Esk,** Irish **esc,** water.

Iona – misreading of **Ioua** (of uncertain meaning).

Kilbarchan – G. **cill,** cell/church, **Bearchain** (Berchan, the saint).

Kilbirnie – G. **cill,** cell/church, **Brenainn** (Brennan, the saint).

Kilmarnock – G. **cill,** cell/church, **mor,** big, **cnoc,** knoll: or G. **cill,** cell/church, **Mernoc,** the saint.

Kincardine – G. **cinn chardain,** at the head of the wood.

Kinlochleven – G. **cinn** – Loch Leven (as for Kincardine).

Kinross – G. **cinn ros,** at the head of the wood.

Kirkconnel – Scots **kirk,** church, **Convall,** the saint.

Kirkintilloch – Br. Celtic **caer,** fort, G. **cinn,** at the head, **tulach,** hillock.

Kyle – the district in Ayrshire, called after **King Coel,** reigned early fifth century.

Kyles of Bute – see 'Bute'.

Kirkton – Scots **kirk,** church, Anglo-Saxon **ton**/Scots **toun,** farm.

Lanark – Br. Celtic **llanerch,** clearing in forest.

Langholm – Scots **lang,** long, **howm,** holm, stretch of low-lying land.

Lerwick – O. Norse **leir,** mud, **vik,** bay.

Leven, Loch – G. **loch,** lake, **leamhan,** elm (uncertain).

Linlithgow – W. **llan,** lake, **llyth,** damp, **cau,** hollow (uncertain).

Lochaber – Irish **eabar,** marsh.

Lomond, Loch – G. **lo,** Old G. for water, **monadh,** mountain: or G. **loch laomuinn,** the beacon loch.

Mearns, The – G. **an mhaoirne,** the stewartry.

Menstrie – Br. Celtic **maes tref,** open field homestead.

Moncrieff – G. **monadh,** hill, **craobh,** tree.

Montrose – G. **monadh,** moorland, **ros,** promontory.

Morar – G. **mor,** big, **dhobhar,** water.

Moray – G. **muir,** sea: place by the sea.

Morvern/Morven – G. **muir,** sea, **bearna,** gap.

Muirkirk – Scots **muir,** moor, **kirk,** church.

Newton – Anglo-Saxon **ton**/Scots **toun,** farm.

Oban – G. **ob,** bay – **an** (diminutive) – little bay.

Ochil Hills – W. **uchel,** high.

Ochiltree – W. **ucheldref,** high settlement.

Orkney – from the name given to the Picts of Orkney – the **Orcs.**

Pentland Firth – O. Norse **Pettaland,** Pictland, **fjiorthr,** arm of sea, fiord.

Perth – W. **perth,** a brake, thicket.

Pitcairn – Br. Celtic **pit,** a part, G. **carn,** stony hill.

Pitlochry – Br. Celtic **pit,** allotment, Irish **cloichreach,** stony ground.

Pittenweem – G. **peit na h'uamha,** allotment by the cave.

Prestwick – Anglo-Saxon **preost,** priest, **wic,** farm.

Rannoch – G. **raithneach,** bracken.

Rhinns of Galloway – W. **rhyn,** point, cape. See also 'Galloway'.

Sanquhar – **sean cathair,** old fort.

Schiehallion – G. **sidh,** fairy hill, **Chailleann,** of the Caledonians.

Scotia – Latin for 'land of the Scots' – also used as an alternative to Hibernia as name for Ireland.

Skye – G. **sgiath,** wing (used of Skye in the sense of a cut, or divided, island).

Sorn – G. **sorn,** kiln.

Stair – G. **stair,** stepping stones.

Stenhousemuir – Scots **stane,** stone, **muir,** moor.

Stornoway – O. Norse **stjorn,** steering, **vagr,** bay.

Strathearn – G. **srath,** valley, **Eireann,** of Ireland.

Symington – Anglo-Saxon **ton**/Scots **toun,** farm: Simon's farm.

Tarbert/Tarbet – G. **tairbeart,** isthmus.

Tarff, River – G. **tarbh,** bull.

Taynuilt – G. **tigh,** house, **allt,** stream.

Thurso – O. Norse **thjorsa,** bull's water.

Tinto/Tintock Hill – G. **teinteach,** place of fire.

Tobermory – G. **tiobar Moire,** Mary's well.

Tomatin – G. **tom aitionn,** juniper-tree hillock.

Tomintoul – **tom an t'sabhail,** barn knoll.

Torness – G. **torr,** mound, O. Norse **nes,** headland.

Torphin – G. **torr,** mound, **fionn,** white.

Tranent – W. **tref yr nent,** settlement of the brooks.

Traquair – W. **tref,** settlement, **Quair,** the river Quair.

Troon – W. **trwn,** snout, cape.

Trossachs – G. **na troiseachan,** the cross places.

Tullochgorum – G. **tulach,** hill, **gorm,** blue.

Tyndrum – G. **tigh,** house, **druim,** ridge.

Urquhart – W. **ar,** near, **carrden,** wood.

Whitburn – Scots **burn,** brook – white brook.

Wick – O. Norse **vik,** bay, creek.

Some Common Place-Name Prefixes and Suffixes

Aber – Br. Celtic **aber** (a) joining of (river) waters, (b) outflow into sea, mouth of river (Aberdeen, mouth of river Don).

Ach, Auch, Auchen – G. **achadh,** field (Achnacarry, Auchencairn, Auchinleck).

Alt – G. **allt,** stream (Altnaharra).

Ard, Aird – G. **aird,** height, promontory (Ardgour, Airdrie).

Auchter – G. **uachdair,** upper part (Auchterarder).

– ay – O. Norse **ey,** island (Raasay).

Bal – G. **baile,** hamlet (Balmoral).

Balloch – G. **bealach,** pass, gap (Balloch, Ballochmyle).

Barr – G. **barr,** crest (Barrhead).

Ben – G. **beinn,** peak, horn (Beinn Mac Duibh – Ben McDhui).

– bie – O. Norse **byr,** farm, hamlet (Lockerbie).

Blair – G. **blar,** piece of land, plain (Blairgowrie).

Caer, Car – Br. Celtic **caer,** fort (Caerlaverock, Carmichael).

Cambus – G. **camus,** bay (Cambuslang).

Carn – G. **carn,** cairn (Carnwath).

Carse – Scots **carse,** stretch of alluvial land by river (Carse of Gowrie).

Close – see Street Names.

Craig – G. **creag,** rock (Craiglockhart).

Dol, Dal – Br. Celtic **dol,** meadow (Dollar, Dalserf).

– dour – W. **dwr,** water (Aberdour).

Drum – G. **druim,** ridge (Drumnadrochit).

Dun, Dum – G. **dun,** fortress (Dunbar, Dumbarton).

Fauld – Scots **fauld,** fold, enclosed piece of ground (Fauldhouse).

– fell – O. Norse **fjall,** hill (Goatfell).

Firth – O. Norse **fiorthr,** arm of sea (Pentland Firth).

Gart – Br. Celtic **garth,** yard, enclosure (Gartcosh).

– gate – see Street Names.

Glas – G. grey, green (Glasgow).

Glen – G. **gleann,** glen (Glencoe).

Howe – Scots **howe,** hollow, vale (Howe of the Mearns).

Inch – G. **innis,** island (Inchinnan).

Inver – G. **inbhir,** river mouth (Inverness).

Kil – G. **cill,** cell/church (Kilbirnie).

Kin – G. **cinn,** head (Kinlochleven).

Kirk – Scots **kirk,** church (Kirkoswald).

Knock – G. **cnoc,** knoll (especially in Galloway e.g. Knockdolian).

Kyle – G. **caol,** narrow (Kyle of Lochalsh).

Lang – Scots **lang,** long (Langholm).

Law – Scots **law,** prominent rounded hill (Broad Law).

Links – Scots **links,** sandy, bent-covered shore (Lundin Links).

Linn – G. **linn,** pool (Loch Linnhe).

Long – G. **long,** ship (Loch Long).

Machair – G. **machair,** a plain (Machrihanish).

Mains – Scots **mains,** an estate home farm (Newmains).

Mon – G. **monadh,** hill, moor (Moncreiff, Montrose).

– **more** – G. **mor,** big (Aviemore).

– **ness** – O. Norse **nes,** headland (Caithness).

Pen – Br. Celtic **pen,** head (Penicuik).

Pin – G. **peinn,** hill (especially in Galloway e.g. Pin-more).

Pit – Br. Celtic **pit,** part, share (Pitkenny).

Ros – **ross** – G. **ros,** projection, cape (Rosneath, Kin-ross).

Strath – G. **srath,** broad valley (Strathpeffer).

Stron – G. **sron,** point, headland (Stronachlachar).

Tobar – G. **tobar,** a well (Tobermory).

Tulloch, Tillie – G. **tulach,** hill (Tullochgorum, Tilli-coultry).

Vennel – see Street Names.

– **way** – O. Norse **vagr,** bay (Stornoway).

– **wick** – (a) O. Norse **vik,** bay (Lerwick).

      (b) Anglo-Saxon **wic,** settlement (Prestwick).

SOME TOWN STREET and PLACE NAMES

Close, a courtyard, alleyway, or lane between houses (Brodie's Close, Edinburgh; The Little Close and Big Close, Strathaven).

– gate, a road, street (Trongate, Glasgow; Cowgate, Mauchline; Watergate, Perth).

Port (Latin porta, a gate), a town gate, or its former position (West Ports in Lanark, Dundee, Edinburgh).

Land, formerly a site which was part of a plot of land, or 'tenement', taken over for building purposes; or the building erected on this site (Gladstone's Land, Edinburgh).

Bow, formerly an arched gateway (West Bow, Nether-bow Port, Edinburgh).

Loan, a lane into a common pasture; a narrow street (Dobbie's Loan, Glasgow; Majors Loan, Falkirk; Hood's Loaning, Dumfries).

Mercat Cross, formerly a town's commercial centre (many examples in Glasgow, Edinburgh – where public proclamations are still read out – Aberdeen, Stirling, Dundee etc.).

Tolbooth, formerly the town jail (the Edinburgh Tolbooth, the Heart of Midlothian, the site of whose entrance door is marked with a heart on granite blocks outside St Giles; the Tolbooth Steeple, Glasgow; The Tolbooth, Dundee; among many others).

Tron, formerly the public weighing machine, then the place where it stood (Tron Steeple and Trongate, Glasgow).

Vennel, a lane between houses (The North and South Vennels, Lanark; The School Vennel, Maybole; Friars Vennel, Dumfries).

Wynd, a narrow side street (Limond's Wynd, Ayr; Kirk Wynds in Falkirk and Kirkcaldy; Castle Wynd, Perth; Smalls Wynd, Dundee).

SCOTS-ENGLISH VOCABULARY

Aa, aw, all: **aabody,** everybody: **aathegither,** altogether: **aathing,** everything.

ablow, below; under.

abune (abin), above; over.

ach, expression of impatience.

ackwart, awkward.

acquant/acquent, to acquaint; acquainted.

adae, fuss.

ae/yae, one.

aff, off; from: **aff-haun,** brusque: **aff-loof,** extempore: **aff-pittin,** dilatory.

afore, before.

aft/aften, often.

agee (ajee), askew.

aglee, askew; off the straight road.

aheid (aheed), ahead.

ahin/ahint, behind.

aicht (ai as in may), eight: **aichty,** eighty.

aik, oak: **aiknit,** acorn.

ain, own; private; personal.

airt, to direct; take the road to; a direction.

aix, axe.

alane, alone: **lay/let alane,** leave undisturbed.

alowe, afire.

amna, am not.

ane/yin, one (pronoun).

apairt, apart.

appearinly, apparently.

argie-bargie, to dispute; a dispute.

ashet, a large meat plate.

asklent, askance, askew.

athout (athoot), without.

auld, old.

awa, away: **awa wi't,** done for.

awfu, disgraceful; very.

ay (as in buy), yes.
aye (as in mile), always.
ayont, beyond.

Baa/baw, ball.
baw-siller, coins thrown to children at a wedding.
babidoozler, a very showy object.
baffs, slippers.
bag, to bulge; to swell.
bailie, a magistrate; farm steward.
bairn, a child.
baith, both.
ballop, trousers flap.
bamboozle, to amaze; to confuse.
bane, a bone.
bannet, bonnet.
bannock, an oatcake.
bap, a baker's roll.
bare-fuit (bare-fit), barefoot: **bare-nakit/scuddie,** quite
   naked.
barra, a barrow.
bash, to beat; to bruise; a blow.
bauchle, a worn-out shoe; an old feeble person.
baudrons, a cat.
baukie-bird, a bat.
baun, a musical band.
baurley, barley: **baurley-bree,** whisky.
baurley, a breathing space.
bawbee, a halfpenny: **bawbees,** money.
beadle, a church officer.
beast, a creature: **beasts,** farm animals.
beezer, a very big/good person or thing.
begeck/begowk, betray; deceive; a betrayal.
behauden, indebted; obliged.
beil (beel), to fester.
beld, bald.
bellises, bellows.
bellythraw, stomach-ache.
belt, to flog.
ben, a mountain.
ben, inner part of a house; inside; within.

best maid, bridesmaid.

bield, to shelter; a shelter.

bien (been), affluent; cosy.

big, to build: **biggin,** a building.

binch, a bench.

bing, a heap.

birk, a birch tree.

birkie, alert, animated; an alert youth.

birl, to rotate; a whirl; a dance.

birr, to whir; force; animation.

birse, bristle; a fit of bad temper.

birsle, to broil; to roast; to toast.

bizz, buzz; bustle; to hiss; to zoom.

bizzum, a broomstick; a loose woman; a mischief-making female.

blae, blue-grey: **blaeberry,** a bilberry: **blaes,** blue-grey clay.

blagyaird, a blackguard.

blashy, wet and windy.

blast, to boast.

blate, diffident; timid.

blaw, to blow; to boast; a respite: **blaw-out** (oot), a feast.

bleck, black; a negro; a rascal; to make dirty; to defame.

bleize (bleeze), to blaze; a blaze.

blether, to babble; to chatter; a gossip: **blethers,** chatter; nonsense.

blin, blind.

bluid (blid), blood.

boke, to gush forth; to retch.

body, a human being; a person.

boggle, to protrude, of eyes.

boggle, a ghost; an object of terror; a scarecrow.

bole-hole, a hole in wall for ventilation.

bonspiel, a curling match.

bool, to play bowls; a bowl; a marble.

bootch, to bungle; a muddle.

boss, empty; hollow.

bothy, farm servants' quarters.

bou-hocht (boo), bandy-legged.

bouk (book), bulk; size; volume.

bourtree, a shrub elder.

bowf, to bark; a bark.
bowlie-leggit, bandy-legged.
box-bed, a wall bed.
brace, mantelshelf.
brae, a steep road; a river bank: **brae-face,** a hill slope.
braid, broad; downright.
brainch, to branch, a branch.
braisant, bold; insolent.
braith, breath; opinion.
brak/brek, to break.
brammle, bramble; blackberry.
brander, to broil; to grill; a gridiron; a sieve.
bravely, exceedingly well.
braws, best (Sunday) clothes.
breckan, bracken.
bree, liquid; broth; gravy; juice.
breeks, trousers.
breid (breed), bread.
breinge (breenj), push forward impetuously; a violent
    rush forward.
breird (breerd), germinate; sprout.
breist, a breast; a slipway.
bricht (as in loch), bright.
bridie, a meat pie, originally made in Forfar.
brig, a bridge.
brither, a brother; an equal; a match.
brock, a badger.
brog, an awl; a gimlet.
brose, porridge made with meal, water, salt and butter:
    brosy-faced, fat-faced.
brou (broo), brow.
broukit, tear-stained.
brounkaties, bronchitis.
bruckle, brittle; friable, of soil.
bruit (brit), brute.
bubblyjock, male turkey.
bucht, a fold; a shelter; put (sheep) in a shelter.
buit (bit), a boot.
bul, a bull.
bullox, make a mess of; spoil; a mess.
bum, to buzz; hum: **bumbee,** a bumble-bee.

bum, backside.
bumbaze, to amaze; to bewilder.
bung, throw violently.
burd, a bird: **burdie,** a little bird; a child.
burn, a brook.
buroo, bureau; Labour Exchange.
busk/buss, to clothe; dress; make ready.
buss, a bush; a shelter.
by, done for; past; compared with.
by-ornar, extraordinary.
byde, dwell; remain; endure.
byke, a beehive; wasp's nest.
byle, to boil: **byler,** a boiler.
byre, a cattle-shed.

Caa, caw, to call; call (noun); need (noun).
caber, a tree trunk; a pole from fir tree trunk.
cadger, a pedlar; a hawker.
cahoutchy (ou as in loose), india-rubber.
caird, a card.
cairn, a heap of stones; a pyramid of stones marking a grave.
cairry, to carry.
cairt, a cart.
callan, a boy; a lad.
caller, cool; fresh.
camsteerie, giddy; unruly.
cangle (ng as in sing), to quibble.
canna, cannot.
canny, cautious; gentle; gradual; pleasant; fortunate.
cantraip, a trick; a prank; a spell.
canty, contented; comfortable; merry.
capercailzie, a very large kind of grouse.
careous (care-ous), curious.
carnaptious, bad-tempered.
carse, a rich flat stretch of land by a river.
cast out, disagree: **cast up,** to recall spitefully.
cauf, a calf.
cauld, cold: **the cauld,** a dose of cold.
caunle, a candle.
caurry-haundit, left-handed.

causey, a cobbled street: **causey-stane,** a cobble.

cavie, to coop up; a hen-coop.

certes, assuredly.

chaft, a cheek, a jaw.

chaip, cheap.

chaipel, chapel.

chairge, to charge; cost of anything.

champ, to mash; to pound.

channer, to complain; fret; scold.

chanty, a chamberpot.

chap, to knock; hammer; to strike; of a clock; a knock.

chapman, a packman; a pedlar.

chaumer, a bedroom; a chamber.

chaw, to provoke; vex; disappoint.

cheatrie, deceit; fraud.

cheeny, china.

cheip (cheep), to chirp.

chiel, a child; a lad; a man.

chirl, to chirp; warble.

chitter, to shiver; tremble; flicker.

chookie, a chicken; a hen.

chowk, a cheek; a jaw.

chuckie, a small pebble.

chynge, to change; become sour; a change; a vicissitude.

clachan, a hamlet.

claes, clothes: **claes-raip,** clothes-rope.

clag, to clog; a sticky lump: **claggy,** sticky.

claith, cloth.

claiver, to chatter; to gossip: **claivers,** chatter; tittle-tattle.

clamjamfry, a crowd; a rabble.

clap, to pat; a pat.

clappit, shrunken.

clart, to befoul; smear; work in wet, dirty conditions; a slovenly person: **clarty,** dirty; messy.

clash, to gossip; to chatter; scandal.

clatty, slimy; muddy.

claut, to scrape; a scraper.

cleckin, a brood; a family; a litter.

cleg, a gadfly.

cleid/cleed, to clothe: **cleidin,** dress; garb.

cleik/cleek, to clutch; seize; walk arm in arm; a hook; a crook.

cless, a class.

cley (as in bite), clay.

clippin, sheep-shearing.

clishmaclaver, gossip.

clock, to sit on eggs to hatch.

cloot, a hoof: **Auld Clootie,** the devil (the hoofed one).

clout/cloot, a rag; a garment: **clouts,** clothes.

clowt, to slap; strike; a blow; a slap.

clud, a cloud.

clype, to blab; tell tales; a tale-bearer.

coble, a flat-bottomed fishing-boat.

cockabendie/cockiedandie, a small lively person.

cockieleekie, leek and chicken soup (served at Burns suppers).

cockieleerie, a cock: **cockieleerielaw,** the crow of the cock.

coddled aipple, roasted apple.

coggle, to move unsteadily; to rock: **coggly,** unsteady.

come back on, to repeat, of food eaten.

concait, conceit; opinion.

confab, to chat; a chat.

cookie, a soft bun.

corbie, a raven.

corn, grain; oats: **cornkister,** a farm-worker's song.

corrie, a hollow in the hills.

cou/coo, a cow.

coum/coom, soot.

courie/coorie, to bend; cower: **courie doun/doon,** to snuggle; to nestle.

courss/coorse, course; stormy.

couthy/coothy, congenial: **couthiness,** graciousness.

cow, to cut; a haircut.

cowp, to capsize; a tumble; a rubbish dump.

crabbit, bad-tempered.

craig, a cliff; a headland.

craik, to grumble; to keep on complaining.

cranreuch, hoarfrost.

crap, to crop; a crop.

cratur, creature: **the cratur,** whisky.

craw, to crow; to boast: **craw-steps,** steps on a house gable.

creddle, a cradle.

creel, a basket carried on the back.

creish/creesh, to grease; grease.

crock, an earthenware vessel.

croun/croon, to crown; a crown.

crouse (crooss), cheerful; jaunty.

crowdie, oatmeal and water porridge.

crunkle, to contract; to wrinkle.

cry, to call: **cry back,** to recall: **cry names,** to miscall.

cuddie, a horse; a donkey; a trestle.

cuddle, to fondle.

cumseil, attic ceiling.

cundy, a conduit; a culvert.

curfuffle, to disarrange; excitement; disorder.

currie, a small stool.

curriehunker, to squat on hams.

cushat/cushie doo (cooshie), a wood pigeon.

Dad, to bang; beat; drive.

dae, to do.

daft, foolish; doting.

daith, death.

dander, anger.

darg, labour; a day's labour.

daud, a lump of material.

dauner, to stroll.

daur, to dare.

daurk, dark.

daurlin, darling.

deave, to deafen; to bore.

dee, to die: **deid,** dead.

deif (deef), deaf; void.

deil/deevil, devil.

denner, dinner.

deoch-an-dorus, a stirrup-cup; a parting drink.

dern, to darn.

deuk (duke and dyuck), a duck.

dicht (as in loch), to wipe; to wash superficially; a rub; a wipe.

diffy, dull; stupid.

ding, to dash down; to surpass; to rain heavily.

dinna, do not.

dirdum, a fuss; an uproar.

dirl, to clatter; to reverberate; to throb; a blow; a vibration.

disna, does not.

divot, a sod.

dizzen, a dozen.

dochter (as in loch), a daughter.

docken, a dock, the plant.

dodge on, plod on.

doitit, absentminded; crazed.

dominie, a schoolmaster.

donnert, stupefied; stupid.

doo, a dove: **dooket,** a dovecot.

douce (to rhyme with loose), decorous; sedate.

douk/dook, to bathe; to dip: **sour douk** (soor dook), sour milk.

doun/doon, down; sown, of seed: **doun-by,** down the road.

dowp, buttocks; cigarette end.

dour (doo-r), obstinate; austere; severe; arduous: **dourness,** obstinacy.

dout (doot), to doubt; to suspect; a doubt.

dover, to doze; to drowse.

dozent, bewildered; stupefied.

draigle, to bedraggle.

draigon, a kite.

dram, a drink of liquor.

drap, to drop; a drop: **a drappie,** a small amount of liquor.

dree, to endure; suffering.

dreep/dreip, to drip; a drip; a soft, spiritless person.

droll, eccentric; strange.

drouk/drook, to drench; to soak: **droukit,** soaked.

droun (droon), to drown.

drouth (drooth), thirst; drought; a heavy drinker.

dub, a bog; a pond of stagnant water.

duds, clothes; rags.

dug, a dog.

dumfouner (dumfooner), to amaze; to stun: **dumfounert,** amazed.

dunch, to bump; to butt; to push.

dunner, to clatter; to reverberate.

dunny, a basement.

dunt, to bump; to knock; a blow; a bump.

dwall, to dwell.

dwam, a stupor; a trance.

dwinnle, to dwindle.

dwyne, to decline in health; to wane.

dyke, a wall.

Edder, an adder.

ee, an eye.

eemock, an ant.

eeran, an errand; a shop purchase.

efter, after.

eild (eeld), age; old age.

elba, an elbow.

eldritch, frightful, unearthly.

eleiven/eleeven, eleven.

en, end; an apartment.

ettle, to intend; to conjecture; to expect.

evens, quits.

excaise, to excuse.

eydence, diligence: **eydent,** diligent.

eyntment, ointment.

Faa/faw, to fall; to happen; a fall; a share.

factor, an agent; an estate steward.

fae/frae, from.

fail, to decline in health.

fain, glad; fond: **fidgin-fain,** anxiously eager.

fair, dry, of weather.

faither, father.

falderal, a bauble; an excuse; a whim.

fankle, entangle; ravel; a muddle; a tangle.

fantoosh, pretentious; showy.

farl, an oatcake.

fash, to disturb; to fret; to annoy.

faucht (as in loch), fight.

faur, far.

fause, false.

feart, afraid: **feartie,** a coward.

feckless, incompetent; worthless.

fegs, expression of surprise.

fell, keen; harsh; severe; appetising.

fent, to faint; a faint.

ferm, a farm.

fettle, strength; state of mind.

feu, land held on payment of feu duty; a building site.

fidge, to fidget.

fient, devil, as in **fient haet,** devil a thing.

fier, a companion; a spouse; a match.

fin/find (as in bit), to find; grope.

fine, comfortable; pleasant; well; nicely; very well.

fissle, to rustle; a rustle.

fitter, to dodder; to fidget with feet.

fizzin drink, a showy person.

flae, a flea.

flaff, to blow fitfully; to flutter; to explode.

flair, a floor.

flaucht (as in loch), flight of birds.

flauchter, to flap; to flutter; to shine fitfully.

flea-luggit, capricious; eccentric.

flee, a fly.

fleetch, to flatter.

flet, flat; a saucer; a flat.

flicht, flight.

flichter, to flutter; glimmer.

fling, to caper; to dance; a dance.

flit, to move from place to place: **flittin,** a house removal.

flouer (flooer), a flower; a bouquet.

flow, a morass; a quicksand.

flunkie, a lackey; a male servant.

flype, to turn inside out.

flyte, to scold: **a flytin,** a scolding.

foggie, an old, out-of-date person.

foggie-bee, a wild bee.

for aa/aw that, nevertheless.

forby, besides.

forenuin (forenin), forenoon.

forfairn, destitute, exhausted.

forfochen (as in loch), exhausted.

forgether, to meet together.

forgie, to forgive; to pardon.

forjeskit, exhausted.

forrit, to foster; to promote; forward; ahead; at hand.

fou (foo), full; drunk.

foumart (foomart), a polecat.

found (foond), to lay the foundation of; a foundation.

fousome (foosome), fulsome; cloying.

foost/foust, to decay; mildew; mould: **foosty,** fusty.

fouter/footer, to potter about; to fuss with little effect.

fower, four: **fowersome,** a company of four.

fozie, flabby; spongy.

fraucht, a burden.

fremmit, alien; foreign; strange.

fricht, to frighten; fright.

frien (freen), a friend; a relation.

fud, a rabbit's tail; buttocks.

fuil (fil), a fool.

fuit (fit), a foot: **fuit-licker,** a toady.

fummle, to fumble; to grope.

fung, to cuff; kick; a cuff; a kick.

furr, a furrow.

furth, abroad: **furth o,** beyond the boundaries of.

fushionless, dull; tasteless.

futrat/whitrat, a weasel.

fyke, to fidget; to fuss: **fykie,** fussy; exacting.

fyle, to befoul.

Gab, to chatter; chatter; mouth.

gae, to go: **gae back,** to deteriorate.

gaird, to guard; a sentinel; a warder.

gairten, a garter.

gallimaufry, a hodge-podge.

gallivant, to gad about; to flirt.

gallowses, trouser braces.

gallus, daring; rash; wild.

galore, plenty; in plenty.

gang, to go.

gant, to yawn.

gar, to cause; to compel.

gate, manner; way; knack.

gate, a way; a street.

gaucy, plump; cheerful; big and jolly.

gawk, to stare open-mouthed: **gawkie,** a fool; clumsy; stupid.

geal/jeel, to freeze; to coagulate.

gean (gee-an), a wild cherry tree.

gear, effects; equipment; money.

geck, to mock; to toss head derisively.

geggie, a show at a fair; a travelling theatre show.

gemm, a game.

gemm, deformed: **gemm-leggit,** lame.

gemmie, a gamekeeper.

get, to be allowed; to beget; to find; a bastard.

gether, to gather: **weill/weel gethert,** wealthy.

gey, big; very.

gie (gee), to give.

gill, a gully; a narrow valley.

gimmer, a ewe in its second year.

gin, before; by, of time; if.

ginger, aerated waters.

gird/girr, a hoop.

girdle, a griddle; iron plate for baking scones.

girn, to complain; to fret; to snarl.

girnel, a granary; a meal bin.

girse, grass.

girsle, gristle.

gitter, to gabble; a silly talker.

glaikit, foolish; giddy.

glamourie, enchantment.

glaur, mud; slime.

gled, a hawk.

gleg, alert; nimble; intelligent.

gless, glass.

glib-gabbit, glib-tongued; eloquent.

glint, glance; gleam; peep (verb and noun).

glit, slime; phlegm.

gloamin, dusk: **gloamin-staur,** evening star.

glower, to stare; to frown.

glunch (glunsh), to frown; to sulk.

goave, to stare stupidly.

gob/gab/gub, a mouth.

golach, a beetle: **forkie/hornie golach,** an earwig.

gollop, to gulp down; a gulp.

gomeril, a stupid person.

goun (goon), a gown.

govie-dick, expression of surprise.

gowan, a daisy.

gowd, gold: **gowdspink,** a goldfinch.

gowk, a cuckoo; a fool; a dunce.

gowf, to strike; golf.

graip, a manure fork.

graith, commodities; equipment; harness; lather.

gralloch (as in loch), to disembowel.

grammar, learning; scholarship.

gran/grand, excellent; splendid.

grane, to groan.

grannie, grandmother; a chimney cowl.

gravat/grauvat, a scarf; a cravat; the hangman's noose.

gray-daurk, dusk: **gray-licht,** dawn.

gree, prize; social rank: **bear the gree,** to excel; to win.

green, a lawn; callow; youthful.

greens, vegetables in general.

greit/greet, to weep.

gress, grass.

grieve, a farm bailiff; a steward.

grip/grup, to grasp; to seize.

growe, to grow.

growth (as in now), growth; weeds.

grozet, a gooseberry.

grue, to shiver from aversion; creep, of flesh: **gruesome,** abhorrent, repulsive.

grummle, to grumble; to find fault.

grumph, to grunt: **grumphy,** ill-natured.

grun, ground.

grunsel, groundsel.

grup, to grip.

grush, gravel; grit.

grushie, fast-growing; thriving; lush.

gub/gob/gab, a mouth.

guff, odour; taste.

guid, Guid, good; God: **guidbrither,** brother-in-law:
    guid-gaun, in good working order: **the unco guid,**
    the self-righteous people.

guiser, a mummer.

gullie, a large knife.

gumption, intelligence.

gurl, to growl: **gurly,** inclement.

gushet, a gusset; a triangular piece of ground between
    adjacent properties.

guts, stomach; a glutton: **gutsy,** glutonous; roomy.

guttie, rubber: **gutties,** gym shoes.

gyte, crazed: **gang gyte,** to go off one's head.

Haar, sea fog.

habble, to limp; confusion.

habnab, to hobnob; to fraternise.

haddie, a haddock.

hae, to have.

haet, an iota; a particle; a whit.

haffers, half-shares.

hag, a peat hole.

haggis, a pudding of onions, oatmeal, sheep's lung, heart
    and liver.

haggle, to cut unevenly.

hain, to save; to enclose; to protect.

hainch, a haunch.

hairse, hoarse.

hairst, harvest.

haiver, to talk nonsense: **haivers,** nonsense.

hale, whole; sound; unharmed.

halie, holy.

hame, home: **hamely,** homely; domestic; simple.

hammer, to thrash.

handsel, to celebrate with a gift.

hanker efter, to desire; yearn for.

hanky, handkerchief.

hantle, a handful.

hap, to cover; wrap; a cover; a screen.

hap, to hop.

hard, strong, of drink: **hard-wrocht,** hard-worked.

hash, to abuse; to mangle; a mess.

hashy, rough; untidy; stormy, of weather.

haud, to hold: **haud on,** to wait.

hauf, half: **hauf-fou,** half drunk: **a wee hauf,** a small whisky.

haun, a hand: **haunless,** handless.

haunle, to handle; a handle.

haurly, hardly.

haurl, a slatter; a slut.

haw, hawthorn; berry of hawthorn.

hear tell o, get news of.

hech ay, expression of weariness.

hech-how, the auld hech-how, the old routine.

heels-ower-gowdie/heid, upside down.

heh, here!

heich, high; tall.

heid (heed), head: **heid bummer,** boss: **heidstane,** a grave stone.

heize/heeze/heist, to hoist; to heave.

help ma bob, expression of surprise.

hen, affectionate term for a female: **hen-pen,** hen droppings: **hen-taed,** intoed.

herry, to rob; to rape.

hert, a heart: **hert-sair,** heartsore.

het, hot.

heuch (hyooch/hyuch, ch as in loch), a cleft; a crag; a gully; a quarry.

heuk (hyook/hyuk), a hook; a sickle.

hey, hay,

hicht (as in loch), height.

hielan (heelan), highland; awkward.

high-bendit, ambitious.

hin-en(d), backside.

hing, to hang: **hing in,** to persevere: **hing on,** to linger.

hinmaist, final; ultimate.

hinner, latter: **at the hinner end,** eventually.

hinner, to hinder.

hinnie, honey; darling.

hinside, the rear.

hippit, lamed through strain in the thigh.

hird, a herd.

hirple, to hobble.

hizzie, a hussy; a charwoman.

hoast, to cough.

hoch, the lower thigh; a joint of beef from hind leg.

hoch ay, expression of resignation.

hog, a yearling sheep not shorn.

Hogmanay, New Year's Eve.

hokery-pokery, sculduggery.

honest, decent; worthy.

hooch (as in loch), expression of exhilaration.

hoodie-craw, a hooded crow.

hoot awa, expression of incredulity.

horny, lascivious.

hotch, to fidget.

hou (hoo), how.

houghmagandy (hooch, as in loch), whoring.

houlet/hoolet, an owl.

hous (hooss), house: **black hous,** a dry-stone and turf house.

howe, a hollow; a plain by a river: **howe-dumb-deed,** depth of night; winter.

howff, a haunt; a sanctuary.

howk, to dig; to burrow; to excavate.

hull, a hill.

hum and hae, to prevaricate.

humph, a hump: **humphy-backit,** hump-backed.

hunker, to squat: **hunkers,** haunches.

hunt-the-gowk, April fool.

hurdies, haunches; buttocks.

hure (hoor), whore.

hurl, to bowl along; to wheel; a vehicle ride: **hurl-barra,** a wheelbarrow: **hurly-bed,** a truckle-bed.

hyne, a harbour.

Ile, oil.

ilk/ilka, each; every.

ill, evil; harm; evil (adj.), difficult: **ill-daein,** profligate: **ill-done-to,** badly treated: **ill-faured,** ugly: **ill-will,** dislike: **tak ill,** to become ill.

inby, indoors; inside.

inch, an island; low land by a river mouth.

ingether, to collect.

ingle, a room fire.
inklin, an allusion; a hint; a rumour; a propensity.
insteid, instead.
intae/intil, into.
inver, a river mouth.
ither, other.
itsel, itself.

Jad/jaud, a jade; a perverse woman.
jag, to prick; a prick: **jaggy,** prickly.
jaiket, a jacket.
jalouse (jalooz), to conjecture; imagine; suspect.
janitor, a school caretaker.
jant, to go on an outing; an outing.
Janwar, January.
jauner, to go about aimlessly.
jaup, to splash; a splash; a spot.
jaur, a jar.
jaurie, a large clay marble.
jawbox, a kitchen sink.
jee/gee, to swerve.
jeelie, jelly; jam.
jeist/jeest, a joist.
jenny-hunder-feet, a centipede: **jenny-lang-legs/jenny-meggie,** a cranefly.
jenny-wran, a wren.
jessie, an effeminate man.
jimp, close-fitting; short; slender; neat.
jink, to dodge; to frolic.
jo, a lover; a sweetheart.
johnnie-aa-thing, a small general merchant.
joug (joog), a jug; a mug.
jouk (jook), to duck; to elude; to swerve; to stoop:
   joukerie-pawkerie, roguery.
jow, to ring; to toll.
juist/jist, just: **juist that,** precisely; quite so.
jummle, to jumble.
jumpin-jaik, a kind of toy; an unreliable person: **jumpin-rope,** a skipping rope.
jyle, jail.
jyne, to join; **jyner,** a joiner: **jynerin,** carpentry.

Kail, soup: **kail-pat,** soup-pot: **kail runt,** a cabbage stalk.

kaim, a comb.

kebbuck, a cheese.

keckle, to cackle; to giggle.

keech (as in loch), to defecate; excrement.

keek, to glance; to peep: **keekin-gless,** a mirror.

keelie, a kestrel or other hawk; a town rough.

ken, to know; recognise: **kennin,** knowledge; understanding; a little bit.

kennle, to kindle.

kenspeckle, prominent; remarkable.

kill, a kiln.

kilter, high spirits.

kiltie, a wearer of the kilt.

kin, kind; lineage.

kink, to twist; a twist; a quirk.

kirk, a church: **kirkyaird,** a cemetery.

kirn, a churn.

kiss-ma-loof, a sycophant; a flatterer.

kist, a box; a coffin; a corn bin; the thorax.

kitchen, sauce; appetiser.

kittle, to tickle; to itch; a tickle; a stimulus; difficult; abstruse; precarious.

kittlin, a kitten.

kizzen, a cousin.

knab, a bigwig: **knabbery,** gentry.

Knacky, adroit; deft; skilful.

knackers, testicles.

knotless, aimless; futile.

knowe, an incline; a small hill.

kye (as in buy), cows.

Lab, to walk with long heavy steps.

laddie, a boy.

lade, a water channel.

lae, to leave.

laft, a loft; an attic.

laich (ch as in loch), low: **laich-set,** stocky.

lair, a grave.

laird, a landowner; a lord.

laith, loath.

lallan, lowland.

Lammas, the term beginning 1st August.

lan, land.

lane, solitary; isolated.

lang, long; tall: **lang-nebbit,** nosy: **langsyne,** days of long ago.

lappert milk, curdled milk.

lashins, plentiful supply.

lass, a girl; a sweetheart.

lauch (as in loch), to laugh.

laud, a lad; a boy friend.

lave, the rest; the residue.

laverock, the lark.

lay aff, to hold forth.

lazy, bone/horn lazy, very lazy.

lea rig, a ridge of unploughed grass.

leal, faithful.

leatherin, a flogging.

leddy, a lady.

lee, to lie; a lie: **leear,** a liar.

leed, lead, the metal; a pendulum.

lee-lang, livelong.

leet, a list of candidates.

leeve, to live.

leid, a dialect; a language.

leir (leer), to learn; to teach; learning.

len, to loan; a loan.

let bug, disclose: **let on,** divulge.

leuk (luck), to look.

lib, to castrate.

licht, to light; a light: **licht-heidit,** dizzy: **lichtsome,** gay.

lichtnin (as in loch), lightning.

lick, to thrash; to defeat; to surpass.

lick-ma-loof, obsequious.

liff/lith, an orange segment; a slice.

lilt, to sing softly.

line, a certificate; a diploma; a prescription; written authorisation.

link at, to act energetically towards.

links, a sandy, bent-covered shore; sausages strung together.

linn, a cliff over which water falls; a waterfall.
lint, flax.
lintie, a linnet.
loan/loaning, a lane; a milking place; a paddock.
loch, a lake.
loonie, a lunatic.
losh, expression of surprise.
love-bairn, a bastard.
lowe, to blaze; a flame: **tak lowe,** to catch fire.
lown, calm; peaceful; sheltered.
lowp, to leap; a leap.
lowse (lowz), to loosen: **lowss,** loose: **lowsin** time, end of
    day's work.
ludge, to lodge.
luewarm (a as in arm), lukewarm.
lug, an ear.
luif (lif)/**loof,** palm of hand; a paw.
lum, a chimney: **lum-hat,** a top hat.
lyart, grizzled.

Machair, low land by shore covered with bent grass.
maggie-rab, a brawling woman.
maggoty-heidit (heedit), eccentric; scatter-brained.
mail, a meal.
mainner, manner.
mains, a home farm.
mair, more.
mairch, a boundary.
maister, master.
maitter, a matter.
mak, to make; to create; to mature, of manure: **makar,** a
    bard; a composer.
mammy, mother.
man, a husband: **man-body,** a male adult.
mang, among.
manna, may not.
mant, to have an impediment in speech.
marl, to mottle.
mart, a building for livestock auction; a market.
mask, to brew; infuse tea.

maun, must.

maut, mault; ale.

maw, mother.

maukit, infested with maggots; putrid.

mealy-moud (moo-d), plausible.

meat, food.

meedie, a meadow.

meenit, a minute.

meikle, much.

mennen, a minnow.

mercat, a market.

messages, shop purchases.

messan, a cur; a mongrel.

micht (as in loch), might: **michty,** mighty.

midden, a refuse dump; a dunghill.

mill, a factory.

mim-moud (moo-d), prim; affected in speech.

mirk, darkness.

misdout (doot), to mistrust.

mither, mother.

mittens, knuckle gloves.

mixter-maxter, confusion: **mixtie-maxtie,** a confused mixture; jumbled.

mochie, clammy.

moger, to bungle; a bungle; a mess.

molligrant, to grumble; to lament.

mooch/mouch (ch as in child), to idle around: **moocher,** an idler.

moodge, to budge; to cause to budge.

morn, the morn, tomorrow.

moss, a bog; a marsh.

mou (moo), mouth.

mountain-dew, whisky.

moup (moop), to nibble; to graze.

mous (mooss), a mouse.

mowdie/mowdiewort, a mole.

muck, to clean out (a byre); dirt; dung.

muckle, much; big; a great deal.

muir (mare), moor.

mummle, to mumble.

mump, to mumble.

mune (min), moon: **munelicht flittin,** removal by night to escape creditors.

murly, crumbly.

murn, to mourn.

mynd/mind, to call to mind; to evoke; to look after: **myndin,** a memento.

Nae, no.

nait, neat; smart.

naither, neither.

naitur, nature: **naitral,** a halfwit; natural; normal.

nakit/bare nakit, naked/quite naked.

nane, none.

near-the-bit, miserly.

neb, beak; nose: **nebby,** inquisitive.

ned, a stupid person.

neeger, a nigger.

ne'er-dae-weill, a rake; a profligate.

neibour, a neighbour: **neibourless stockin,** a stocking that doesn't match.

neip/neep, a swede turnip.

nerra, narrow.

nesty, nasty.

neuk (nyook/nyuk), a corner; a recess, an alcove.

new-fanglt (ng as in sing), novel.

nicht (as in loch), night: **nichtgoun,** a nightgown.\

nick, to grab; to steal; to snip: **the nick,** the jail.

nicks, knuckles.

nieve (neeve), a fist: **nieve-shakin,** a golden handshake.

nippers, forceps.

nippit, stingy.

nit, a nut.

nit, a louse egg.

no, not: **no weill** (weel), ill.

nocht, nothing.

norie, a fad; a whim.

notion, a liking.

nou (noo), now: **the nou,** just now.

nyaff, a contemptible person.

O, of; about.

obleege, to oblige.

ocht (as in loch), aught.
odds, difference; disparity.
offish, frigid in manner.
ongauns, happenings.
onie, any.
oo, wool.
oor, hour.
oorie, eerie.
ooss, carpet sweepings; fluff.
or, until.
ornar, ordinary.
orra, abnormal; occasional: **orra body,** a vagrant: **orra-man,** an odd-job man.
ower/owre, above; over; too (overmuch).
oxter, armpit.

Pack, intimate.
packie, a packman.
paidle, to paddle.
painch, a paunch; a stomach.
pairt, to part; a part.
paitrick, a partridge.
palin, a fence.
paper, a newspaper.
parritch, porridge.
partan, a crab.
pat, a pot.
pauchle, to embezzle; to wangle.
pauchtie, arrogant.
pawkie, astute; guileful.
pawm, palm of hand; to foist: **pawmie,** a stroke with a strap.
pawns, curtains for wall bed.
pech, to gasp.
pee, to piddle: **peeins,** urine: **pee-the-bed,** a dandelion.
peel, a Borders tower.
peel, a pill.
peel, to equal: **be peels,** to have the same score.
peelie-wallie, delicate; sickly.
peen, a pin.
peenie, a pinafore.

peenie-rose, a peony.

peerie, a spinning top.

peesie/peesweep, a peewit; a lapwing.

peevers, hopscotch.

peer/peir, a pear.

penny jo, a prostitute: **penny wheep,** weak ale.

pent, paint.

perjink, a fastidious person; fastidious.

pernickety, fastidious.

pey, to pay.

pick, to eat little.

pickle, an indefinite amount; a little: **a wee pickle,** a small amount.

piece, a snack.

pig, an earthenware bowl/pot.

pirn, a bobbin.

pish, to urinate; a rush of water.

pit, to put: **pit about** (aboot), to disconcert: **pit by,** to hoard: **pit doun** (doon), to kill: **pit in for,** to apply for: **pit tae yin's haun,** to lend a hand: **pit up to,** to incite.

plainstane, a paving stone: **plainstanes,** a pavement.

plaister, plaster.

plantin, a plantation.

plenish, to furnish: **plenishin,** a furnishing.

plicht, plight.

ploo/plou, to plough; a plough.

plook/plouk, a pimple; a blotch: **plookie/ploukie,** pimply.

ploom/ploum, a plum.

plowter, to potter; to splash about aimlessly; a muddle.

ploy, an escapade; an undertaking; a social gathering.

plunk, to propel a marble from thumb and forefinger.

plyde, a plaid.

po, a chamberpot.

poke/pock, a bag.

polis, a policeman.

post, mail; postage; postman.

potty, putty.

potty-heid, potted meat.

pou (poo), to pull.

pouch/pooch, a pocket.

pouer/pooer, power; a large number.

pouk/pook, to pluck; to twitch: **poukit,** pinched; emaciated: **in the pouk,** in the moult.

pourie (poorie), a cream jug.

pouther (poother), powder.

pownie, a pony.

powter, to work aimlessly.

prap, a prop.

pree, to sample; to prove.

preen, a pin.

press, a cupboard.

prickmadentie, an affected person.

prig, to beg; to bargain contentiously; to insist.

primsy, demure.

privy, a privet.

puddock, a frog.

puir (pare), poor.

pun/pund, pound, weight or sterling.

pyne/pine, pain; hardship.

pynt, to point; a point.

Quaich (as in loch), a drinking cup.

quait, quiet; calm.

quakin bog, a shifting bog.

quat, to quit.

quean, a girl; a woman; a hussy.

quey (ey as in bite), a heifer.

quicken, to ferment.

quyne, see **quean.**

Rack, to sprain; to wrench; to worry; a sprain; worry.

ragnail, torn skin at base of fingernail.

raik, a roving person.

raip, a rope.

rair, to roar.

raither, rather.

raivel, to dishevel; to entangle.

rale, real; genuine.

rammy, a disturbance; an uproar.

ramstam, to rush headlong; a headstrong person.

ramsteegerous, boisterous.

randy, a brawling woman; dissipated.

rant, to rampage; to revel; a sprightly tune.

rape, a rope.

rare, exquisite.

rasp, a raspberry.

rattan, a rat.

raucle, bluff; coarse; unruly.

rax, to extend; to sprain; to wrench: **rax for,** to reach for.

ream, to foam; to effervesce.

redd, to clean up; to set in order: **redd o,** rid of.

reek, smoke, vapour.

reel-rall, in a disordered manner.

reenge, to rummage; search.

reive, to grab; to plunder; to rob.

remeid, remedy; redress.

renaig, to shirk.

renunce, to renounce; to abdicate.

resurrector, a body-snatcher.

rib, a fire bar.

richt (as in loch), right; exceedingly: **no richt,** abnormal; simple-minded.

rickle, a loose pile.

rid/reid, red.

rift, to make wind.

rig, a ridge of land between furrows: **rigbane,** a backbone: **riggin,** rafters.

rigwiddie, lean; tough and bony-looking.

rin, to run; to melt; the tide; a current.

rink, an arena; a tournament; a demarcation line.

rise, a hoax: **tak a rise out** (oot) **o,** to hoax.

rive, to rend; to rip; to wrench.

road, direction; route; method.

roarie, garish: **roarin fou** (foo), very drunk.

rodden-tree, a rowan tree.

rone, an air funnel; a gutter for drawing off water.

roun/roon, round.

roust/roost, rust.

rowe, to roll; to enfold.

rowp, to sell/a sale by auction.

rowth, abundance, abundant.

rozet, resin.

ruch/rouch (as in loch), rough; hoarse; unshaven; abundant; affluent.

ruction, a brawl; a quarrel.

rue, to repudiate; repentance: **tak the rue,** to regret.

ruif (riff), a roof; a ceiling.

ruit, a root.

rummle, to rumble; to shake up violently; a clumsy person.

runchie, crunchy.

runkle, to wrinkle; to crease.

runt, rump; stump of plant; a dwarfish person.

ryne/rine, a rein.

rype/ripe, to ransack; to plunder.

Sab, to sob.

sae, so: **sae be,** if it so happens.

saft, soft; rainy, of weather: **saft-skinned,** sensitive.

saicont, second; a second.

sain, to bless; a blessing.

saip, soap.

sair, sore; badly; greatly: **sair heid,** a headache.

sait, a chair; a seat.

sang, a song; a fuss: **auld sang,** an old story.

sappy, moist; juicy.

saps, sops: **sapsy,** effeminate.

sark, a shirt.

sarkin, wood roof lining.

sauch (as in loch), a willow: **greitin** (greetin) **sauch,** a weeping willow.

saul, a soul.

saum, a psalm.

saumon, a salmon.

saun, sand.

saunt, a saint.

saut, salt: **saut dish,** a salt-cellar.

sax, six.

scad, to burn; scald; scorch.

scaffie, a scavenger.

scant, scarcity; poverty.

scart, to scratch.

scaud, to scald.

scaur, to scar; a scar; a cliff.

schuil/schule (skil), a school: **wee schuil,** an infant school.

scliff, to scuff feet on ground in walking.

sclim, to climb; a climb.

scoor/scour (scoor), to clean out; to purge; diarrhoea.

scouth (scooth)**/scowth,** room; scope; freedom.

scraich/screich/screech (as in loch), to shreik.

scran, to scrape together; to scrounge; provisions; loot.

scranky, lean; gaunt.

scrape, to scrawl; to shave: **scrape o the pen,** a letter.

screed, a letter; a harangue.

screenge, to glean; to scour vigorously.

screw, a salary.

scrieve/screive, to write.

scrimpit, frugal; undersized.

scud, to beat; to move quickly: **bare scuddy,** naked.

scunner, to cause/get a feeling of aversion; loathing: **scunnersome,** disgusting.

seck, to dismiss from a job; a sack.

see awa, to outlive: **see me,** give me.

seep, to ooze; to percolate; to leak.

seiven/seeven, seven.

sel, self.

semmit, undershirt; vest.

sen, to send.

ser, to serve; to suit; to satisfy.

serviette, a table napkin.

set, to congeal.

sgian-dhu, a dirk.

shae, a shoe.

shair, sure; certain.

shairn, cow dung.

shak, to shake.

shalla, shallow.

shan-gabbit, lantern-jawed.

shank, a leg.

shauchle (as in loch), to shuffle; to shamble.

shaup, to shell peas; a peapod.

shaw, a grove; a coppice; a turnip/potato leaf.

shed, to divide; to part the hair; a hair parting.

sheddae, a shadow.

sheepie-meh, child's name for a sheep.

sherp/shairp, sharp; frosty.

sheuch (shyuch/shooch, as in loch), to trench; a ditch; a gutter.

shew (shoo), to sew.

shieling, a temporary summer abode for shepherds.

shilpit, emaciated; puny; shrunken.

shock, a stroke of paralysis.

shog, to nudge; to push; a nudge; a push.

shop-door, trousers flap.

shouer (shooer), a shower.

shouder/shouther (shoother), a shoulder.

shuil (shill), a shovel.

shunkie, a latrine.

shut tae, to close.

sib, kin; related.

sic, such: **sicca/sicna,** such a.

siccar, sure; staunch; true: **mak siccar,** to make certain.

sicht (as in loch), sight.

siller, silver; money.

silly, flimsy; frail, innocent.

simmer, summer.

single, to thin out seedlings.

sit in, to take a seat at the table: **sit still,** to sit at peace.

skail, to spill; upset; disperse: **skailin time,** stopping time.

skaith, hurt; damage.

skech (as in loch), to cadge; to purloin.

skeich (as in loch), gay; frisky.

skelf, a sliver; a splinter.

skellie, lopsided; squint-eyed.

skellum, a rogue.

skelp, to slap: **skelpin,** a thrashing.

skelp, to hurry; to race.

skep, a bee-hive: **get skeppit,** to go to bed.

skiddle, to dabble in water; slop.

skimmer, to shimmer.

skin-a-louse, a miser.

skinkle, to gleam; to glitter.

skip, the peak of a cap; **skippit bannet,** a peaked cap.

skirl, to shriek; to scream.

skirl, to frizzle; to fry; to sizzle: **skirl-i-the-pan,** oatmeal-onion fry.

skite, to fly off obliquely; to ricochet.

sklent, to slant; to glance; to move sideways.

slabber, to dribble; to slaver; slop; slush.

slaister, to bedaub; a sloppy mess.

slaiver, to dribble; to slobber; saliva.

slater, a woodlouse.

slee, sly.

sleekit, unctuous; hypocritical.

sleep, to go numb.

slip awa, to die: **slippy,** slippery; speedy.

slitter, to splash aimlessly in water; a sloppy mess.

slogger, to dawdle; to walk in a slovenly manner.

slorp, to eat dirtily; to swallow noisily.

slounge (sloonj), to drench; a drenching.

sma/sma-boukit (bookit), small/small in stature: **sma drink,** a nonentity.

smeddum, pith; vigour.

smeek/smeik, to smoke; smoke; fumes, odour.

smert, smart.

smiddy, a smithy.

smirr, to drizzle; a drizzle.

smit, to infect; to taint; contagion.

smithereens, small fragments.

smowt, a young salmon; anything small.

snash, impertinence; abuse.

snaw, snow.

sneck, to bolt; to latch; a bolt; a latch.

sned, to chop off.

snell, cold; biting, of wind: **snell-gabbit,** sharp-tongued.

snib, to bolt; a door latch.

snicker, to sneer; to titter.

snod, to trim; to tidy up; trim; tidy.

snood, a hair ribbon; a hair net.

snool, to cringe.

snotter, to snivel: **snotters,** nasal mucus.

snowk, to sniff; to pry.

sodger, a soldier.

sole, a sill.

sonsy, plump.

sook/souk, to suck; a suck.

soom, to swim; a swim.

soople/souple, supple; limp.

sour (soor), sour: **sour douk** (dook), buttermilk.

soutar (sootar), a cobbler; a shoemaker.

sowl, a soul.

sowther, to solder; to weld.

spadin, a spade-depth.

spaik, a batten; a slat.

spail, a lath; a splinter.

sparra, a sparrow.

spate, a river torrent.

spaur, a perch.

speeder, a spider.

speel/speil, to climb.

speir, to ask; to investigate: **speir at,** to inquire of.

spence, a parlour; a sitting room.

speug (spyug), a sparrow.

spicket, a spigot.

spinnle, a spindle: **spinnle-shanks,** long thin legs.

spital, a hospital.

spitten image, exact likeness.

splairge. to besmear.

splitter, to splutter; a splutter; a fuss.

splore, a prank; an exploit.

splounge (sploonj), to splash about.

sprauchle/sprachle (as in loch), to sprawl; to flounder.

spreckle, to speckle; a speckle; a spot.

spree, a carouse; a frolic.

spud, a potato.

spune (spin), a spoon.

spunk, animation; bravery.

spurtle, a porridge stick.

spile/spyle, to spoil, to pamper.

squatter, a crowd; a swarm.

squeegee, out of shape.

stab, a pole; a stake.

stacher, to stagger.

stamack, stomach; to tolerate.

stance, a street trader's pitch; a bus-halt.

stane, a stone: **stany,** stony.

stap, to cram.

staun, to stand.

staur, a star.

stave, to sprain.

staw, to cloy; nausea.

steamie, a public wash-house.

steek/steik, to stitch; to sew; a stitch.

steer/steir, to stir; to disturb: **steerin,** active; mischievous.

steeve/stieve, firm; stiff; steep.

step aside, to err morally.

sterk, stark.

stert, to start.

sterve, to starve.

stey (as in bite), to dwell; to remain; a sojourn.

stey (as in bite), steep.

stibble, stubble.

stick in, to persist: **stick up to,** to stand up to.

sticks, furniture.

still and on, notwithstanding.

stippit, stupid.

stirk, a bullock.

stirlin, a starling.

stirrup-dram, a parting drink.

stook, a group of sheaves set up to dry.

stop, to dwell; to remain.

stot, to bounce; to stagger.

stoun (stoon), to ache; to throb; an ache.

stour (stoor), dust: **stour o words,** bombast.

stovies, potatoes stewed with onions.

stow (as in now), to cram; to gorge.

strae, straw: **strae daith,** a natural death.

stramash, a fuss; a brawl.

strang, strong.

strappin, stalwart; burly.

strath, a broad river valley.

straucht/stracht (as in loch), straight.

stravaig, to gad; to stroll.

straw basher, a straw hat.

streetch/streitch, to stretch; a stretch; a spell; a turn.
stroup/stroop, a spout; a faucet.
stuckie, a starling.
stuck up, conceited.
stuffy, hardy; healthy.
stuil (stil), a stool.
stummle, stumble.
stushie (stooshie), a squabble; tumult.
Suddron/Southron, English; southern.
sugaraulie, licorice.
sumph, a simpleton; a stupid fellow.
Sunday braws, Sunday clothes; best clothes.
sune/shune (sin/shin), soon.
swack, active; spry; supple.
swall, to swell; to bloat.
swalla, a swallow, the bird.
swally, to swallow.
swank, spry; supple: **swankie,** an active lad.
swatch, a sample.
swats, ale; beer.
swaw, to undulate; undulation.
swee, to swing; a pivot used to suspend pots over fire.
sweetie, a sweet: **sweetie wife,** a purveyor of gossip.
sweir (sweer), to swear; an expletive.
sweir/sweirt (sweer), loath.
sweit/sweet, to sweat; sweat.
swick, a fraud.
switchpoll, an earwig.
swither, to doubt; to hesitate; doubt; hesitation.
swurl, to swirl; a swirl.
swipe, a sweeping blow.
sybie, a spring onion.
syke, a ditch; a gutter.
syle, soil.
syne (sine), to rinse; a rinse.
syver (as in eye), a drain; a gutter; a sink.

Tacket, a hobnail: **tackety-buits** (bits), hobnailed boots.
tae, a toe; a tine.
tae, too; also: **tae-sided,** biased.

taigle, to delay; to detain: **taiglesome,** hindering, tedious.

tairge, a virago.

tairt, a tart.

tait, a wee tait, a small quantity.

tak, to take.

Tallie, an Italian.

tane, the tane . . . the tither, the one . . . the other.

tangs, tongs.

tap, top: **tap-coat,** overcoat: **tappit-hen,** decanter topped with hen's comb.

tapsalteerie, topsy-turvy; chaotic.

tare, a frolic; a piece of fun.

targe, an ill-tempered woman.

tash, to soil; to fray.

tattie, a potato; **champit tatties,** mashed potatoes: **tattie bing,** a potato pit: **tattie-bogle,** a scarecrow.

taur, tar.

tawpie, a foolish person.

tawse, a strap.

tea-skiddle, a tea-party.

tedisome, boring; tiresome.

teem, to pour heavily.

teir (teer), to tear: **teirin,** violent.

tent, to listen to; to care for: **tentie,** attentive: **tentless,** thoughtless: **tak tent,** to heed; to take note.

teuch (tyuch, as in loch), tough: **teuch jean,** a jujube.

teuchat (tyoochat, as in loch), a lapwing; a peewit.

Teuchter, a Highlander, contemptuous.

thack/theek, to thatch, thatch.

thae, these; those.

thaim, them.

that, who; whom; so, to such an extent.

thegither, together.

theirsels, themselves: **their lane,** by themselves.

thir, these.

thirl, to bind; to enslave.

thocht (as in loch), thought.

thole, to endure; to undergo; to permit.

thon, that; those; yon.

thoom, a thumb.

thorn, a hawthorn.

thowe, to thaw; a thaw.

thowless, listless; weak; spineless.

thrab, to throb.

thrang, to throng; to crowd; bustle; busy; crowded.

thrapple, to strangle; a throat; a windpipe.

thraw, to twist; to distort: **thrawn,** stubborn; surly; adverse.

thresh, to thrash.

thrissle, a thistle.

throu, finished: **throu time,** gradually.

thrum, to hum; to purr.

thummle, a thimble.

thunner, thunder: **thunner-plump,** a sudden downpour.

ticht (as in loch), tight.

tid, a propitious time; a season; a mood.

til, to; towards.

timorsome, fearful; nervous; timid.

tink/tinkler, a tinker; a gipsy; a vagabond.

tint, lost.

tip/tup, a ram.

tippy, stylish.

tip, a rubbish dump.

tirl, to strip off.

tirrivee, a bustle; a tantrum; a rage.

tits, expression of impatience.

tocher (as in loch), a purse; a dowry.

tod, fox.

toddle, to waddle; to saunter.

tolbooth, a town jail.

toll, a turnpike.

tollie, a lump of excrement.

tongue-deavin, deafeningly loquacious: **tongue-tackit,** tongue-tied.

toom/tuim (tim), empty.

toun (toon), a town; a hamlet; a farm.

toorie, a tassel; a tuft.

tousy (toozy), unkempt; blustery.

tosh, tidy: **tosht up,** smartly dressed.

tottie, tiny.

towt, to tease; to vex; a tantrum.

traik, to gad; to trudge.

tramp, to tread down.

trap, a hatch; a pothole.

trashery, rubbish: **trashtrie,** riff-raff.

trauchle (as in loch), to overburden; to trudge; hard, tiring work.

tred, a trade.

trekkle, treacle.

trevel/traivel, to travel.

trewan, a trowel.

trig, neat; smart.

trinch, to trench; a trench.

troch (as in loch), a trough.

troke wi, to associate with.

tron, a public weighing machine.

trowe (as in brow), to roll; to spin/cause to spin.

trummle, to tremble: **trummlin tam,** potted meat.

tryst, to fix a meeting with; a rendezvous: **trysted,** betrothed.

tuim (tim)/**toom,** empty.

tuin (tin), tune.

tuith (tith), a tooth.

tumfie, a boring, insensible person.

tumshie, a turnip.

turn, to curdle, of milk; a bent; an inclination; a walk.

twa/twae, two: **twa-three,** a few.

twal, twelve.

tweel, twill.

tyauve, to struggle; a struggle.

tyke, a dog; a mongrel.

tyler, a tailor.

tyne/tine, to lose.

Uncanny, unlucky; unearthly.

unchancy, unlucky; ill-omened.

unco, strange; extraordinary; exceedingly.

unctioneer, an auctioneer.

Vaunty, conceited; jaunty; gay.

veesit, to visit; a visit.

vennel, a lane between houses.

vex, to fret; vexation; **vext,** sorry.
vieve/veeve, lively.
virr, force; vigour.
vyce, a voice.

Waa/waw, a wall.
wabster, a weaver.
wabbit, exhausted.
wad, would.
waddin, a wedding.
waefu/waesome, woeful.
wae's me, woe is me.
waff, to wave; to flap; to flutter; a blast of air; a puff; aroma.
waffle, to shilly-shally.
wag-at-the-waa, a wall-clock with a pendulum.
waik, weak.
wairsh, insipid; lacking salt.
wal, a well; a water tap.
wale, to select: **the wale o,** the pick of.
wallie-dug, a china dog ornament.
wallop, to beat; to strike; a blow.
wallop, to gallop; to flutter.
wally-draigle, the weakest fledgling; a puny person.
wallies, ornaments: **a wally close,** a tiled entry to a block of flats.
wame, a stomach; a womb.
wan, one.
wanchancy, ill-fated.
want (as in man), to want; to be deficient in; to seek; a mental defect: **wantin,** without: **dae wantin,** to do without.
wark, to work; to ferment; to purge.
warld, world: **warld's gear,** worldly wealth.
warse, worse.
warsle, to contend; to wrestle: **warsle on,** to struggle forward: **warsle through,** to overcome adversity.
wast, west: **wastlins,** westwards.
waster, a ne'er-do-well: **wastrie,** extravagance.
wat, wet.

water, a river: **watergaw,** an incomplete rainbow: **water-waggie,** a water-wagtail.

wather, weather: **saft wather,** wet weather.

waucht (as in loch), a draught of liquor: **guidwillie waucht,** a hearty draught of liquor.

wauchle (as in loch), to shamble; to stagger.

wauk, to awake: **wauken,** to arouse; awake (adj.).

wauner, to wander.

waur, worse.

waxcloth, linoleum.

wean (wane), a child; an infant.

weary on, to long for.

wecht (as in loch), weight: **wechts,** scales.

wee, small: **wee pickle,** a small amount: **wee yin,** a child.

weel/weill, well: **weel-aff,** prosperous: **weel-daein,** well-behaved: **well-gethert,** well-off: **weel-kent,** well-known.

weir, to wear: **weir-in,** to pass slowly, of time: **weir-on,** to grow late.

weit, wet, moisture.

werena, were not.

wey (as in bite), way; direction; manner; mood; reason.

wha/whae, who.

whalp, a whelp.

whan, when.

whang, a band; a leather bootlace; a thong.

whase, whose.

whatna, what sort of.

whaup, a curlew.

whaur, where.

wheasel, a weasel.

wheech (as in loch), stink.

wheen, a wheen, a small number of.

wheenge, to whine.

wheeple, to whistle shrilly; a shrill whistle.

wheesht, hush!

whigmaleerie, a bauble; a gimmick; a whim.

whit, what: **whitna,** what kind of.

whitrat/futrat, weasel.

whittle, an abscess near finger nail.

whuff, to whiff; a whiff.

whummle, to capsize; an upset.

whun/whin, furze; gorse.

whun/whunstane, whinstone.

whup, to whip; a whip.

whurl, to whirl: **whurly,** a chimney cowl; a pulley.

whurr, to whir.

whussle, to whistle; a whistle.

whiles/whyles, sometimes.

wi, with.

wick, a sea inlet.

wife, a woman: **the wife,** my wife.

wimple, to ripple; to meander.

win, to gain; to earn; to reach; to dwell: **win awa,** to die:
    win throu, to survive.

win, wind.

winch, to go sweethearting; a wench.

windae, window: **windae sole,** window sill.

winna/willna, shall not; won't.

wis (wiz), was.

wishie-washie, weak and watery.

wizzen, to shrink: **wizzent,** shrunken.

word, notice; report.

wrack, couchgrass.

wrang, wrong.

wrastle/warsle, to wrestle; to strive.

wricht (as in loch), a carpenter; a joiner.

writer, an attorney; a lawyer.

wud, crazed.

wuid (wid), wood.

wulcat, wildcat.

wulk, a whelk.

wumman, woman.

wunner, to wonder; a wonder.

wur, were.

wurset, worsted.

witch, a witch.

wyce, shrewd; intelligent.

wynd, a lane between houses.

Yabble, to gabble; to speak incoherently.

yae, one: **yae man,** a certain man.

yaird, a yard: **kailyaird,** a kitchen garden.
yaise, to use.
yammer, to fret; to complain.
yank, to pluck; to twitch.
yap, to yelp; to nag.
yatter, to chatter.
ye, you.
yeld/yell, barren; not yielding milk.
yella, yellow.
yer, your: **yersel,** yourself.
yestreen, yesterday evening.
yett, a gate.
yeuky, itchy.
yill, ale.
yin, one: **yin's lane,** by oneself.
yird, to bury; earth.
yiss, use.
yon, that; those.
yowe, a ewe.
yowl, to howl; yell.

SOME HANDY QUICK-REFERENCE LISTS

TYPICAL SCOTS FOODS

Arbroath Smokies – small haddocks smoked over oak or birch chips.

Bannocks – round oatmeal cakes baked on a griddle.

Black Bun – a spiced fruit cake with very rich ingredients baked specially for the Scots Hogmanay (New Year's Eve).

Brose – porridge made with boiling water (or milk) and oatmeal, with salt added.

Cauld Steerie – oatmeal and cold water stirred together.

Cockieleekie Soup – soup made from leeks and chicken stock, and generally served at Burns Suppers on 25th January.

Coddled Aipples – apples roasted in oven or before fire.

Drogget Scones – oatmeal-and-potato scones.

Forfar Bridies – pasties originally made in Forfar, with mince filling and added onions and seasoning.

Finnan Haddies – haddocks smoked in peat reek; name derived from the fishing village of Findon on the north-east coast.

Haggis – a dish also served at Burns Suppers, and made of sheep's offal, oatmeal, suet, onions, herbs, with salt and pepper added.

Mince Collops – slices of steak or hare or venison, minced and cooked with oatmeal, onions, butter and seasoning.

Pancakes – soft round scones made with a soft batter of flour, egg, sugar and milk, dropped on to a hot griddle or pan.

Parkins – biscuits made of flour, oatmeal, treacle, spice and sugar, mixed together, flattened and baked in oven.

Shortbread – a crisp type of biscuit made from flour, butter and sugar; a favourite offering with sherry etc. during the New Year festive season.

Skink – soup made from shin of beef, with potatoes and onion added. **Cullen Skink** substitutes haddock for beef.

Skirlie/Skirl-i-the-pan – oatmeal and onions fried in suet or dripping.

Stovies – stewed potatoes and onions.

Tattie Scones – scones made from champit tatties (mashed potatoes), butter, flour and salt.

PARTS OF THE BODY

Adam's Apple – knot o the craig (throat).
Armpit – oxter.
Belly – painch; kyte.
Brain – harns.
Buttocks – hurdies.
Cheeks – chowks; chafts.
Chest – kist.
Ear – lug.
Fist – nieve.
Foot – fuit (fit).
Hand – haun.
Haunch – hainch.
Hips – hurdies.
Hip-bone – hurkle-bane.
Head – heid (heed).
Internal organs – intimmers.
Knee-cap – knap.
Little finger – pinkie.
Neck – craig; hause.
Palm of hand – loof.
Pubic bone – shear-bane.
Shoulder – shouther (shoother).
Shoulder-bone – spaul-bane.
Sole of foot – howe o the fuit.
Spinal column – backbane links.
Thigh (lower) – hoch.
Toe – tae.

Windpipe – wizzen.
Wrist – shackle.
Wrist-bone – shackle-bane.

AILMENTS

Bandy-legged – bou-hocht (boo).
Bellyache, Colic – belly-thraw.
Boil – byle.
Bronchitis – brounkaties (broon).
Corn on foot; bunion – weerock.
Diarrhoea – the scoot.
Heartburn – water-brash.
Heart pain – stoun (stoon).
Hernia – rimburst.
Hooping-cough – kink-hoast.
Hump-backed – bou-backit (boo); humphy-backit.
Infection – smit.
Lame through thigh strain – hippit.
Lockjaw – jawlock.
Misshapen teeth, having – gam-teetht.
Pain – pyne.
Physically exhausted – forfochen (as in loch).
Pimple – plook.
Rash – the nirls.
Scarlet fever – rush; fivver.
Silicosis – miner's asthma.
Skin eruption in child – hives.
Slight illness – a towt.
Smallpox – pock.
Sprained joint – wrocht bane.
Whooping-cough – kink-hoast.

HOUSE AND HOUSEHOLD

Basement – dunny.
Chimney – lum.
Clock – knock.
Coal bucket – baikie.
Crossbeam – bauk.

Cupboard; pantry – aumry.
Door latch – sneck.
Door mat – bass.
Doorway – door-cheek.
Eaves – easin.
Fire – ingle.
Floor – flair.
Joist – jeist (jeest).
Kitchen work – scodgie wark.
Loft – laft.
Pillow – cod.
Plate rack on wall; kitchen sideboard – bink.
Rafters – kebars.
Roof ridge – riggin.
Room – chaumer.
Sill – sole.
Sink – jawbox.
Spare room; sitting-room – spence.
Wall cupboard – press.
Window – windae; winnock.
Window sash – chess.

ANIMALS

Badger – brock.
Bat – bawkie.
Bullock – stot.
Calf – cauf.
Cow – coo (plural kye).
Ewe – yowe.
Fox – tod.
Hare – mawkin.
Heifer – quey (ey as in bite).
Kitten – kitlin.
Mole – mowdie.
Pony – pownie.
Ram – tip.
Rat – rattan.
Sow – soo.
Steer – stirk.
Weasel – whitrat.

AND OTHERS

Ant – eemock.
Bumble-bee – bumbee.
Caterpillar – kailworm.
Earwig – hornie-golach.
Flea – flae.
Fly – flee.
Frog – puddock.
Ladybird – clockleddy.
Louse – poolie.
Maggot – mawk.
Moth – moch (as in loch).
Toad – tade.
Woodlouse – slater.

BIRDS

Bullfinch – bullie (u as in bus).
Carrion crow – hoodie-craw.
Chaffinch – shulfie.
Cuckoo – gowk.
Curlew – whaup.
Eagle – earn.
Fieldfare – skittery-feltie.
Goldfinch – gowdspink.
Greenfinch – green-lintie.
Jackdaw – kae.
Kite – gled.
Lapwing – peesweep; teuchat.
Magpie – pyat.
Owl – hoolet.
Partridge – paitrick.
Puffin – tammie-norie.
Raven – corbie.
Seagull – sea-maw.
Skylark – laverock.
Snipe – earn-bleater.
Sparrow – speug (spyug).
Starling – stirlin; stuckie.

Wood-pigeon – cushat; cushie-doo (cooshie).
Yellow-hammer – yella-yite.

TREES, PLANTS AND FLOWERS

Ash – aish.
Birch – birk.
Dahlia – dally.
Daisy – gowan.
Dandelion – bumpipe; pee-the-bed.
Elder – bourtree.
Foxglove – witches' thummles.
Hydrangea – hedereenge.
Oak – aik.
Ragwort – benweed.
Rowan – rodden.
Sorrel – soorock.
Thistle – thristle.
Wild cherry – gean.
Willow – sauch (ch as in loch).
Yellow Iris – seg.

MIXTIE-MAXTIE QUIZ

(Answers on page 77)

1. A piggie bank is so-called because of its shape. True or false?
2. If scart-free in Scots means free of scratches, scot-free will mean free of what?
3. Many a mickle maks a muckle. Right or wrong?
4. Believe it or not, old people used to take a pig to bed with them to keep themselves warm. True or false?
5. "Caller oo!" was the cry of itinerant buyers of fresh season's wool for making into "raploch", a coarse woollen cloth. True or false?
6. The merle and the blackbird,
   The laverock and the lark,
   The goldie and the gowdspink –
   How many birds is that?
7. A pibroch is a miniature bagpipe used by a learner before graduating to the bagpipe proper. True or false?
8. What metallic element was called after a place in Argyll from having been found in a leadmine there?
9. Why is Buckhaven called Buckhyne locally?
10. Whose aim was it to set up a school in every Scottish parish?
11. Why was a spinning-top called a peerie in Scotland?
12. Why was a certain kind of wedding called a penny waddin in former times?
13. What have Princes Street, Portobello, Kelvinside and a pan loaf got in common?
14. What is Edinburgh's nickname?
15. Norn was a language spoken in Orkney and Shetland till the end of the eighteenth century. True or false?
16. The unit of electricity, the watt, got its name from the Scots inventor, James Watt. True or false?

17. Is it wrang, or is it richt?
    Yestreen I saw an unco (strange) sicht –
    Pigs and grannies fleein doon
    Frae twa lumheids (chimney-heads) in a skirl o win (wind).

18. Which Scottish town does a Doonhamer come from? – and a Bairn? – and a Rid-lichtie?

19. A teuch (tyuch – tough) jean was the name commonly given in Glasgow primary schools to a hard-bitten female teacher. True or false?

20. How many of these words do you think were borrowed by English from Scots: gillie, flunkey, caddie, hostel, palliase?

21. What is the meaning of, to gie somebody his coffee?

22. "That's the end o an auld sang," said the Scottish Chancellor, The Earl of Seafield. What was the end of an auld sang?

23. This is the tree that never grew;
    This is the bird that never flew;
    This is the bell that never rang;
    And this is the fish that never swam.
    To what does this rhyme refer? Clue – a city.

24. St Johnstoun is the name sometimes given to which Scottish town?

25. What are the Daft Days in Scotland?

ANSWERS TO QUIZ

1. False. "Piggie" in Scots means made of "pig" (earthenware).
2. Tax. "Scot" here comes from the Old Norse word "skat" meaning tax.
3. Wrong. Both "mickle" and "muckle" mean the same thing – much, which renders the saying meaningless. For "mickle" read "pickle".
4. True. A pig was an earthenware hot-water bottle.
5. False. "Caller oo!" means "Fresh oysters!" and was the cry of the fishwives selling oysters in the street in the nineteenth century.
6. Three. There are two names for the same bird in each line.
7. False. The pibroch is a form of bagpipe music with variations on a theme.
8. Strontium, from Strontian in Argyll.
9. "Hyne" is the Scots word for haven.
10. John Knox's.
11. Because it is shaped like a pear (Scots "peer").
12. A penny waddin was one at which guests paid for their food and drink. One at which guests did not contribute was called a private wedding.
13. People in all three places are said to speak "pan loaf" – in other words, speak English in a highly affected manner. "Pan loaf" because that sort of loaf is always dearer than a plain one.
14. Edinburgh's nickname is Auld Reekie.
15. True. Norn is a kind of Norwegian.
16. True. Watt was born in Greenock.
17. Right. Pigs were earthenware chimney-pots. Grannies were chimney-cowls.
18. A Doonhamer from Dumfries, a Bairn from Falkirk, a Rid-lichtie from Arbroath.
19. False. A teuch jean was a lozenge made of sugar and gum in imitation of the fruit of the jujube tree.
20. All of them.

21. It means to give someone a scolding.
22. The Union of Parliaments in 1707.
23. The rhyme refers to the arms of Glasgow, consisting of a tree, a bird, a bell, and a fish.
24. Perth.
25. The twelve days from Christmas Eve to 6th January.

also by

WILLIAM GRAHAM

The Scots Word Book

An essential handbook for everyone interested in the Scots language, *The Scots Word Book* includes chapters on grammar, spelling and pronunciation, and much space is devoted to a vocabulary of Scots words in regular conversational or literary use. Of particular value is the English-Scots section which greatly simplifies the finding of comparable Scottish words and at last fills a deeply felt need.

Hardback £7.50   ISBN 0 902859 71 4

THE RAMSAY HEAD PRESS

The Scots Language:

Planning for Modern Usage

J. DERRICK McCLURE, A. J. AITKEN
JOHN THOMAS LOW

An examination of the problems involved in preserving and developing the Lowland Scottish tongue.

Hardback £3.95   ISBN 0 902859 62 5

THE RAMSAY HEAD PRESS

Introduction: Theories of myth

Let me be clear from the outset: this book is an introduction not to myths but to approaches to myth, or theories of myth, and it is limited to modern theories. Theories of myth may be as old as myths themselves. Certainly they go back at least to the Presocratics. But only in the modern era – specifically, only since the second half of the nineteenth century – have those theories purported to be scientific. For only since then have there existed the professional disciplines that have sought to supply truly scientific theories of myth: the social sciences, of which anthropology, psychology, and to a lesser extent sociology have contributed the most. Some social scientific theories of myth may have earlier counterparts, but scientific theorizing is still different from earlier theorizing. Where earlier theorizing was largely speculative and abstract, scientific theorizing is based far more on accumulated information. The differences summed up by the anthropologist John Beattie apply to the other social sciences as well:

> Thus it was the reports of eighteenth- and nineteenth-century missionaries and travellers in Africa, North America, the Pacific and elsewhere that provided the raw material upon which the first anthropological works, written in the second half of the last century, were based. Before then, of course, there had been plenty of conjecturing about human institutions and their origins ... But although their speculations were often brilliant, these thinkers were

not empirical scientists; their conclusions were not based on any kind of evidence which could be tested; rather, they were deductively argued from principles which were for the most part implicit in their own cultures. They were really philosophers and historians of Europe, not anthropologists.

(Beattie, *Other Cultures*, pp. 5-6)

Some modern theories of myth hail from the hoary disciplines of philosophy and literature, but they, too, reflect the influence of the social sciences. Even Mircea Eliade, who pits his theory from religious studies against those from the social sciences, enlists data from the social sciences to support his theory!

Each discipline harbours multiple theories of myth. Strictly, theories of myth are theories of some much larger domain, with myth a mere subset. For example, anthropological theories of myth are theories of culture *applied* to the case of myth. Psychological theories of myth are theories of the mind. Sociological theories of myth are theories of society. There are no theories of myth itself, for there is no discipline of myth in itself. Myth is not like literature, which, so it has or had traditionally been claimed, must be studied as *literature* rather than as history, sociology, or something else nonliterary. There is no study of myth as myth.

What unite the study of myth across the disciplines are the questions asked. The three main questions are those of origin, function, and subject matter. By 'origin' is meant why and how myth arises. By 'function' is meant why and how myth persists. The answer to the why of origin and function is usually a need, which myth arises to fulfil and lasts by continuing to fulfil. What the need is, varies from theory to theory. By 'subject matter' is meant the referent of myth. Some theories read myth literally, so that the referent is the straightforward, apparent one, such as gods. Other theories read myth symbolically, and the symbolized referent can be anything.

2

Theories differ not only in their answers to these questions but also in the questions they ask. Some theories, and perhaps some disciplines, concentrate on the origin of myth; others, on the function; still others, on the subject matter. Only a few theories address all three questions, and some of the theories that address origin or function deal with either 'why' or 'how' but not both.

It is commonly said that theories of the nineteenth century focused on the question of origin and that theories of the twentieth century have focused on the questions of function and subject matter. But this characterization confuses historical origin with recurrent origin. Theories that profess to provide the origin of myth claim to know not where and when myth first arose but why and how myth arises wherever and whenever it does. The issue of recurrent origin has been as popular with twentieth-century theories as with nineteenth-century ones, and interest in function and subject matter was as common to nineteenth-century theories as to twentieth-century ones.

There is one genuine difference between nineteenth- and twentieth-century theories. Nineteenth-century theories tended to see the subject matter of myth as the natural world and to see the function of myth as either a literal explanation or a symbolic description of that world. Myth was typically taken to be the 'primitive' counterpart to science, which was assumed to be wholly modern. Science rendered myth not merely redundant but outright incompatible, so that moderns, who by definition are scientific, had to reject myth. By contrast, twentieth-century theories have tended to see myth as almost anything but an outdated counterpart to science, either in subject matter or in function. Consequently, moderns are not obliged to abandon myth for science.

Besides the questions of origin, function, and subject matter, questions often asked about myth include: is myth universal? is

myth true? The answers to these questions stem from the answers to the first three questions. A theory which contends that myth arises and functions to explain natural processes will likely restrict myth to societies supposedly bereft of science. By contrast, a theory which contends that myth arises and functions to unify society may well deem myth acceptable and perhaps even indispensable to all societies.

A theory which maintains that myth functions to explain natural processes is committed to the falsity of myth if the explanation given proves incompatible with a scientific one. A theory which maintains that myth functions to unify society may circumvent the issue of truth by asserting that society is unified when its members *believe* that the laws they are expected to obey were established long ago by revered ancestors, whether or not those laws really were established back then. This kind of theory sidesteps the question of truth because its answers to the questions of origin and function do.

Definition of myth

I have attended many a conference at which speakers fervently propound on 'the nature of myth' in novel X or play Y or film Z. Yet so much of the argument depends on the definition of myth. Let me make explicit my own proposed one.

To begin with, I propose defining myth as a story. That myth, whatever else it is, is a story may seem self-evident. After all, when asked to name myths, most of us think first of *stories* about Greek and Roman gods and heroes. Yet myth can also be taken more broadly as a belief or credo – for example, the American 'rags to riches myth' and the American 'myth of the frontier'. Horatio Alger wrote scores of popular novels illustrating the rags to riches myth, but the credo itself does not rest on a story. The same is true of the myth of the frontier.

4

All of the theories considered in this book deem myth a story. True, E. B. Tylor turns the story into a tacit argument, but the argument is still conveyed by a story. True, Claude Lévi-Strauss ventures beyond the story to the 'structure' of myth, but again the structure is conveyed by the story. Theories that read myth symbolically rather than literally still take the subject matter, or the meaning, to be the unfolding of a story.

If, then, myth is to be taken here as a story, what is the story about? For folklorists above all, myth is about the creation of the world. In the Bible only the two creation stories (Genesis 1 and 2), the Garden of Eden story (Genesis 3), and the Noah story (Genesis 6–9) would thereby qualify as myths. All the other stories would instead constitute either legends or folk tales. Outside the Bible the Oedipus 'myth', for example, would actually be a legend. I do not propose being so rigid and will instead define myth as simply a story about something significant. The story can take place in the past, as for Eliade and for Bronislaw Malinowski, or in the present or the future.

For theories from, above all, religious studies, the main characters in myth must be gods or near-gods. Here, too, I do not propose being so rigid. If I were, I would have to exclude most of the Hebrew Bible, in which all the stories may *involve* God but, apart from only the first two chapters of Genesis, are at least as much about human beings as about God. I will insist only that the main figures be personalities – divine, human, or even animal. Excluded would be impersonal forces such as Plato's Good. Among theorists, Tylor is the most preoccupied with the personalistic nature of myth, but all the other theorists to be discussed assume it – with the exception of Lévi-Strauss. At the same time the personalities can be either the agents or the objects of actions.

Save for Rudolf Bultmann and Hans Jonas, all of the theorists considered address the function of myth, and Malinowski focuses on it almost exclusively. Theorists differ over what the function of myth is. I do not propose to dictate what the function of myth must somehow

be. I note only that for all the theorists the function is weighty – in contrast to the lighter functions of legend and folk tale. I thereby propose that myth accomplishes something significant for adherents, but I leave open-ended what that accomplishment might be.

In today's parlance, myth is false. Myth is 'mere' myth. For example, in 1997 historian William Rubinstein published *The Myth of Rescue: Why the Democracies Could Not Have Saved More Jews from the Nazis*. The title says it all. The book challenges the common conviction that many Jewish victims of the Nazis could have been saved if only the Allies had committed themselves to rescuing them. Rubinstein is challenging the assumption that the Allies were indifferent to the fate of European Jews and were indifferent because they were anti-Semitic. For him, the term 'myth' captures the sway of the conviction about the failure to rescue more fully than would tamer phrases like 'erroneous belief' and 'popular misconception'. A 'myth' is a conviction false yet tenacious.

By contrast, the phrase 'rags to riches myth' uses the term myth positively yet still conveys the hold of the conviction. A blatantly false conviction might seem to have a stronger hold than a true one, for the conviction remains firm even in the face of its transparent falsity. But a cherished conviction that is true can be clutched as tightly as a false one, especially when supported by persuasive evidence. Ironically, some Americans who continue to espouse the rags to riches credo may no longer refer to it as a 'myth' because the term has *come* to connote falsity. I propose that, to qualify as a myth, a story, which can of course express a conviction, be held tenaciously by adherents. But I leave open-ended whether the story must in fact be true.

The myth of Adonis

In order to drive home the differences among theories, I propose taking a familiar myth – that of Adonis – and showing how it looks from the standpoint of the theories discussed. I choose this myth,

first, because it is extant in such varying versions, thereby showing the malleability of myth. The main sources of the myth are the Greek Apollodorus' *Library* (Book III, chapter 14, paragraphs 3–4) and the Roman Ovid's *Metamorphoses* (Book X, lines 298–739).

According to Apollodorus, who himself cites a version of the story from the epic poet Panyasis, Adonis' mother, Smyrna, was irresistibly attracted to her father and became pregnant with his child. When her father discovered that it was Smyrna with whom he was nightly having sex, he immediately drew his sword, she fled, and he pursued her. On the verge of being overtaken, she prayed to the gods to become invisible, and they, taking pity, turned her into a myrrh (smyrna) tree. Ten months later the tree burst open, and Adonis was born.

Even as an infant, Adonis was preternaturally beautiful, and Aphrodite, who apparently had kept watch over him, was irresistibly smitten with him, just as Smyrna had been with her father. To have him all to herself, Aphrodite hid Adonis in a chest. When Persephone, queen of the Underworld (Hades), opened the chest, which Aphrodite had entrusted to her without revealing its contents, she too fell in love with Adonis and refused to return him to Aphrodite. Each goddess wanted Adonis exclusively for herself. The king of the gods, Zeus, was appealed to by both sides, and he ruled that Adonis should spend a third of the year with Persephone, a third with Aphrodite, and a third alone. Adonis readily conceded his third to Aphrodite and was thereby never outside the custody of a goddess. One day, while hunting, he was gored to death by a boar. According to another, unnamed version of the story recounted by Apollodorus, the goring was the work of Ares, god of war, who was angry at having been bested by Adonis as the lover of Aphrodite.

Ovid similarly takes the story of Adonis back to incest between his mother, Myrrha, and her father, here Cinyras. Myrrha was on the

point of hanging herself to be free from her distress when she was saved by her old nurse, who pried loose the source of Myrrha's despair and, as in Apollodorus, arranged for Myrrha to bed her father without discovery. But when, on the third night, he called for light to discover who it was who loved him so, he, as in Apollodorus, drew his sword and she fled. For nine months the pregnant Myrrha wandered. Also as in Apollodorus, the worn-out Myrrha prayed and was turned by the pitying gods into a tree – though here at the end, not the beginning, of her pregnancy. Yet Myrrha remained human enough to weep, and from her tears came the perfume myrrh. The baby, still alive in her, had to fight its way out of the tree to be born.

In Ovid, in contrast to Apollodorus, Venus (the Roman name for Aphrodite) encountered Adonis only as a young man but was likewise immediately smitten. There was no rivalry with other goddesses, so that Venus had him all to herself. They went hunting together. While Venus continually warned him to stick to small game, he heedlessly took on big game and, as in Apollodorus' version, was gored to death by a boar, though not one sent by any rival for Venus' love.

Where Apollodorus' story ends with Adonis' death, Ovid's continues with Venus' mourning for him. As a memorial, she sprinkled nectar over his blood, from which sprouted the flower anemone. Like Adonis, it is short-lived.

Where for Apollodorus the annual cycle of death and rebirth *antedates* Adonis' 'final' death, for Ovid the annual cycle, in the form of the flower, *follows* Adonis' death. The planting of the flower anticipates the ritual associated with the myth of Adonis – a connection absent from Apollodorus.

Where for Apollodorus the main spur to events is anger, for Ovid it is love. Where for Apollodorus Adonis is the innocent victim of warring parents and of rival deities, for Ovid the inconsolable Aphrodite is as much the victim as Adonis.

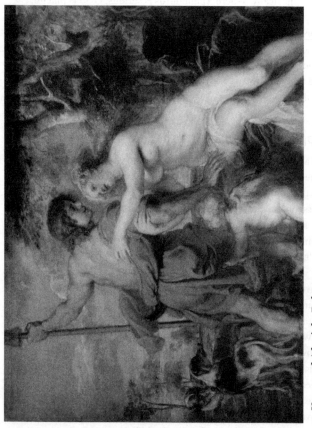

1. *Venus and Adonis* by Rubens

Where Apollodorus presents the story as true, Ovid presents it as fictional. Where Apollodorus tells it straight, Ovid twists it to fit larger themes – notably, that of transformation, as in Myrrha's becoming a tree and Adonis' becoming a flower. Where Apollodorus intends his story to be taken literally, Ovid intends his to be read metaphorically. Where Apollodorus is serious, Ovid is playful.

I propose using the myth of Adonis not only because it is extant in versions so disparate but also because it has proved so popular with modern theorists of myth. It has been analysed by J. G. Frazer, by the then-Lévi-Straussian Marcel Detienne, and by C. G. Jung and his followers.

Applying theories to myths

To analyse a myth is to analyse it from the viewpoint of some theory. Theorizing is inescapable. For example, handbooks of classical mythology that matter-of-factly connect Adonis' annual trek to Persephone and return to Aphrodite with the course of vegetation presuppose a view of myth as the primitive counterpart to science. Being sceptical of the universality of any theory is one thing. Being able to sidestep theorizing altogether is another.

Theories need myths as much as myths need theories. If theories illuminate myths, myths confirm theories. True, the sheer applicability of a myth does not itself confirm the theory, the tenets of which must be established in their own right. For example, to show that Jung's theory, when applied, elucidates the myth of Adonis would not itself establish the existence of a collective unconscious, which, on the contrary, would be presupposed. But one, albeit indirect, way of confirming a theory is to show how well it works *when* its tenets are assumed – this on the grounds that the theory must be either false or limited if it turns out not to work.

Chapter 1
Myth and science

In the West the challenge to myth goes back at least to Plato, who rejected Homeric myth on, especially, ethical grounds. It was above all the Stoics who defended myth against this charge by reinterpreting it allegorically. The chief modern challenge to myth has come not from ethics but from science. Here myth is assumed to explain how gods control the physical world rather than, as for Plato, how they behave among themselves. Where Plato bemoans myths for presenting the gods as practitioners of immoral behaviour, modern critics dismiss myth for explaining the world unscientifically.

Myth as true science

One form of the modern challenge to myth has been to the scientific credibility of myth. Did creation really occur in a mere six days, as the first of two creation stories in Genesis (1:1–2:4a) claims? Was there really a worldwide flood? Is the earth truly but six or seven thousand years old? Could the ten plagues on the Egyptians actually have happened? The most unrepentant defence against this challenge has been to claim that the biblical account is correct, for, after all, the Pentateuch was revealed to Moses by God. This position, known as 'creationism', assumes varying forms, ranging, for example, from taking the days of creation to mean exactly six days to taking them to mean 'ages'. Creationism arose in reaction to

Darwin's *Origin of Species* (1859), which contends that species gradually emerged out of one another rather than being created separately and virtually simultaneously. Surprisingly, creationism has become ever more, not ever less, uncompromisingly literalist in its rendition of the biblical account of creation.

At the same time creationists of all stripes vaunt their views as scientific *as well as* religious, not as religious *rather than* scientific. 'Creationism' is shorthand for 'creation science', which appropriates scientific evidence of any kind both to bolster its own claims and to refute those of secular rivals like evolution. Doubtless 'creation scientists' would object to the term 'myth' to characterize the view they defend, but only because the term has come to connote false belief. If the term is used neutrally for a staunchly held conviction, creationism is a myth that claims to be scientific. For creation scientists, it is evolution that is untenable scientifically. In any clash between the Bible and modern science, modern science must give way to biblical science, not vice versa.

Myth as modern science

A much tamer defence against the challenge of modern science has been to reconcile myth with that science. Here elements at odds with modern science are either removed or, more cleverly, reinterpreted as in fact modern and scientific. Myth is credible scientifically because it *is* science – modern science. There might not have been a Noah able singlehandedly to gather up all living species and to keep them alive in a wooden boat sturdy enough to withstand the strongest seas that ever arose, but a worldwide flood did occur. What thus remains in myth is true because scientific. This approach is the opposite of that called 'demythologizing', which *separates* myth from science. Demythologizing will be considered in the next chapter.

In their comment on the first plague, the turning of the waters of the Nile into blood (Exodus 7:14–24), the editors of the *Oxford*

Annotated Bible epitomize this rationalizing approach: 'The plague of blood apparently reflects a natural phenomenon of Egypt: namely, the reddish color of the Nile at its height in the summer owing to red particles of earth or perhaps minute organisms.' Of the second plague, that of frogs (Exodus 8:1–15), the editors declare similarly: 'The mud of the Nile, after the seasonal overflowing, was a natural place for frogs to generate. Egypt has been spared more frequent occurrence of this pestilence by the frog-eating bird, the ibis.' How fortuitous that the ibis must have been on holiday when Aaron stretched out his hand to produce the plague and must have just returned when Moses wanted the plague to cease! Instead of setting myth *against* science, this tactic turns myth *into* science – and not, as is fashionable today, science into myth.

Myth as primitive science

By far the most common response to the challenge of science has been to abandon myth for science. Here myth, while still an explanation of the world, is now taken as an explanation of its own kind, not a scientific explanation in mythic guise. The issue is therefore not the scientific credibility of myth but the compatibility of myth with science. Myth is considered to be 'primitive' science – or, more precisely, the pre-scientific counterpart to science, which is assumed to be exclusively modern. Myth is here part of religion. Where religion apart from myth provides the sheer belief in gods, myth fills in the details of how gods cause events. Because myth is part of religion, the rise of science as the reigning modern explanation of physical events has consequently spelled the fall of not only religion but also myth. Because moderns by definition accept science, they cannot also have myth, and the phrase 'modern myth' is self-contradictory. Myth is a victim of the process of secularization that constitutes modernity.

The relationship between religion and science has actually been anything but uniform, and works with tendentious titles like *A*

13

History of the Warfare of Science with Theology in Christendom
express a one-sided viewpoint. Still, religion and science, and so
myth and science, were more regularly opposed in the nineteenth
century than in the twentieth century, when they have more often
been reconciled.

E. B. Tylor

The pioneering English anthropologist E. B. Tylor (1832–1917)
remains the classic exponent of the view that myth and science are
at odds. Tylor subsumes myth under religion and in turn subsumes
both religion and science under philosophy. He divides philosophy
into 'primitive' and 'modern'. Primitive philosophy is identical
with primitive religion. There is no primitive science. Modern
philosophy, by contrast, has two subdivisions: religion and science.
Of the two, science is by far the more important and is the modern
counterpart to primitive religion. Modern religion is composed of
two elements – metaphysics and ethics – neither of which is present
in primitive religion. Metaphysics deals with nonphysical entities,
of which 'primitives' have no conception. Ethics is not absent from
primitive culture, but it falls outside primitive religion: 'the
conjunction of ethics and Animistic philosophy, so intimate and
powerful in the higher culture, seems scarcely yet to have begun in
the lower' . Tylor uses the term 'animism' for religion per se, modern
and primitive alike, because he derives the belief in gods from the
belief in souls (*anima* in Latin means soul). In primitive religion
souls occupy all physical entities, beginning with the bodies of
humans. Gods are the souls in all physical entities *except* humans,
who themselves are not gods.

Primitive religion is the primitive counterpart to science because
both are explanations of the physical world. Tylor thus characterizes
primitive religion as 'savage biology' and maintains that
'mechanical astronomy gradually superseded the animistic
astronomy of the lower races' and that today 'biological pathology
gradually supersedes animistic pathology'. The religious

2. E. B. Tylor, by G. Bonavia

explanation is personalistic: the decisions of gods explain events.
The scientific explanation is impersonal: mechanical laws explain
events. The sciences as a whole have replaced religion as the
explanation of the physical world, so that 'animistic astronomy' and
'animistic pathology' refer only to primitive, not modern, animism.
Modern religion has surrendered the physical world to science and
has retreated to the immaterial world, especially to the realm of life
after death – that is, of the life of the soul after the death of the
body. Where in primitive religion souls are deemed material, in
modern religion they are deemed immaterial and are limited to
human beings:

> In our own day and country, the notion of souls of beasts is to be
> seen dying out. Animism, indeed, seems to be drawing in its
> outposts, and concentrating itself on its first and main position,
> the doctrine of the human soul.... The soul has given up its
> ethereal substance, and become an immaterial entity, 'the shadow

15

of a shade.' Its theory is becoming separated from the investigations of biology and mental science, which now discuss the phenomena of life and thought, the senses and the intellect, the emotions and the will, on a ground-work of pure experience. There has arisen an intellectual product whose very existence is of the deepest significance, a 'psychology' which has no longer anything to do with 'soul.' The soul's place in modern thought is in the metaphysics of religion, and its especial office there is that of furnishing an intellectual side to the religious doctrine of the future.

(Tylor, *Primitive Culture*, vol. II, p. 85)

Similarly, where in primitive religion gods are deemed material, in modern religion they are deemed immaterial. Gods thereby cease to be agents in the physical world – Tylor assumes that physical effects must have physical causes – and religion ceases to be an explanation of the physical world. Gods are relocated from the physical world to the social world. They become models for humans, just as they should be for Plato. One now turns to the Bible to learn ethics, not physics. One reads the Bible not for the story of creation but for the Ten Commandments, just as for Plato a bowdlerized Homer would enable one to do. Jesus is to be emulated as the ideal human, not as a miracle worker. The epitome of this view was expressed by the Victorian cultural critic Matthew Arnold.

This irenic position is also like that of the late evolutionary biologist Stephen Jay Gould, for whom science, above all evolution, is compatible with religion because the two never intersect. Science explains the physical world; religion prescribes ethics and gives meaning to life:

> Science tries to document the factual character of the natural world, and to develop theories that coordinate and explain these facts. Religion, on the other hand, operates in the equally important, but utterly different, realm of human purposes, meanings, and values.

(Gould, *Rocks of Ages*, p. 4)

exemplar of Tylor's position is the American anthropologist David Bidney.

One reason Tylor pits myth against science is that he subsumes myth under religion. For him, there is no myth outside religion, even though modern religion is without myth. Because primitive religion is the counterpart to science, myth must be as well. Because religion is to be taken literally, so must myth be.

Another reason Tylor pits myth against science is that he reads myth literally. He opposes those who read myth symbolically, poetically, or metaphorically – for him, interchangeable terms. He opposes the 'moral allegorizers', for whom the myth of Helios' daily driving his chariot across the sky is a way of instilling self-discipline. Likewise he opposes the 'euhemerists', for whom the myth is simply a colourful way of describing the exploits of some local or national hero. (Euhemerus was an ancient Greek mythographer who established the tradition of seeking an actual historical basis for mythical events.) For Tylor, the myth of Helios is an explanation of why the sun rises and sets, and the explanatory function *requires* a literal reading. For both the allegorizers and the euhemerists, myth is not the primitive counterpart to science because, read symbolically, it is about human beings rather than about gods or the world. For the allegorizers, it is also unscientific because, read symbolically, it prescribes how humans ought to behave rather than explains how they do behave.

As interpretations of myth, moral allegory and euhemerism alike go back to ancient times, but Tylor sees contemporary exponents of both as motivated by a desire to preserve myth in the face of the distinctively modern challenge of science. While Tylor dismisses as 'euhemerists' those who interpret gods as mere metaphors for human beings, ancient euhemerists themselves conventionally granted that gods, once postulated, were interpreted as gods and merely argued that gods *arose* from the magnification of humans, as Tylor himself allows. Ancient euhemerists maintained that the first

gods were really great kings, who were deified after their deaths. Euhemerus himself maintained that the first gods were kings deified during their lives.

Opposite to Tylor stands his fellow Victorian, the German-born Sanskritist Friedrich Max Müller (1823–1900), who spent his career at Oxford. Where for Tylor moderns misread myth by taking it symbolically, for Müller ancients themselves eventually came to misread their own myths, or mythical data, by gradually taking them literally. Originally symbolic descriptions of natural phenomena came to be read as literal descriptions of the attributes of gods. For example, the sea described poetically as 'raging' was eventually taken as the characteristic of the personality responsible for the sea, and a myth was then invented to account for this characteristic. Mythology for Müller stems from the absence or near-absence in ancient languages of abstract nouns and of a neuter gender. Thus any name given the sun – say, 'the giver of warmth' – invariably turned an abstract, impersonal entity into an actual personality, and later generations invented myths to fill in the life of this male or female god.

A Tylorian approach to Adonis would see the myth as an explanation – for its own sake – of something striking that has been observed. For Tylor, Apollodorus' and Ovid's versions would offer an account of the origin of myrrh. Ovid's would, in addition, offer an account of the origin of the flower anemone. Further, Ovid's would account for the notable brevity of the lifespan of the flower, which would be symbolic of Adonis'. If one could generalize from the anemone to flowers and other vegetation, the myth could be explaining why these entities do not just die but also get reborn. For Tylor, Adonis would have to be a god, not a human being, and the myth would have to be attributing the annual course of flowers and of vegetation as a whole to his annual trip to Hades and back. Adonis' final death would be ignored. The stress would be on Adonis' power to control the natural entities for which he was responsible. The payoff of the myth would be wholly intellectual:

one would know why crops behave so quirkily – dying and then coming back to life, and not once but forever.

Yet the myth itself does not connect Adonis' annual trip to the course of vegetation, though the ritual of planting seeds in the quick-growing and quick-dying 'gardens of Adonis' does. And even if the myth did link the trip to the course of vegetation, the effect on vegetation would come not from any decision on Adonis' part, as Tylor would require, but as the automatic consequence of his actions.

Moreover, much in the myth would still be left out. Tylor's theory simply cannot cover the issues of incest, love, jealousy, and sexuality. More precisely, it can do so only as motives on the part of Adonis. But in the myth they are, rather, motives on the parts of the figures around him. He himself is more passive object than agent. And however miraculous the events in Adonis' life, he is still just a human being, not a god. Overall, the myth seems interested more in his relations with others than in either his or their impact on the physical world.

Tylor's theory seems geared more to a myth that is explicitly an account of the creation and, even better, the ongoing operation of physical phenomena. Take Genesis 1, which for Tylor would easily qualify as a myth by this criterion. To cite a few passages:

> And God said, 'Let the waters under the heavens be gathered together into one place, and let the dry land appear.' And it was so. God called the dry land Earth, and the waters that were gathered together he called Seas. And God saw that it was good.
>
> (Genesis 1:9–10 [Revised Standard Version])

> And God said, 'Let the waters bring forth swarms of living creatures, and let birds fly above the earth across the firmament of the heavens.' So God created the great sea monsters and every living creature that moves, with which the waters swarm, according to

their kinds, and every winged bird according to its kind. And God
saw that it was good.

(Genesis 1:20–21)

Then God said, 'Let us make man in our image, after our likeness; and
let them have dominion over the fish of the sea, and over the birds of
the air, and over the cattle, and over all the earth, and over every
creeping thing that creeps upon the earth.' So God created man in his
own image, in the image of God he created him; male and female he
created them. And God blessed them, and God said to them, 'Be
fruitful and multiply, and fill the earth and subdue it' . . . And God saw
everything that he had made, and behold, it was very good.

(Genesis 1:26–31)

Tylor's theory would better fit those elements of the world that not
merely are set in order once and for all, such as dry land and seas,
but also recur, such as rainfall, the change of seasons, and (in the
story of Noah) the rainbow. Genesis 1 covers many recurrent
phenomena: day and night, sun and moon, and all living things.
Still, Tylor's theory would require that recurring phenomena come
from the recurring decisions of gods. For Tylor, gods are to the
physical world as humans are to the social world: each time they
decide anew to do the same thing. They do not set up things that
simply carry on, the way gods do for such theorists as Bronislaw
Malinowski and Eliade.

What of phenomena that have never been observed, such as sea
monsters? How can myth serve to account for them? Tylor's easy
answer would surely be that the creators of Genesis assumed that
somebody had seen, or assumed to have seen, them. Sea monsters
would be no different from UFOs.

Even if Tylor's theory fitted snugly the process of creation in Genesis 1,
much of the myth would remain beyond the ken of the theory. The myth
does not just explain creation but also evaluates it, continually
pronouncing it good. Because Tylor so insistently parallels myth to

science, he allows no room in myth for morality, as his objection to the moral allegorizers attests. For him, Genesis 1 should merely explain, not assess, creation. Similarly, the story does not just explain the creation of human beings but also elevates them above the rest of creation, according them at once the right and the duty to oversee the physical world. If, further, the 'image' of God in which humans are created is more than anatomical, then here, too, Tylor's theory falls short.

Finally, even if Tylor's theory worked, what would it illuminate? It is one thing for a theory to fit a myth. It is another for a theory to elucidate whatever it fits. What would Tylor's theory tell us that we would not know without it? One could not, in fairness, ask of Tylor what a myth *means*, for Tylor stands committed to a literal rendition of myth: a myth means what it says. Tylor's contribution would be to the origin and the function of myth. Genesis 1, he would contend, arose not from wild speculations about the world but from steady observations about recurrent, if still striking, natural processes that call for an explanation. Tylor would find an appreciative audience among creationists – not because he would consider Genesis 1 the correct account of the origin of the world but because he would consider it *an* account, and a distinctively religious one. Tylor would offer a corrective to those twentieth-century theologians who, intent on making the Bible palatable to moderns, maintain that Genesis 1 is anything but an account of creation – a view like that of Rudolf Bultmann on the New Testament, as we shall see in the next chapter.

J. G. Frazer

Tylor's is but one view of the relationship between myth and science, or between religion and science. Closest to Tylor stands J. G. Frazer (1854–1941), the Scottish-born, Cambridge-affiliated classicist and fellow pioneering anthropologist. For Frazer, as for Tylor, myth is part of primitive religion; primitive religion is part of philosophy, itself universal; and primitive religion is the counterpart to natural science, itself entirely modern. Primitive

religion and science are, as for Tylor, mutually exclusive. Primitive religion is false, science true. But where for Tylor primitive religion, including myth, functions as the counterpart to scientific *theory*, for Frazer it functions even more as the counterpart to *applied* science, or technology. Where for Tylor primitive religion serves to *explain* events in the physical world, for Frazer it serves even more to *effect* events, above all the growth of crops. Where Tylor treats myth as an autonomous text, Frazer ties myth to ritual, which enacts it.

Frazer takes the myth of Adonis as one of the main examples, for him, of the chief myth among all mythologies: the biography of the chief god, the god of vegetation. For Frazer, the myth of Adonis would have been acted out, and that ritualistic enactment would have been believed to work magically to effect whatever had been acted out. To have acted act out the resurfacing of Adonis would have been to effect it and in turn the resurfacing of the crops. The myth would have served not simply to explain why the crops had died – they had died because Adonis, in descending to the land of the dead, had died – but actually to revive the crops. For Frazer, the payoff of myth could scarcely have been more practical: avoiding starvation. Frazer's interpretation of Adonis will be considered in detail in Chapter 4.

The biggest difficulty for Tylor's and Frazer's view of myth as the primitive counterpart to science is that it conspicuously fails to account for the retention of myth in the wake of science. If myth functions to do no more than science, why is it still around? Of course, Tylor and Frazer could promptly reply that whatever remains is not myth, and exactly because it is not serving a scientific-like function. By contrast, the contemporary German philosopher Hans Blumenberg (1920–96) maintains that the survival of myth alongside science proves that myth has *never* served the same function as science. Yet neither Blumenberg nor Tylor and Frazer ever explain why myth, or religion as a whole, is still invoked *alongside* science to explain physical events.

For example, whenever a handful of passengers survives a plane crash, the crash itself gets explained scientifically, but the survival often gets credited to intervention by God and not to, say, the location of the seats. Tylor and Frazer would doubtless reply that the survivors have simply not faced up to the incompatibility of their religious explanation with a scientific one, but this appeal to consistency is apparently outweighed by some more pressing need that only a religious explanation can fulfil.

Lucien Lévy-Bruhl

Reacting against the views of Tylor, Frazer, and other members of what he imprecisely calls 'the English school of anthropology', the French philosopher and armchair anthropologist Lucien Lévy-Bruhl (1857–1939) insisted on a much wider divide between myth and science. Where for Tylor and Frazer primitives think like moderns, just less rigorously, for Lévy-Bruhl primitives think differently from moderns. Where for Tylor and Frazer primitive thinking is logical, just erroneous, for Lévy-Bruhl primitive thinking is plainly nonlogical—or, in his preferred term, 'prelogical'.

According to Lévy-Bruhl, primitives believe not, as for Tylor, that all natural phenomena possess individual, human-like souls, or gods, but that all phenomena, including humans and their artefacts, are part of an impersonal sacred, or 'mystic', realm pervading the natural one. Primitives believe, further, that the 'participation' of all things in this mystic reality enables phenomena not only to affect one another magically but also to become one another, yet remain what they are: 'objects, beings, phenomena can be, though in a way incomprehensible to us [moderns], both themselves and something other than themselves'. The Bororo of Brazil declare themselves red araras, or parakeets, yet still human beings. Lévy-Bruhl calls this belief prelogical because it violates the law of noncontradiction: the notion that something can simultaneously be both itself and something else.

Where for Tylor and Frazer myth involves the same processes of observation, inference, and generalization as science, or at least of science as they think of it, for Lévy-Bruhl mythic thinking is the opposite of scientific thinking. Where for Tylor and Frazer primitives *perceive* the same world as moderns but simply *conceive* of it differently, for Lévy-Bruhl primitives see and in turn conceptualize the world differently from moderns – namely, as identical with themselves.

For Lévy-Bruhl, as for Tylor and Frazer, myth is part of religion, religion is primitive, and moderns have science rather than religion. But where Tylor and Frazer subsume both religion and science under philosophy, Lévy-Bruhl associates philosophy with thinking freed from mystical identification with the world. Primitive thinking is nonphilosophical because it is not detached from the world. Primitives have a whole mentality of their own, one evinced in their myths.

Even the use to which myth is put is for Lévy-Bruhl one of emotional involvement rather than, as for Tylor and Frazer, one of intellectual detachment. Primitives use religion, especially myth, not to explain or to control the world but instead to commune with it – more precisely, to restore the 'mystic' communion that has gradually begun to fade:

> Where the participation of the individual in the social group is still directly felt, where the participation of the group with surrounding groups is actually lived – that is, as long as the period of mystic symbiosis lasts – myths are meagre in number and of poor quality. . . . Can myths then likewise be the products of primitive mentality which appear when this mentality is endeavouring to realize a participation no longer felt – when it has recourse to intermediaries, and vehicles designed to secure a communion which has ceased to be a living reality?

> (Lévy-Bruhl, *How Natives Think*, p. 330)

Myth

Presented with the myth of Adonis, Lévy-Bruhl would surely focus on Adonis' mystic relationship to the world. Ovid's Adonis is oblivious to all warnings about the dangers of the world because he imagines himself at home in the world, and at home because one with the world. He is unable to resist the goddesses because he sees them as his mother, with whom he seeks not intercourse but womb-like absorption. Between him and the goddesses there exists the primordial state of oneness that Lévy-Bruhl calls *participation mystique*.

Bronislaw Malinowski

One reaction to Lévy-Bruhl was to reassert the philosophical nature of myth – a reaction to be considered in the next chapter. The key theorists here were Paul Radin and Ernst Cassirer. Another reaction was to accept Lévy-Bruhl's separation of myth from philosophy but not his characterization of myth as pre-philosophical or pre-scientific. The key figure here was the Polish-born anthropologist Bronislaw Malinowski (1884–1942), who early on moved to England. Where Lévy-Bruhl asserts that primitives seek to commune with nature rather than to explain it, Malinowski asserts that primitives seek to control nature rather than to explain it. Both associate a philosophical approach with an explanatory, or intellectualist, one, and both associate that view with the British – for Malinowski, with Tylor but not also with Frazer. Both attribute this contrived notion of myth and, in general, of religion to a contrived notion of primitives.

Invoking Frazer, for whom myth and religion are the primitive counterpart to applied science, Malinowski argues that primitives are too busy scurrying to survive in the world to have the luxury of reflecting on it. Where for Frazer primitives use myth *in place of* science, which, again, is exclusively modern, for Malinowski primitives use myth as a *fallback* to science. Primitives possess not just the counterpart to science but science itself:

If by science be understood a body of rules and conceptions, based on experience and derived from it by logical inference, embodied in material achievements and in a fixed form of tradition and carried on by some sort of social organization – then there is no doubt that even the lowest savage communities have the beginnings of science, however rudimentary.

(Malinowski, 'Magic, Science and Religion', p. 34)

Primitives use science to control the physical world. Where science stops, they turn to magic.

Where magic stops, primitives turn to myth – not to secure further control over the world, as Frazer would assume, but the opposite: to reconcile themselves to aspects of the world that cannot be controlled, such as natural catastrophes, illness, ageing, and death. Myths, which are not limited to religion, root these woes in the irreversible, primordial actions of either gods or humans. According to a typical myth, humans age because two forebears did something foolish that introduced old age irremediably into the world:

The longed-for power of eternal youth and the faculty of rejuvenation which gives immunity from decay and age, have been lost by a small accident which it would have been in the power of a child and a woman to prevent.

(Malinowski, 'Myth in Primitive Psychology', p. 137)

Myth explains how, say, flooding arose – a god or a human brought it about – but primitive science and magic try to do something about it. By contrast, myth says that nothing can be done about it. Myths that serve to resign primitives to the uncontrollable are about physical phenomena. Myths about *social* phenomena, such as customs and laws, serve to persuade primitives to accept what *can* be resisted, as will be considered in Chapter 8.

What would Malinowski say of the myth of Adonis? He would likely concentrate on the myth as an expression of the ineluctability of

death for all, would see Adonis as a human and not a god, and would take Adonis' obliviousness to his mortality as a lesson for others. But Malinowski's theory would truly work only if the myth *accounted for* mortality rather than presupposed it. Myth for Malinowski – and, as we shall see, for Eliade – is about origins. Malinowski would be left with Ovid's version of the myth as an elongated account of the flower anemone, and Malinowski would have to show that the flower mattered to the lives of ancient Greeks or Romans. Like Tylor, he would take the myth literally.

Claude Lévi-Strauss

Reacting both against Malinowski's view of primitives as practical rather than intellectual and against Lévy-Bruhl's view of primitives as emotional rather than intellectual, the French structural anthropologist Claude Lévi-Strauss (b. 1908) has boldly sought to revive an intellectualist view of primitives and of myth. At first glance Lévi-Strauss seems a sheer throwback to Tylor. For myth for Lévi-Strauss, just as for Tylor, is at once an exclusively primitive, yet nevertheless rigorously intellectual, enterprise. In declaring that primitives, 'moved by a need or a desire to understand the world around them, . . . proceed by intellectual means, exactly as a philosopher, or even to some extent a scientist, can and would do', Lévi-Strauss seems indistinguishable from Tylor.

Yet in fact Lévi-Strauss is severely critical of Tylor, for whom primitives create myth rather than science because they think less critically than moderns. For Lévi-Strauss, primitives create myth because they think differently from moderns – but, contrary to Lévy-Bruhl, still think and still think rigorously. For both Tylor and Lévi-Strauss, myth is the epitome of primitive thinking.

Where for Tylor primitive thinking is personalistic and modern thinking impersonal, for Lévi-Strauss primitive thinking is concrete and modern thinking abstract. Primitive thinking deals with phenomena qualitatively rather than, like modern thinking,

quantitatively. It focuses on the observable, sensible aspects of phenomena rather than, like modern thinking, on the unobservable, insensible ones:

> For these men [i.e. primitives] . . . the world is made up of minerals, plants, animals, noises, colors, textures, flavors, odors. . . . What separates the savage thought from [modern] scientific thought is perfectly clear – and it is not a greater or lesser thirst for logic. Myths manipulate those qualities of perception that modern thought, at the birth of modern science, exorcised from science.
>
> (Lévi-Strauss, in André Akoun et al., 'A Conversation with Claude Lévi-Strauss', p. 39)

Yet antithetically to Tylor, Lévi-Strauss considers myth no less scientific than modern science. Myth is simply part of the 'science of the concrete' rather than of the science of the abstract:

> [T]here are two distinct modes of scientific thought. These are certainly not a function of different stages of the human mind but rather of two strategic levels at which nature is accessible to scientific enquiry: one roughly adapted to that of perception and the imagination: the other at a remove from it.
>
> (Lévi-Strauss, *The Savage Mind*, p. 15)

Where for Tylor myth is the primitive counterpart to science per se, for Lévi-Strauss myth is the primitive counterpart to *modern* science. Myth *is* primitive science, but not thereby inferior science.

If myth is an instance of primitive thinking because it deals with concrete, tangible phenomena, it is an instance of thinking itself because it classifies phenomena. Lévi-Strauss maintains that all humans think in the form of classifications, specifically pairs of oppositions, and project them onto the world. Many cultural phenomena express these oppositions. Myth is distinctive in resolving or, more accurately, tempering the oppositions it expresses. Where for Tylor myth is like science precisely because it

30

goes beyond observation to explanation, for Lévi-Strauss myth is outright scientific because it goes beyond the recording of observed contradictions to the tempering of them. Those contradictions are to be found not in the plot or myth but in what Lévi-Strauss famously calls the 'structure', and the approach to myth that is thereby called 'structuralist' will be accorded a chapter of its own, Chapter 7, in which the myth of Adonis will be analysed at length.

Robin Horton

Tylor's preoccupation with mythic and religious explanations as personalistic and with scientific explanations as impersonal has been challenged by the English anthropologist Robin Horton (b. 1932), who has spent his career in Nigeria. Horton follows Tylor so much that he is called a 'neo-Tylorian' – a label intended to be pejorative but one accepted by him with pride. Like Tylor, Horton deems both religion and science explanations of the physical world. Like Tylor, Horton deems the religious explanation primitive, for which he prefers the less offensive term 'traditional', and deems the scientific one modern. Like Tylor, Horton deems the explanations mutually exclusive. While Horton does not focus on myth in particular, myth for him, as for Tylor, is part of religion.

Horton does not contest Tylor's equation of religion with personalistic explanations and of science with impersonal ones. But he breaks with Tylor in relegating the matter – an obsession for Tylor – to a mere 'difference in the idiom of the explanatory quest'. Antithetically to Tylor, Horton considers the use of personal causes to explain events no less empirical than the use of impersonal ones – though, as with Tylor and as against Lévi-Strauss, still not scientific.

Tylor attributes personalistic explanations to the less critical thinking of primitives. They take the first kind of explanation at hand. Like children, they analogize to the familiar explanations of human behaviour. Horton also assumes that primitives draw on

what they are familiar with, but he maintains that moderns do so as well. For Horton, familiar phenomena are ones that evince order and regularity. Because in 'complex, rapidly changing industrial societies the human scene is in flux', order and regularity are to be found instead 'in the world of inanimate things'. Therefore the mind in quest of explanatory analogies turns most readily to the inanimate'. By contrast, in African societies order and regularity 'are far less evident' in the inanimate world than in the human one, where 'being less at home with people than with things is unimaginable'. Therefore 'the mind in quest of explanatory analogies turns naturally to people and their relations'. That African religion credits events to the decisions of person-like entities thus makes solid theoretical sense.

Horton departs most fully from Tylor in distinguishing between religious and scientific explanations on the grounds of *context* rather than of *content*. Adopting the terminology of Karl Popper, Horton argues that religious explanations operate in a 'closed' society, where scientific explanations operate in an 'open' one. In a closed, or uncritical, society 'there is no developed awareness of alternatives to the established body of theoretical tenets'. An open society is a self-critical one, in which 'such awareness is highly developed'. In a closed society the prevailing tenets, because never challenged, assume a sacred status, any challenge to which would constitute blasphemy. In an open society the existing beliefs, because subject to challenge, possess no sacred aura and can therefore legitimately be assessed.

Like Tylor, Horton would have little to say about the myth of Adonis and would have far more to say about Genesis 1, which, like Tylor, he would take unabashedly as a pre-scientific account of the origin of the physical world – an account that moderns cannot retain alongside the scientific one. Moderns could retain it only by re-characterizing either its function or its meaning, but just like Tylor, Horton bars either option.

In contrast to Horton, American anthropologist Stewart Guthrie revives Tylor's preoccupation with personalistic, or anthropomorphic, explanations in religion. For Guthrie, as for Tylor, anthropomorphism constitutes the heart of the religious, including mythic, explanation. But Guthrie breaks with Horton as well as with Tylor in finding anthropomorphism in science as well as in religion. Where for both Horton and Tylor anthropomorphism is an exclusively primitive way of explaining the world, for Guthrie it is a nearly universal one.

Karl Popper

Karl Popper (1902–94), the Viennese-born philosopher of science who eventually settled in England, breaks even more radically than Horton with Tylor. First, Tylor never explains how science ever emerged, for religion, including myth, provides a comprehensive and seemingly nonfalsifiable explanation of all events in the physical world. Second, science for Tylor does not build on myth but simply replaces it. For Popper, science emerges *out of* myth – not, however, out of the *acceptance* of myth but out of the *criticism* of it: 'Thus, science must begin with myths, and with the criticism of myths'. By 'criticism' Popper means not rejection but assessment, which becomes scientific when it takes the form of subjection to attempts to falsify the truth claims made.

Going even further, Popper maintains that there are scientific as well as religious myths – this antithetically to Tylor, himself never cited by Popper. The difference between scientific and religious myths is not in their content but in the attitude towards them. Where religious myths are accepted dogmatically, scientific myths are questioned:

> My thesis is that what we call 'science' is differentiated from the older myths not by being something distinct from a myth, but by being accompanied by a second-order tradition – that of critically discussing the myth. Before, there was only the first-order tradition.

33

A definite story was handed on. Now there was still, of course, a story to be handed on, but with it went something like a silent accompanying text of a second-order character: 'I hand it on to you, but tell me what you think of it. Think it over. Perhaps you can give us a different story.' . . . We shall understand that, in a certain sense, science is myth-making just as religion is.

(Popper, *Conjectures and Refutations*, p. 127)

Popper even maintains that scientific theories *remain* myth-like, for theories, like myths, can never be proved, only disproved, and therefore 'remain essentially uncertain or hypothetical'.

It is not clear what Popper would be able to say of the myth of Adonis. The myths that grab him are creation myths, for they make bold conjectures about the origin of the world and thereby start the process of scientific theorizing. For the proverbial record, the same Popper wrote a book entitled *The Myth of the Framework* and by 'myth' there means what William Rubinstein means in *The Myth of Rescue*: a staunchly held false conviction, one not to be further tested but to be abandoned!

Like Popper, the English classical philosopher F. M. Cornford (1874–1943) argued that Greek science grew out of myth and religion, but he limits himself to the content and considers not at all the attitude. For Cornford, science perpetuates, albeit in secular form, religious and mythical beliefs. Cornford contends that Greek science only subsequently severed its ties to religion and became empirical science. Cornford later argued that Greek science never severed its ties to religion and never became empirical science.

Tylor himself does contrast the testability of science to the untestability of myth, but he never specifies the nature of the test:

We are being trained to the facts of physical science, which we can test and test again, and we feel it a fall from this high level of proof when we turn our minds to the old records which elude such testing,

34

and are even admitted on all hands to contain statements not to be relied on.

(Tylor, *Primitive Culture*, vol. I, p. 280)

Yet Tylor must grant primitives some capacity for criticism, for how else to account for the eventual replacement of myth by science? Who save the last generation of primitives was present to create science, to substitute it for myth, and to forge modernity?

Chapter 2
Myth and philosophy

The relationship between myth and science overlaps with the relationship between myth and philosophy, so that many of the theorists considered in the previous chapter could have been considered here instead. Yet there is an even greater array of positions held on the relationship between myth and philosophy: that myth is part of philosophy, that myth *is* philosophy, that philosophy is myth, that myth grows out of philosophy, that philosophy grows out of myth, that myth and philosophy are independent of each other but serve the same function, and that myth and philosophy are independent of each other and serve different functions.

Paul Radin

Recall that where Tylor and Frazer alike subsumed both myth and science under philosophy, Lévy-Bruhl, in reaction, set myth against both science and philosophy. For him, primitive identification with the world, as evinced in myth, is the opposite of the detachment from the world demanded by science and philosophy.

In turn, the most abrupt reaction to Lévy-Bruhl came from the Polish-born anthropologist Paul Radin (1883–1959), who arrived in America as an infant. The title of his key book, *Primitive Man as Philosopher*, is self-explanatory. Though oddly Radin never

mentions Tylor here, he in effect revives Tylor's view, while at once qualifying and extending it. Radin grants that *most* primitives are far from philosophical but observes that so are most persons in any culture. He distinguishes between the average person, the 'man of action', and the exceptional person, the 'thinker':

> The former [i.e. the man of action] is satisfied that the world exists and that things happen. Explanations are of secondary consequence. He is ready to accept the first one that comes to hand. At bottom it is a matter of utter indifference. He does, however, show a predilection for one type of explanation as opposed to another. He prefers an explanation in which the purely mechanical relation between a series of events is specifically stressed. His mental rhythm – if I may be permitted to use this term – is characterized by a demand for endless repetition of the same event or, at best, of events all of which are on the same general level. . . . Now the rhythm of the thinker is quite different. The postulation of a mechanical relation between events does not suffice. He insists on a description couched either in terms of a gradual progress and evolution from one to many and from simple to complex, or on the postulation of a cause and effect relation.
>
> (Radin, *Primitive Man as Philosopher*, pp. 232–3)

Both 'types of temperament' are to be found in all cultures, and in the same proportion. If Lévy-Bruhl is therefore wrong to deny that any primitives are thinkers, Tylor is equally wrong to assume that all are. But those primitives who are get credited by Radin with a philosophical prowess far keener than that granted even myth-makers by Tylor, who calls them 'savage philosophers'. For Radin, primitive speculations, found most fully in myths, do more than account for events in the physical world, as, alas, the myth of Adonis could at most be said to do. Myths deal with metaphysical topics of all kinds, such as the ultimate components of reality. Contrary to Tylor, primitives, furthermore, are capable of rigorous criticism:

> it is manifestly unfair to contend that primitive people are deficient

either in the power of abstract thought or in the power of arranging these thoughts in a systematic order, or, finally, of subjecting them and their whole environment to an objective critique.

(Radin, *Primitive Man as Philosopher*, p. 384)

Likely for Radin, as definitely for Karl Popper and Robin Horton, the capacity for criticism is the hallmark of thinking.

Ernst Cassirer

A far less dismissive reaction to Lévy-Bruhl came from the German-born philosopher Ernst Cassirer (1874–1945). For Cassirer, wholly following Lévy-Bruhl, mythic, or 'mythopoeic', thinking is primitive, is laden with emotion, is part of religion, and is the projection of mystical oneness onto the world. Yet Cassirer claims to be breaking sharply with Lévy-Bruhl in asserting that mythic thinking has its own brand of logic. In actuality, Lévy-Bruhl says the same and invents the term 'prelogical' exactly to avoid labelling mythic thinking 'illogical' or 'nonlogical'. Cassirer also claims to be breaking with Lévy-Bruhl in stressing the autonomy of myth as a form of knowledge – language, art, and science being the other main forms:

> But though a subordination of myth to a general system of symbolic forms seems imperative, it presents a certain danger. . . . [I]t may well lead to a leveling of the intrinsic [i.e. distinctive] form of myth. And indeed there has been no lack of attempts to explain myth by reducing it to another form of cultural life, whether knowledge [i.e. science], art, or language.
>
> (Cassirer, *The Philosophy of Symbolic Forms*, vol. II, p. 21)

Yet Cassirer simultaneously maintains, no differently from Lévy-Bruhl, that myth is incompatible with science and that science succeeds it: 'Science arrives at its own form only by rejecting all mythical and metaphysical ingredients.' For both Cassirer and Lévy-Bruhl, myth is exclusively primitive and science exclusively modern. Still, Cassirer's characterization of myth as a form of

knowledge – as one of humanity's symbol-making, world-creating activities – puts myth in the same genus as science, which is not quite where Lévy-Bruhl would put it.

Subsequently, Cassirer came to see myth as not merely primitive but also modern. Fleeing to America from Hitler's Germany, he came to focus on modern political myths, above all those of Nazism. Myth here amounts to ideology. Having previously concentrated on ethereal, epistemological issues, Cassirer now turns to brute, social scientific ones: how do political myths take and keep hold? Having previously scorned Lévy-Bruhl's supposed stress on the irrationality of myth, Cassirer now embraces it:

> In all critical moments of man's social life, the rational forces that resist the rise of the old mythical conceptions are no longer sure of themselves. In these moments the time for myth has come again.
>
> (Cassirer, *The Myth of the State*, p. 280)

Tying myth to magic and magic to a desperate effort to control the world, Cassirer applies to *modern* myths the explication of *primitive* myths by, especially, Bronislaw Malinowski:

> This description [by Malinowski] of the role of magic and mythology in primitive society applies equally well to highly advanced stages of man's political life. In desperate situations man will always have recourse to desperate means.
>
> (Cassirer, *The Myth of the State*, p. 279)

Cassirer departs from Malinowski in making the uncontrollable world the social rather than the physical one, in conferring on myth itself magical potency, and most of all in seeing myth as modern. But there is a catch: modern myths constitute an atavistic revival of primitivism.

Where previously Cassirer analysed myth as quasi-philosophy, now he cuts off myth from philosophy. Myth now is anything but a form

Ancient Egyptians and Mesopotamians, argue the Frankforts, lived in a wholly mythopoeic world. The move from mythopoeic to philosophical thinking began with the Israelites, who fused many gods into one god and placed that god outside of nature. The Israelites thereby paved the way for the Greeks, who transformed that personal god into one or more impersonal forces underlying nature, or appearance. The final 'demythicizing' of nature awaited only the transformation of Presocratic imagination into experimental science.

There are many problems with the Frankforts' thesis. First, at times mythopoeism seems no more than Tylor's animism, which credits primitives with the same mentality as that of moderns. Second, Buber's I–Thou does not involve the experience of a *thing* as a person, only of a *person* as a person. Third, any phenomenon can surely be experienced as both an It and a Thou: consider, for example, a pet and a patient. Fourth, no culture could engage nature exclusively as Thou yet be detached enough to, say, raise crops. Fifth, the characterization of ancient Near Eastern cultures as wholly mythopoeic, of Israel as largely nonmythopoeic, and of Greece as wholly scientific is embarrassingly simplistic, as F. M. Cornford on Greek science makes clear.

Still, the Frankforts are to be commended for trying to apply Lévy-Bruhl's abstract theory to specific cases. Following Lévy-Bruhl and Cassirer, they at heart argue that myths, while themselves stories, presuppose a distinctive mentality. Ironically, the Frankforts' strongest criticism of Lévy-Bruhl is the same as Cassirer's and is equally misplaced: it is Lévy-Bruhl himself who insists that primitive thinking is distinctive but not illogical. The application of the Frankforts to the myth of Adonis would be the same as Lévy-Bruhl's: it would focus on Adonis' emotional identification with the world and consequent inability to see the world straight.

Rudolf Bultmann and Hans Jonas

As philosophical as the approach to myth of especially earlier
Cassirer is, he never contends that myth *is* philosophy. The
theorists who do so are the German theologian Rudolf Bultmann
(1884–1976) and the German-born philosopher Hans Jonas
(1903–93), who eventually settled in the United States. The two
not only take the meaning of myth from philosophy – from early,
existentialist Martin Heidegger – but also confine themselves to the
issue of meaning. Neither the origin nor the function of myth
interests them. Myth is for them part of no activity. Like some
armchair anthropologists, they treat myth as an autonomous text,
but unlike Tylor, they do not even speculate from their armchairs
about how myth arose or worked.

Undeniably, both Bultmann and Jonas translate myth into
existentialist terms in order to make its meaning palatable to
moderns, but they do not consider why myth is needed, especially
when the message is the same as that conveyed by philosophy. They
do not, for example, propose that myth, like literature for Aristotle,
is a more accessible way of conveying abstract truths. Because
the mythologies they study – the New Testament for Bultmann,
Gnosticism for Jonas – are nevertheless religious and not merely
philosophical, their theories will be considered more fully in the
next chapter, on myth and religion.

Albert Camus

A more concrete example of the reduction of myth to philosophy
is to be found in the celebrated interpretation of the Greek myth of
Sisyphus by Albert Camus (1913–60), the French existentialist
writer. Among the figures whom the hero Odysseus encounters in
Tartarus, the part of Hades reserved for those who have offended
Zeus, is Sisyphus, whose eternal punishment is to have to push a
huge stone up a steep hill, only for it to roll back down every time
just as he nears the top. As Odysseus describes the sight,

Also I saw Sisyphos. He was suffering strong pains,
and with both arms embracing the monstrous stone, struggling
with hands and feet alike, he would try to push the stone upward
to the crest of the hill, but when it was on the point of going
over the top, the force of gravity turned it backward,
and the pitiless stone rolled back down to the level. He then
tried once more to push it up, straining hard, and sweat ran
all down his body, and over his head a cloud of dust rose.

(Homer, *The Odyssey*, lines 593–600)

Homer does not disclose what Sisyphus' misdeed was, and ancient authorities differ. Still, for all ancients, Sisyphus was to be pitied. For Camus, he is to be admired. Rather than embodying the fate that awaits those few human beings who dare to defy the gods, Sisyphus symbolizes the fate of all humans who find themselves condemned to live in a world without gods. He is admirable because he accepts the absurdity of human existence, which is less unfair than pointless. Instead of giving up and committing suicide, he toils on, even while fully aware that his every attempt will prove futile. His is the only kind of heroism that a meaningless, because godless, world allows. Camus uses the myth of Sisyphus to dramatize the human condition.

The myth of Sisyphus was no less a part of a religion than the myths analysed by Bultmann and Jonas were – and for Bultmann still are. But Camus, just like Bultmann and Jonas, treats myth as an autonomous text, severed from any practising, institutionalized religion. For all three, myth is a philosophical tale, for after all, myth for them *is* philosophy.

SISYPHE CONDAMNÉ A ROULER UNE PIERRE SUR LE HAUT
D'UNE MONTAGNE, D'OU ELLE RETOMBE A L'INSTANT.

Sisyphus's Stone.

Der Sisyphus unaufhörliches Steinwälzen.
De opgewerkte steen van Sisyphus rolt 'telkens te rug.

B. Picart. del.

3. Sisyphus in Tartarus, 18th-century engraving by B. Picart

Chapter 3
Myth and religion

To approach myth from the field of religious studies is naturally to subsume myth under religion but is thereby to expose myth to the challenge to religion from science. Twentieth-century theories from religious studies have sought to reconcile myth with science by reconciling religion with science.

There have been two main strategies for reconciling the two. One tactic has been to re-characterize the subject matter of religion and therefore of myth. Religion, it has been argued, is not about the physical world, in which case religion is safe from any encroachment by science. The myths considered under this approach to religion are traditional myths, such as biblical and classical ones, but they are now read symbolically rather than literally. Myth, it is claimed, has been taken to be at odds with science because it has been misread. Tylor's tirade against the moral allegorizers and the euhemerists for taking myth other than literally epitomizes this misreading of myth – by Tylor himself!

The other tactic has been to elevate seemingly secular phenomena to religious ones. As part of this elevation, myth is no longer confined to explicitly religious ancient tales. There are now overtly secular modern myths as well. For example, stories about heroes are at face value about mere human beings, but the humans are raised so high above ordinary mortals as to become virtual gods. At

the same time the actions of these 'gods' are not supernatural and are thus not incompatible with science. This approach retains a literal reading of myth but re-categorizes the literal status of the agents in myth.

There is a third tactic: replacing religious myths with secular ones. This strategy saves myth from the fate of religion by severing myth from religion. It is thus the opposite of the second tactic: turning secular myths into religious ones. In uncoupling myth from religion, this tactic conspicuously falls outside the present chapter.

Rudolf Bultmann

The grandest exponents of a symbolic rendition of traditional religious myths have been Rudolf Bultmann and Hans Jonas, both discussed briefly in the previous chapter. As noted, the two confine themselves to their specialities, Christianity and Gnosticism, but nevertheless apply to them a theory of myth per se.

Taken literally, myth for Bultmann is exactly what it is for Tylor: a primitive explanation of the world, an explanation incompatible with a scientific one, and an explanation therefore unacceptable to moderns, who by definition accept science. Read literally, myth for Bultmann should be rejected as uncompromisingly as Tylor rejects it. But unlike Tylor, Bultmann reads myth symbolically. In his celebrated, if excruciatingly confusing, phrase, he 'demythologizes' myth, which means not eliminating, or 'demythicizing', the mythology but instead extricating its true, symbolic meaning. To seek evidence of an actual worldwide flood, while dismissing the miraculous notion of an ark harbouring all species, would be to *demythicize* the Noah myth. To interpret the flood as a symbolic statement about the precariousness of human life would be to *demythologize* the myth.

Myth and religion

Demythologized, myth ceases to be about the world and turns out to be about the human *experience* of the world. Demythologized, myth ceases to be an explanation at all and becomes an expression, an expression of what it 'feels' like to live in the world. Myth ceases to be merely primitive and becomes universal. It ceases to be false and becomes true. It depicts the human condition. In Bultmann's words,

> The real purpose of myth is not to present an objective picture of the world as it is, but to express man's understanding of himself in the world in which he lives. Myth should be interpreted not cosmologically, but anthropologically, or better still, existentially.
>
> (Rudolf Bultmann, 'New Testament and Mythology', p. 10)

Taken literally, the New Testament in particular describes a cosmic battle between good and evil beings for control of the physical world. These supernatural figures intervene not only in the operation of nature, as for Tylor, but also in the lives of human beings. The beneficent beings direct humans to do good; the malevolent ones compel them to do evil. Taken literally, the New Testament describes a pre-scientific outlook:

> The world is viewed as a three-storied structure, with the earth in the centre, the heaven above, and the underworld beneath. Heaven is the abode of God and of celestial beings – the angels. The underworld is hell, the place of torment. Even the earth is more than the scene of natural, everyday events, of the trivial round and common task. It is the scene of the supernatural activity of God and his angels on the one hand, and of Satan and his daemons on the other. These supernatural forces intervene in the course of nature and in all that men think and will and do. Miracles are by no means rare. Man is not in control of his own life. Evil spirits may take possession of him. Satan may inspire him with evil thoughts. Alternatively, God may inspire his thought and guide his purposes.
>
> (Bultmann, 'New Testament and Mythology', p. 1)

Demythologized, the New Testament still refers in part to the physical world, but now to a world ruled by a single, non-anthropomorphic, transcendent God, who does not look like a human being and who does not intervene miraculously in the world:

> Mythology expresses a certain understanding of human existence. It believes that the world and human life have their ground and their limits in a power which is beyond all that we can calculate or control. Mythology speaks about this power inadequately and insufficiently because it speaks about it as if it were a worldly [i.e., physical] power. It [rightly] speaks of gods who represent the power beyond the visible, comprehensible world. [But] it speaks of gods as if they were men and of their actions as human actions . . . It may be said that myths give to the transcendent reality an immanent, this-worldly objectivity.
>
> (Bultmann, *Jesus Christ and Mythology*, p. 19)

Demythologized, God still exists, but Satan becomes a mere symbol of the evil inclinations within humans. Damnation refers not to a future place but to one's present state of mind, which exists as long as one rejects God. Salvation refers to one's state of mind once one accepts God. There is no physical hell. Hell symbolizes despair over the absence of God. Heaven refers not to a place in the sky but to joy in the presence of God. The Kingdom comes not outwardly, with cosmic upheavals, but inwardly, whenever one embraces God.

Overall, the New Testament, when demythologized, presents the opposing ways in which the world is experienced: the alienation from the world felt by those who have not yet found God versus the at-homeness in the world felt by those who have found God. For those without God, the world is cold, callous, and scary. For those with God, the world is warm, inviting, and secure.

Taken literally, myth, as a personalistic explanation of the physical world, is incompatible with science and is therefore unacceptable to moderns:

> Man's knowledge and mastery of the world have advanced to such an extent through science and technology that it is no longer possible for anyone seriously to hold the New Testament view of the world – in fact, there is no one who does. . . . We no longer believe in the three-storied universe which the creeds take for granted.
>
> (Bultmann, 'New Testament and Mythology', p. 4)

Once demythologized, however, myth is compatible with science because it now refers at once to the transcendent, nonphysical world – as modern religion *without* myth does for Tylor – and, even more, to humans' experience of the physical one.

Bultmann the theologian does not merely urge modern Christians to accept the New Testament but actually shows them how to do so – by translating the New Testament into existentialist terms. His justification for the translation is not, however, that otherwise moderns could not accept the Christian Bible but that its true meaning has always been existential.

Still, to say that myth is acceptable to scientifically minded moderns is not to say why it should be accepted. In providing a modern *subject matter* of myth, Bultmann provides no modern *function*. Perhaps for him the function is self-evident: describing the human condition. But why bother describing that condition, and why use myth to do so? Bultmann cannot contend that myth *discloses* the human condition, for he himself enlists philosophy to find the same meaning in myth.

Moreover, myth, even when demythologized, is acceptable to moderns only if the existence of God is. As eager as Bultmann is to make myth acceptable to scientifically minded moderns, he is not prepared to interpret away – to demythicize – God altogether. To accept the mythology, one must continue to believe in God, however

sophisticated the conception. Compatibility with science may be necessary for the espousal of myth today, but it is far from sufficient.

What would Bultmann say of the myth of Adonis? Surely he would contrast the worlds in which Adonis finds himself. Adonis, never out of the hovering presence of a smothering goddess, is nurtured in a womb-like world, one wholly safe and sheltering. So immersed in it is he that the dangers from the 'real' world which, in Ovid's version, Venus desperately tries to impress on him simply do not register. Demythologized, the myth describes opposing experiences of the world – here not secular versus religious but infantile versus adult.

For the record, Bultmann is in fact inconsistent. Despite his seeming characterization of myth per se as a symbolic expression of the human condition, he takes literally the ancient mythologies out of which Christianity arose: those of Jewish apocalyptic and of Gnosticism. Bultmann thus seems to be restricting demythologization to Christianity, yet with further inconsistency he acknowledges his debt to fellow existentialist Jonas' pioneering demythologization of Gnosticism!

Hans Jonas

Hans Jonas argues that ancient Gnosticism presents the same fundamental view of the human condition as modern existentialism – but of atheistic rather than, as for Bultmann, of religious existentialism. Both Gnosticism and existentialism stress the radical alienation of human beings from the world:

> the essence of existentialism is a certain dualism, an estrangement between man and the world ... There is [only] one situation ... where that condition has been realized and lived out with all the vehemence of a cataclysmic event. That is the gnostic movement.
>
> (Jonas, *The Gnostic Religion*, p. 325)

But unlike Bultmann, who strives to bridge the gap between Christianity and modernity, Jonas acknowledges the divide between Gnosticism and modernity. He is therefore not seeking to win modern converts to Gnosticism. Because ancient Gnosticism, unlike mainstream Christianity, sets immateriality against matter, humans remain alienated from the physical world even after they have found the true God. In fact, that god can be found only by rejecting the physical world and its false god. Gnostics overcome alienation from this world only by transcending it. But then for Gnostics estrangement is only temporary, where for moderns it is permanent. Yet for Jonas, Gnostic mythology can still speak to moderns, and not to modern believers, as for Bultmann, but to modern sceptics. The mythology can do so because, rightly grasped, it addresses not the nature of the world but the nature of the experience of the world – that is, of this world. Like Bultmann, Jonas seeks to reconcile myth with science by re-characterizing the subject matter of myth.

To make ancient Gnosticism palatable to moderns, Jonas, like Bultmann, must bypass those aspects of the myths that encroach on science by presenting either the origin or the future of the world. The *fact* of human alienation from the world, not the source of it or the solution to it, is the demythologized subject of myth. Ignored, therefore, are Gnostic descriptions of the godhead, the emanations, the creator god, and the material world. Ignored above all is the Gnostic prospect of escape from the material world. In short, the bulk of Gnostic mythology is reduced to mere mythology – to be discarded, or demythicized, just like *all* of mythology for Tylor.

No more than Bultmann does Jonas offer any function of myth for moderns. Even if myth serves to express the human condition, why is it necessary to express that condition at all, let alone through myth, and again when philosophy already does so? Jonas does not say. Both he and Bultmann limit themselves to the meaning, or subject matter, of myth.

Bultmann's and Jonas' approach to myth could scarcely be more opposed to Tylor's. Tylor takes for granted that to be taken seriously, myth must be taken literally. For him, the moral allegorizers and the euhemerists trivialize myth by interpreting it symbolically. Bultmann and Jonas, as well as such other theorists as Joseph Campbell, argue the opposite: that myth must be taken symbolically to be taken seriously. Where Tylor argues that myth is credible to primitives only because they take it literally, Bultmann and Jonas argue that myth was most credible to early Christians and ancient Gnostics because they took it existentially. Where Tylor argues that myth is incredible to moderns precisely because they rightly take it literally, Bultmann and Jonas argue that myth is credible to moderns only in so far as they rightly take it symbolically. Yet Tylor truly objects not to those theorists who read myth symbolically for moderns but to those who read it symbolically for primitives. He would thus berate Bultmann and Jonas far more for what they say of early Christians and ancient Gnostics than for what they say of moderns.

Ironically, Tylor, Bultmann, and Jonas all write in defence of myth. The difference is that for Tylor the defence demands the abandonment of myth in the wake of science, where for Bultmann and Jonas the defence requires the explication of the true meaning of myth in the wake of science. That meaning is not a new one concocted by moderns to save myth. It is the meaning that myth has always had but that, until pressed by the threat from science, has not been fully recognized. By forcing moderns to go back to the hoary text to discover what it has really been saying all along, science has turned a necessity into a virtue.

Mircea Eliade

Hagiographical biographies of celebrated figures transform them into near-gods and their sagas into myths. For example, immediately after the first Gulf War, biographies of the American supreme commander, 'Stormin' Norman' Schwarzkopf, touted him

as the smartest and bravest soldier in the world – so much smarter and braver than anyone else as to make him almost more than human.

The key theorist here is the Romanian-born historian of religions Mircea Eliade (1907–86), who spent the last three decades of his life in the United States. Unlike Bultmann and Jonas, Eliade does not seek to reconcile myth with science by interpreting myth symbolically. He reads myth as literally as Tylor does. Unlike Bultmann and Jonas, Eliade does not alter the apparent function of myth. For him, as much as for Tylor, myth is an explanation, though, strictly, of the origin of a phenomenon and not just of its recurrence. Unlike Bultmann and Jonas, Eliade does not try to update traditional myths. But rather than, like Tylor, sticking to traditional, explicitly religious myths, he turns to modern, seemingly nonreligious ones. Yet instead of trying to reconcile those myths with science, as Bultmann and Jonas would, he appeals to the sheer presence of them to argue for their compatibility with science: if

4. **Mircea Eliade, Paris, 1978**

moderns, who for Eliade no less than for the others have science, also have myth, then myth simply must be compatible with science.

Eliade's criterion for myth is that a story attribute to its subject a feat so exceptional as to turn its subject into a superhuman figure. Myth describes how, in primaeval, 'sacred' time, a god or near-god created a phenomenon that continues to exist. That phenomenon can be social *or* natural – for example, marriage or rain:

> myth tells how, through the deeds of Supernatural Beings, a reality came into existence, be it the whole of reality, the Cosmos, or only a fragment of reality – an island, a species of plant, a particular kind of human behavior, an institution.
>
> (Eliade, *Myth and Reality*, pp. 5–6)

Where outright gods are credited with creating natural phenomena, 'culture heroes' are credited with creating social phenomena. The mythic feat is creation.

While myth for Eliade does explain, it does more. Explanation turns out to be a mere means to an end, which is regeneration. To hear, to read, and especially to re-enact a myth is magically to return to the time when the myth took place, the time of the origin of whatever phenomenon it explains:

> But since ritual recitation of the cosmogonic myth implies reactualization of that primordial event, it follows that he for whom it is recited is magically projected *in illo tempore*, into the 'beginning of the World'; he becomes contemporary with the cosmogony.
>
> (Eliade, *The Sacred and the Profane*, p. 82)

Myth works like a magic carpet, albeit one that goes in a single direction. In returning one to primordial time, myth reunites one with the gods, for it is then when they are nearest, as the biblical case of 'the Lord God['s] walking in the garden in the cool of the

day' typifies (Genesis 3.8). That 'reunion' reverses the post-Edenic separation from the gods and renews one spiritually:

> What is involved is, in short, a return to the original time, the therapeutic purpose of which is to begin life once again, a symbolic rebirth.
>
> (Eliade, *The Sacred and the Profane*, p. 82)

The ultimate payoff of myth is experiential: encountering divinity. No theory of myth could be more rooted in religion than Eliade's.

Clearly, science offers no regenerative function. Science simply explains. Myth, then, can do things that science cannot. Yet Eliade's main argument for the survival of myth is not that it serves a unique function but that it serves that function for moderns as well as for primitives. According to Eliade, moderns fancy themselves scrupulously rational, intellectual, unsentimental, and forward-looking – in short, scientific. Yet even they, maintains Eliade, cannot dispense with myth:

> A whole volume could well be written on the myths of modern man, on the mythologies camouflaged in the plays that he enjoys, in the books that he reads. The cinema, that 'dream factory,' takes over and employs countless mythical motifs – the fight between hero and monster, initiatory combats and ordeals, paradigmatic figures and images (the maiden, the hero, the paradisal landscape, hell, and so on). Even reading includes a mythological function ... because, through reading, the modern man succeeds in obtaining an 'escape from time' comparable to the 'emergence from time' effected by myths. ... [R]eading projects him out of his personal duration and incorporates him into other rhythms, makes him live in another 'history.'
>
> (Eliade, *The Sacred and the Profane*, p. 205)

Plays, books, and films are like myths because they reveal the existence of another, often earlier, world alongside the everyday

one – a world of extraordinary figures and events akin to those found in traditional myths. Furthermore, the actions of those figures account for the present state of the everyday world. Most of all, moderns get so absorbed in plays, books, and films that they imagine themselves back in the time of myth. Where Bultmann and Jonas argue meekly that moderns *can* have myth, Eliade argues boldly that they *do*. If even avowed atheists have myth, then surely myth is not merely acceptable to moderns, as for Bultmann and Jonas, but ineluctable. It is pan-human. Where Tylor and Frazer assume that myth is the victim of the process of secularization, Eliade argues that no real secularization has occurred. Religion and, with it, myth remain, just 'camouflaged'.

How to apply Eliade to the case of Adonis, who seems as far from heroic as can be? Like the other Greek antiheroes Icarus and Phaëthon, Adonis imagines himself omnipotent. In actuality, he, like them, is oblivious to the dangers of the world and dies as a result of his narcissistic foolhardiness.

A modern Adonis would be John F. Kennedy, Jr (1960–99), a beckoning hero to many and an irresistible sex symbol to women, who, ignoring Venus-like warnings, died when he recklessly insisted on flying in weather conditions for which a mere novice like him was in fact egregiously unprepared. In his plunge to earth he was even more akin to Icarus and Phaëthon. The widespread mourning for J. F. K., Jr was exactly for a would-be hero rather than for an accomplished one.

A more suitable figure for Eliade would be the indisputable hero George Washington (1732–99). Revered by all Americans as the father of the country, Washington first served as Commander in Chief of the Continental Army in the war against the British, who were finally defeated in 1781. He then retired from public life but returned to preside over the Constitutional Convention, where his support was considered indispensable for the ratification of the Constitution. Washington was unanimously elected the first

5. John F. Kennedy, Jr, on the front cover of *Us Weekly*, June 2000

President of the United States (by the Electoral College) in 1789, was then unanimously re-elected, and would have been re-elected anew had he been willing to serve. He was held in such awe that many revolutionaries feared that he or his supporters would establish a monarchy and thereby undo the republican goals for which the Revolution had been fought. His resistance to this temptation made him even more revered.

The reverence accorded Washington by Americans in his time and long afterwards bordered on deification, and the treatment of him constituted virtual worship. Even before he became the first President, let alone while and after he served, there were coins bearing his image, an unprecedented number of paintings and sculptures of him, songs and poems praising him, counties and towns named after him, elaborate celebrations of his birthdays, and tumultous receptions for him wherever he went. For Eliade, a myth honours its subject's establishing something

6. **George Washington before Yorktown, 1824–5, by Rembrandt Peale**

in the physical or social world that continues to this day – in the case of Founding Father Washington, America itself. A historian's description of the birthday celebrations during Washington's presidency captures the 'cult' of Washington:

> By 1791, two years after he took office, the 'monarchical' and 'idolatrous' celebration of his birthday had become a national custom. There was hardly a town anywhere too small to have at least one ball or banquet on that day to honor Washington. . . . It was a national event, equaled only by July Fourth in enthusiasm and resplendence. The birth of the nation and the birth of Washington had become commemorative touchstones for the American people. . . . [T]he observance of Washington's Birthday took on the character of a religious rite. . . . Washington's Birthday was indeed a sacred day: a time for communion, a time when the sanctity of the nation, and the strength of the people's attachment to it, could be reaffirmed.

(Schwartz, *George Washington*, pp. 77–9)

Long after his death, the celebration of Washington's birthday, which even today remains a national holiday, served not merely to commemorate his deeds but to bring them, and him, alive. Part of the celebration – the ritual – was the recitation of the highpoints of his biography – the myth. The bandied American line 'George Washington slept here' evinces the ultimate function of myth of Eliade: providing contact with a deity.

Of course, a sceptic can demur. Is a human hero, however revered, quite a divinity? Is celebration quite equivalent to worship? Does the celebration of a dead hero's life really bring the hero back to life? Do celebrants really believe that they have travelled back in reality and not merely in their imagination? And in so far as the social sciences explain the lasting accomplishments of heroes, what is left for myth to explain? As affecting as Eliade's effort to secure a firm place for myth in the modern, scientific world is, is it convincing?

Chapter 4
Myth and ritual

Myth is commonly taken to be words, often in the form of a story. A myth is read or heard. It says something. Yet there is an approach to myth that deems this view of myth artificial. According to the myth and ritual, or myth-ritualist, theory, myth does not stand by itself but is tied to ritual. Myth is not just a statement but an action. The least compromising form of the theory maintains that all myths have accompanying rituals and all rituals accompanying myths. In tamer versions some myths may flourish without rituals or some rituals without myths. Alternatively, myths and rituals may originally operate together but subsequently go their separate ways. Or myths and rituals may arise separately but subsequently coalesce. Whatever the tie between myth and ritual, the myth-ritualist theory differs from other theories of myth and from other theories of ritual in focusing on the tie.

William Robertson Smith

The myth-ritualist theory was pioneered by the Scottish biblicist and Arabist William Robertson Smith (1846–94). In his *Lectures on the Religion of the Semites* Smith argues that belief is central to *modern* religion but not to *ancient* religion, in which ritual was central. Smith grants that ancients doubtless performed rituals only for some reason. But the reason was secondary and could even fluctuate. And rather than a formal declaration of belief, or a creed,

the reason was a story, or a *myth*, which simply described 'the circumstances under which the rite first came to be established, by the command or by the direct example of the god'.

Myth itself was 'secondary'. Where ritual was obligatory, myth was optional. Where ritual was set, any myth would do. And myth did not even arise until the original, nonmythic reason given for the ritual had somehow been forgotten:

> the myth is merely the explanation of a religious usage; and ordinarily it is such an explanation as could not have arisen till the original sense of the usage had more or less fallen into oblivion.
>
> (Smith, *Lectures on the Religion of the Semites*, p. 19)

While Smith was the first to argue that myths must be understood *vis-à-vis* rituals, the nexus by no means requires that myths and rituals be of equal importance. For Smith, there would never have been myth without ritual, whether or not without myth there would have ceased to be ritual.

Because Adonis was a Semitic god, Smith includes him in his *Lectures*. As part of his overall argument that ancient religion had no sense of sin, so that sacrifice – the main ritual – was not penance, he contrasts the amoral, mythic explanation for the ritualistic 'wailing and lamentation' over the dead Adonis to the later, 'Christian idea that the death of the God-man is a death for the sins of the people':

> [I]f, as in the Adonis myth, an attempt is made to give some further account of the annual rite than is supplied by the story that the god had once been killed and rose again, the explanation offered is derived from the physical decay and regeneration of nature. The Canaanite Adonis or Tammuz ... was regarded by his worshippers as the source of all natural growth and fertility. His death therefore meant a temporary suspension of the life of nature ... And this death of the life of nature the worshippers lament out of natural

sympathy, without any moral idea, just as modern man is touched with melancholy at the falling of the autumn leaves.

(Smith, Lectures on the Religion of the Semites, p. 392)

In other words, originally, there was just the ritualistic sacrifice of the god Adonis, plus whatever nonmythic reason was given for it. That ritual involved not only the killing but also the mourning and, too, the hope for Adonis' rebirth. Once the reason for the ritual was forgotten, the myth of Adonis as the dying and rising god of vegetation was created to account for the ritual. As pagan rather than Christian, the myth did not judge the killing sinful.

One major limitation of Smith's theory is that it explains only myth and not ritual, which is simply presupposed. Another limitation is that the theory obviously restricts myth to ritual, though Smith does trace the subsequent development of myth independent of ritual. Yet in so far as myth as even an explanation of ritual typically involves the action of a god, myth from the start is about more than sheer ritual, as Smith himself grants.

E. B. Tylor

In claiming that myth is an explanation of ritual, Smith was denying the standard conception of myth, espoused classically by E. B. Tylor. According to Tylor, let us recall, myth is an explanation of the physical world, not of ritual, and operates independently of ritual. Myth is a statement, not an action, and amounts to creed, merely presented in the form of a story. For Tylor, ritual is to myth as, for Smith, myth is to ritual: secondary. Where for Smith myth presupposes ritual, for Tylor ritual presupposes myth. For Tylor, myth functions to explain the world as an end in itself. Ritual applies that explanation to control the world. Ritual is the *application*, not the *subject*, of myth. The subject remains the world. Both because ritual depends on myth and, even more, because explanation is for Tylor more important than control, myth is a more important aspect of religion than ritual. Smith might as

well, then, have been directing himself against Tylor in stating that 'religion in primitive times was not a system of beliefs with practical applications' but instead 'a body of fixed traditional practices'.

Smith is like Tylor in one key respect. For both, myth is wholly ancient. Modern religion is without myth – and without ritual as well. Myth and ritual are not merely ancient but *primitive*. In fact, for both Tylor and Smith, ancient religion is but a case of primitive religion, which is the fundamental foil to modern religion. Where for Tylor modern religion is without myth and ritual because it is no longer about the physical world and is instead a combination of ethics and metaphysics, for Smith modern religion is without myth and ritual because it is a combination of ethics and creed. For Tylor, modern religion, because bereft of myth, is a come-down from its ancient and primitive height. For Smith, modern religion, because severed from myth and, even more, from ritual, is a leap beyond its ancient and primitive beginnings. The epitome of modern religion for Smith is his own vigorously anti-ritualistic, because anti-Catholic, Presbyterianism. The main criticism to be made of both Tylor and Smith is their confinement of myth and ritual alike to ancient and primitive religion.

J. G. Frazer

In the several editions of *The Golden Bough* J. G. Frazer developed the myth-ritualist theory far beyond that of his friend Smith, to whom he dedicates the work. While *The Golden Bough* is best known for its tripartite division of all culture into the stages of magic, religion, and science, the bulk of the tome in fact concerns an intermediate stage between religion and science – a stage of magic and religion combined. Only in this in-between stage, itself still ancient and primitive, is myth-ritualism to be found, for only here do myths and rituals work together.

Frazer, rarely consistent, actually presents two distinct versions of myth-ritualism. In the first version, the one already discussed in

Chapter 1, myth describes the life of the god of vegetation, the chief god of the pantheon, and ritual enacts the myth describing his death and rebirth. The ritual operates on the basis of the magical Law of Similarity, according to which the imitation of an action causes it to happen. The clearest example of this brand of magic is voodoo. The ritual directly manipulates the god of vegetation, not vegetation itself, but as the god goes, so automatically goes vegetation. That vegetation is under the direct control of a god is the legacy of religion. That vegetation can be controlled, even if only indirectly through the god, is the legacy of magic. The combination of myth and ritual is the combination of religion and magic:

> Thus the old magical theory of the seasons was displaced, or rather supplemented, by a religious theory. For although men now attributed the annual cycle of change primarily to corresponding changes in their deities, they still thought that by performing certain magical rites they could aid the god who was the principle of life, in his struggle with the opposing principle of death. They imagined that they could recruit his failing energies and even raise him from the dead.
>
> (Frazer, *The Golden Bough*, p. 377)

The ritual is performed when one wants winter to end, presumably when stored-up provisions are running low. A human being, often the king, plays the role of the god and acts out what he thereby magically induces the god to do.

In Frazer's second, till now unmentioned, version of myth-ritualism the king is central. Here the king does not merely act the part of the god but is himself divine, by which Frazer means that the god resides in him. Just as the health of vegetation depends on the health of its god, so now the health of the god depends on the health of the king: as the king goes, so goes the god of vegetation, and so in turn goes vegetation itself. To ensure a steady supply of food, the community kills its king while he is

still in his prime and thereby safely transfers the soul of the god to his successor:

> For [primitives] believe ... that the king's life or spirit is so sympathetically bound up with the prosperity of the whole country, that if he fell ill or grew senile the cattle would sicken and cease to multiply, the crops would rot in the fields, and men would perish of widespread disease. Hence, in their opinion, the only way of averting these calamities is to put the king to death while he is still hale and hearty, in order that the divine spirit which he has inherited from his predecessors may be transmitted in turn by him to his successor while it is still in full vigour and has not yet been impaired by the weakness of disease and old age.
>
> (Frazer, *The Golden Bough*, pp. 312–13)

The king is killed either at the end of a short term or at the first sign of infirmity. As in the first version, the aim is to end winter, which now is attributed to the weakening of the king. How winter can ever, let alone annually, ensue if the king is removed at or even before the onset of any debilitation, Frazer never explains.

In any event this second version of myth-ritualism has proved the more influential by far, even though it actually provides only a tenuous link between religious myth and magical ritual. Instead of enacting the myth of the god of vegetation, the ritual simply changes the residence of the god. The king dies not in imitation of the death of the god but as a sacrifice to preserve the health of the god. What part myth plays here, it is not easy to see. Instead of reviving the god by magical imitation, the ritual revives the god by a transplant.

In Frazer's first, truly myth-ritualist scenario myth arises prior to ritual rather than, as for Smith, after it. The myth that gets enacted in the combined stage emerges in the stage of religion and therefore antedates the ritual to which it is applied. In the combined stage myth, as for Smith, explains the point of ritual, but from the outset.

Myth gives ritual its original and sole meaning. Without the myth of the death and rebirth of that god, the death and rebirth of the god of vegetation would scarcely be ritualistically enacted. Still, myth for Frazer, as for Tylor, is an explanation of the world – of the course of vegetation – and not just, as for Smith, of ritual. But for Frazer, unlike Tylor, explanation is only a means to control, so that myth is the ancient and primitive counterpart to applied science rather than, as for Tylor, to scientific theory. Ritual may still be the application of myth, but myth is subordinate to ritual.

The severest limitation of Frazer's myth-ritualism is not only that it, like Smith's, precludes modern myths and rituals but also that it restricts even ancient and primitive myth-ritualism to myths about the god of vegetation, and really only to myths about the death and rebirth of that god.

Where Smith discusses the case of Adonis only in passing, Frazer makes Adonis a key example of the myth and ritual of the dying-and-rising god of vegetation. Consistently or not, Frazer actually places Adonis in all three of his pre-scientific stages of culture: those of magic, of religion, and of magic and religion combined.

Frazer locates the celebrated potted gardens of Adonis in his first, magical stage. In this stage humans believe that impersonal forces rather than gods cause events in the physical world. Ancient Greeks would have been planting seeds in earth-filled pots not to persuade a god to grant growth but, by the magical Law of Similarity, to force the impersonal earth itself to grow: 'For ignorant people suppose that by mimicking the effect which they desire to produce they actually help to produce it.' Because there are no gods in this stage, Adonis can hardly be a god of vegetation. Rather, he is vegetation itself. Vegetation does not symbolize Adonis; Adonis symbolizes vegetation.

In Frazer's second, religious stage gods replace magical laws as the

source of events in the physical world, so that Adonis becomes, at least on the literal level, the god of vegetation. As the god of vegetation, Adonis could, most simply, have been asked for crops. Or the request could have been reinforced by obedience to the god's ritualistic and ethical dictates. Frazer himself writes that rites of mourning were performed for Adonis – not, as in the next stage, to undo his death but to seek his forgiveness for it. For Adonis has died not, as in the next stage, because he has descended to the Underworld but because in cutting, stamping, and grinding the corn – the specific part of vegetation he symbolizes – humans have killed him. Rather than 'the natural decay of vegetation in general under the summer heat or the winter cold', the death of Adonis is 'the violent destruction of the corn by man'. Yet Adonis is somehow still sufficiently alive to be capable of punishing humans, something that the rituals of forgiveness are intended to avert. Since, however, Adonis dies because vegetation itself does, the god is here really, as in the first stage, only a metaphor for the element that he supposedly controls. Again, as vegetation goes, so goes Adonis.

In Frazer's third, combined stage Adonis seems at last a god. If in stage two as vegetation goes, so goes Adonis, now as Adonis goes, so seemingly goes vegetation. Adonis' death means his descent to the Underworld for his stay with Persephone. Frazer assumes that whether or not Adonis has willed his descent, he is too weak to ascend by himself. By acting out his rebirth, humans facilitate it. On the one hand the enactment employs the magical Law of Similarity. On the other hand the enactment does not, as in the first stage, compel but only bolsters Adonis, who, despite his present state of death, is yet hearty enough to revive himself, just not unassisted. In this stage gods still control the physical world, but their effect on it is automatic rather than deliberate. To enact the rebirth of Adonis is to spur his rebirth and, through it, the rebirth of vegetation.

Yet even in this stage the sole aspect of Adonis' life considered by Frazer is that which parallels the annual course of vegetation: Adonis' death and rebirth. Adonis' otherwise *unnatural* life, beginning with

7. The Green Corn fertility dance of the Minatarees of North America, 19th-century illustration by George Catlin

his incestuous birth, is ignored. Ignored above all is Adonis' final death, the unnatural cause – killing, even murder – aside. And so Frazer must do. For if Adonis' life is to symbolize the course of vegetation, Adonis must continually die and be reborn. Yet he does not. By whatever means Adonis in Apollodorus' version overcomes death annually, he does not do so indefinitely. In Ovid's version Adonis has never before died and been reborn, and Venus is disconsolate exactly because he is gone once and for all. How, then, can his short, mortal life symbolize eternal rebirth, and how can he be a god? Frazer never says.

Finally, Frazer, once again oblivious to consistency, simultaneously declares Adonis' life in even the combined stage to be but a symbol of the course of vegetation itself: the myth that Adonis spent a portion of the year in the Underworld

> is explained most simply and naturally by supposing that he represented vegetation, especially the corn, which lies buried in the earth half the year and reappears above ground the other half.
>
> (Frazer, *The Golden Bough*, p. 392)

Adonis now proves to be not the cause of the fate of vegetation but only a metaphor for that fate, so that in stage three as well as in stage two as vegetation goes, so goes Adonis, and not vice versa. How myth-ritualism is possible when there is no longer a god to be ritualistically revived and when there is only a description, not an explanation, of the course of vegetation is not easy to see. In now taking mythology as a symbolic description of natural processes, Frazer is like a group of largely German nineteenth-century theorists known appropriately as nature mythologists.

Jane Harrison and S. H. Hooke

The next stage in the myth-ritualist theory came with Jane Harrison (1850–1928) and S. H. Hooke (1874–1968), the English leaders of the initial main groups of myth-ritualists: classicists and biblicists.

Their positions are close. Both largely follow Frazer's first myth-ritualist scheme, though Hooke, nearly as inconsistent as Frazer, sometimes follows the second scheme. Unlike Frazer, Hooke and Harrison postulate no distinct, prior stages of magic and of religion. Both begin instead with the equivalent of Frazer's combined stage. Like Frazer, they deem myth-ritualism the ancient and primitive counterpart to modern science, which replaces not only myth-ritualism but myth and ritual per se. Harrison and Hooke follow Frazer most of all in their willingness to see heretofore elevated, superior religions – those of Hellenic Greece and of biblical Israel – as primitive. The conventional, pious view had been, and often continues to be, that Greece and Israel stood above the benighted magical endeavours of their neighbours.

Venturing beyond both Frazer and Hooke, Harrison adds to the ritual of the renewal of vegetation the ritual of initiation into society. She even argues that the original ritual, while still performed annually, was exclusively initiatory. There was no myth, so that for her, as for Smith, ritual precedes myth. God was only the projection of the euphoria produced by the ritual. Subsequently, god became the god of vegetation, the myth of the death and rebirth of that god arose, and the ritual of initiation became an agricultural ritual as well. Just as the initiates symbolically died and were reborn as fully fledged members of society, so the god of vegetation and in turn crops literally died and were reborn. In time, the initiatory side of the combined ritual faded, and only the Frazerian, agricultural ritual remained.

Against Smith, Harrison and Hooke alike deny vigorously that myth is an explanation of ritual: 'The myth', states Harrison, 'is not an attempted explanation of either facts or rites.' But she and Hooke really mean no more than Frazer. Myth is still an explanation of what is presently happening in the ritual, just not of how the ritual arose. Myth is like the sound in a film or the narration of a pantomime. Writes Hooke: 'In general the spoken part of a ritual consists of a description of what is being done . . . This is the sense

in which the term "myth" is used in our discussion.' Harrison puts it pithily: 'The primary meaning of myth . . . is the spoken correlative of the acted rite, the thing done'.

Both Harrison and Hooke go further than Frazer. Where for him the power of myth is merely dramatic, for Harrison and Hooke it is outright magical. 'The spoken word', writes Hooke, 'had the efficacy of an act'. 'A myth', writes Harrison, 'becomes practically a story of magical intent and potency.' We have here word magic. Contemporary myth-ritualists like the American classicist Gregory Nagy appeal to the nature of oral, as opposed to written, literature to argue that myth was originally so closely tied to ritual, or performance, as to be ritualistic itself:

> Once we view myth as performance, we can see that myth itself is a form of ritual: rather than think of myth and ritual separately and only contrastively, we can see them as a continuum in which myth is a verbal aspect of ritual while ritual is a notional aspect of myth.
>
> (Gregory Nagy, 'Can Myth Be Saved?', p. 243)

How this position goes beyond that of Hooke and Harrison is far from clear.

Application of the theory

The classicists Gilbert Murray, F. M. Cornford, and A. B. Cook, all English or English-resident, applied Harrison's theory to such ancient Greek phenomena as tragedy, comedy, the Olympic Games, science, and philosophy. These seemingly secular, even anti-religious, phenomena are interpreted as latent expressions of the myth of the death and rebirth of the god of vegetation.

Among biblicists, the Swedish Ivan Engnell, the Welsh Aubrey Johnson, and the Norwegian Sigmund Mowinckel differed over the extent to which ancient Israel in particular adhered to the myth-ritualist pattern. Engnell sees an even stronger adherence

than the cautious Hooke; Johnson and especially Mowinckel, a weaker one.

Invoking Frazer, Bronislaw Malinowski, whose theory was considered in Chapter 1, applied his own, qualified version of the theory to the myths of native peoples worldwide. Malinowski argues that myth, which for him, as for Smith, explains the origin of ritual, gives rituals a hoary past and thereby sanctions them. Society depends on myth to spur adherence to rituals. But if all rituals depend on myth, so do many other cultural practices on which society depends. They have myths of their own. Myth and ritual are therefore not coextensive.

Mircea Eliade, whose theory was discussed in Chapter 3, applied a similar form of the theory, but he goes beyond Malinowski to apply the theory to modern as well as primitive cultures. Myth for him, too, sanctions phenomena of all kinds, not just rituals, by giving them a primaeval origin. For him, too, then, myth and ritual are not coextensive. But Eliade again goes beyond Malinowski in stressing the importance of the ritualistic enactment of myth in the fulfilment of the ultimate function of myth: when enacted, myth acts as a time machine, carrying one back to the time of the myth and thereby bringing one closer to god.

Application of the theory to literature

The most notable application of the myth-ritualist theory outside of religion has been to literature. Harrison herself boldly derived all art, not just literature, from ritual. She speculates that gradually people ceased believing that the imitation of an action caused that action to occur. Yet rather than abandoning ritual, they now practised it as an end in itself. Ritual for its own sake became art, her clearest example of which is drama. More modestly than she, Murray and Cornford rooted specifically Greek epic, tragedy, and comedy in myth-ritualism. Murray then extended the theory to Shakespeare.

Other standard-bearers of the theory have included Jessie Weston on the Grail legend, E. M. Butler on the Faust legend, C. L. Barber on Shakespearean comedy, Herbert Weisinger on Shakespearean tragedy and on tragedy per se, Francis Fergusson on tragedy, Lord Raglan on hero myths and on literature as a whole, and Northrop Frye and Stanley Edgar Hyman on literature generally. As literary critics, these myth-ritualists have understandably been concerned less with myth itself than with the mythic origin of literature. Works of literature are interpreted as the outgrowth of myths once tied to rituals. For those literary critics indebted to Frazer, as the majority are, literature harks back to Frazer's second myth-ritualist scenario. 'The king must die' becomes the familiar summary line.

For literary myth-ritualists, myth becomes literature when myth is severed from ritual. Myth tied to ritual is religious literature; myth cut off from ritual is secular literature, or plain literature. When tied to ritual, myth can serve any of the active functions ascribed to it by myth-ritualists. Bereft of ritual, myth is reduced to mere commentary.

Literary myth-ritualism is a theory not of myth and ritual themselves, both of which are assumed, but of their impact on literature. Yet it is not a theory of literature either, for it refuses to reduce literature to myth. Literary myth-ritualism is an explanation of the transformation of myth and ritual into literature, and it will be considered in detail in the next chapter.

René Girard

In *The Hero*, which will be discussed at length in the next chapter, Lord Raglan extends Frazer's second myth-ritualist scenario by turning the king who dies for the community into a hero. In *Violence and the Sacred* and many subsequent works, the French-born, American-resident literary critic René Girard (b. 1923) offers an ironic twist to the theory of Raglan, himself never cited. Where Raglan's hero is willing to die for the community, Girard's hero is

killed or exiled by the community for having caused their present woes. Indeed, the 'hero' is initially considered a criminal who deserves to die. Only subsequently is the villain turned into a hero, who, as for Raglan, dies selflessly for the community. Both Raglan and Girard cite Oedipus as their fullest example. (Their doing so makes neither a Freudian. Both spurn Freud.) For Girard, the transformation of Oedipus from reviled exile in Sophocles' *Oedipus the King* to revered benefactor in Sophocles' *Oedipus at Colonus* typifies the transformation from criminal to hero.

Yet this change is for Girard only the second half of the process. The first half is the change from innocent victim to criminal. Originally, violence erupts in the community. The cause is the inclination, innate in human nature, to imitate others and thereby to desire the same objects as those of the imitated. Imitation leads to rivalry, which leads to violence. Desperate to end the violence, the community selects an innocent member to blame for the turmoil. This 'scapegoat' can be anyone and can range from the most helpless member of society to the most elevated, including, as with Oedipus, the king. The victim is usually killed, though, as with Oedipus, sometimes exiled. The killing is the ritualistic sacrifice. Rather than *directing* the ritual, as for Frazer, myth for Girard is created *after* the killing to *excuse* it. Myth comes from ritual, as for Smith, but it comes to justify rather than, as for Smith, to explain the ritual. Myth turns the scapegoat into a criminal, who deserved to die, and then turns the criminal into a hero, who has died voluntarily for the good of the community.

Girard's theory, which centres on the place of the protagonist in society, would seem hopelessly inapplicable to the myth of Adonis. Adonis hardly dies willingly or selflessly. The very worlds he inhabits – the woods and the Underworld – seem as far removed from society as can be. In Chapter 8 this myth will nevertheless be interpreted socially, and Girard's own interpretation of the myth of Oedipus will be presented.

While Girard never cites Raglan, he does regularly cite Frazer. Confining himself to Frazer's second myth-ritualist scenario, Girard lauds Frazer for recognizing the key primitive ritual of regicide but berates him for missing its real origin and function. For Frazer, sacrifice is the innocent application of a benighted, pre-scientific explanation of the world: the king is killed and replaced so that the the god of vegetation, whose soul resides in the incumbent, can either retain or regain his health. The function of the sacrifice is wholly agricultural. There is no hatred of the victim, who simply fulfils his duty as king and is celebrated throughout for his self-sacrifice. According to Girard, Frazer thereby falls for the mythic cover-up. The real origin and function of ritual and subsequent myth are social rather than agricultural, as will be discussed in Chapter 8.

Walter Burkert

Perhaps the first to temper the dogma that myths and rituals are inseparable was the American anthropologist Clyde Kluckhohn. The German classicist Walter Burkert (b. 1931) has gone well beyond Kluckhohn in not merely permitting but outright assuming the original independence of myth and ritual. He maintains that when the two do come together, they do not just serve a common function, as Kluckhohn assumes, but reinforce each other. Myth bolsters ritual by giving merely human behaviour a divine origin: do this because the gods did or do it. Conversely, ritual bolsters myth by turning a mere story into prescribed behaviour of the most dutiful kind: do this on pain of anxiety, if not punishment. Where for Smith myth serves ritual, for Burkert ritual equally serves myth.

Like Girard, Burkert roots myth in sacrifice and roots sacrifice in aggression, but he does not limit sacrifice to human sacrifice, and he roots sacrifice itself in hunting – the original expression of aggression. Moreover, myth for Burkert functions not to hide the reality of sacrifice, as for Girard, but on the contrary to preserve it

and thereby to retain its psychological and social effects. Finally, Burkert connects myths not only to rituals of sacrifice but also, like Harrison, to rituals of initiation. Myth here serves the same socializing function as ritual.

Ritual for Burkert is 'as if' behaviour. To take his central example, the 'ritual' is not the customs and formalities involved in actual hunting but dramatized hunting. The function is no longer that of securing food, as for Frazer, for the ritual proper arises only after farming has supplanted hunting as the prime source of food:

> Hunting lost its basic function with the emergence of agriculture some ten thousand years ago. But hunting ritual had become so important that it could not be given up.
>
> (Burkert, *Structure and History in Greek Mythology and Ritual*, p. 55)

8. **Hunting the Calydon Boar, Laconian Greek cup from Cerveteri, 6th century** BC

The communal nature of actual hunting, and of ritualized hunting thereafter, functioned to assuage anxiety over one's own aggression and one's own mortality, and at the same time to cement a bond among participants. The functions were psychological and sociological, not agricultural.

The myth of Adonis would present an ironic case for Burkert. Not only is Adonis' hunting solitary rather than communal, but Adonis is scarcely a real hunter, let alone one racked by anxiety. For him, hunting is more a sport than a life-and-death encounter. Therefore hunting can hardly abet him either psychologically or socially. Yet his saga can still function as a warning to others, as will be proposed in Chapter 8.

Chapter 5
Myth and literature

The relationship between myth and literature has taken varying forms. The most obvious form has been the use of myth in works of literature. A standard theme in literature courses has been the tracing of classical figures, events, and themes in Western literature thereafter – beginning with the Church Fathers, who utilized classical mythology even while warring on paganism, and proceeding through Petrarch, Boccacio, Dante, Chaucer, Spenser, Shakespeare, Milton, Goethe, Byron, Keats, and Shelley, and then down to Joyce, Eliot, Gide, Cocteau, Anouilh, and Eugene O'Neill. The same has commonly been done for biblical myths. Both groups of myths have alternatively been read literally, been read symbolically, been rearranged, and been outright recreated. And they are to be found in all of the arts, including music and film. Freud used the figures Oedipus and Electra to name the most fundamental human drives, and he took from psychiatrists the figure Narcissus to name self-love.

The pervasiveness of classical, or pagan, mythology is even more of a feat than that of biblical mythology, for classical mythology has survived the demise of the religion of which, two thousand years ago, it was originally a part. By contrast, biblical mythology has been sustained by the near-monolithic presence of the religion of which it remains a part. Indeed, classical mythology has been preserved by the culture tied to the religion that killed off classical religion. Till

recently, the very term 'paganism' has had a negative connotation. That classical mythology has survived where the rest of its religion has not is an ironic reversal of Tylor's view of the fates of both, though Tylor is referring to the survival of Christianity, not of paganism, and to the survival of Christianity in the face of modern science, not of a rival religion.

The mythic origin of literature

Another form of the relationship between myth and literature already noted in the previous chapter is the derivation of literature from myth – an approach pioneered by Jane Harrison and her fellow classicists Gilbert Murray and F. M. Cornford. Let's take some examples of this approach.

In *From Ritual to Romance* the English medievalist Jessie Weston (1850–1928) applied Frazer's second myth-ritualist version to the Grail legend. Following Frazer, she maintains that for ancients and primitives alike the fertility of the land depended on the fertility of their king, in whom resided the god of vegetation. But where for Frazer the key ritual was the replacement of an ailing king, for Weston the aim of the Grail quest was the *rejuvenation* of the king. Furthermore, Weston adds an ethereal, spiritual dimension that transcends Frazer. The aim of the quest turns out to have been mystical oneness with god and not just food from god. It is this spiritual dimension of the legend that inspired T. S. Eliot to use Weston in 'The Waste Land'. Weston is not reducing the Grail legend to primitive myth and ritual but merely tracing the legend back to primitive myth and ritual. The legend itself is literature, not myth. Because Frazer's second myth-ritualist scenario is not about the enactment of any myth of the god of vegetation but about the condition of the reigning king, the myth giving rise to the legend is not the life of a god like Adonis but the life of the Grail king himself.

In *The Idea of a Theater* Francis Fergusson (1904–86), an esteemed American theatre critic, applied Frazer's second myth-ritualist

version to the whole genre of tragedy. He argues that the story of the suffering and redemption of the tragic hero derives from Frazer's scenario of the killing and replacement of the king. For example, Oedipus, King of Thebes, must sacrifice his throne, though not his life, for the sake of his subjects. Only with his abdication will the plague cease. But for Fergusson, as for Weston, the renewal sought is less physical than spiritual, and for Fergusson, Oedipus seeks it for himself as well as for his people.

More than most other literary myth-ritualists, Fergusson is concerned as much with the product – drama – as with the source – myth and ritual. He even criticizes Harrison and especially Murray for taking the meaning of tragedy to be the Frazerian act of regicide rather than, say, the theme of self-sacrifice. For Fergusson, as for Weston, the Frazerian scenario provides the background to literature but is itself myth and ritual rather than literature.

In *Anatomy of Criticism* famed Canadian literary critic Northrop Frye (1912–91) argued that not one genre but all genres of literature derive from myth – specifically, the myth of the life of the hero. Frye associates the life cycle of the hero with several other cycles: the yearly cycle of the seasons, the daily cycle of the sun, and the nightly cycle of dreaming and awakening. The association with the seasons comes from Frazer. The association with the sun, never attributed, perhaps comes from Max Müller. The association with dreaming comes from Jung. The association of the seasons with heroism, while again never attributed, may come from Raglan, who will shortly be considered in his own right. Frye offers his own heroic pattern, which he calls the 'quest-myth', but it consists of just four broad stages: the birth, triumph, isolation, and defeat of the hero.

Each main genre of literature parallels at once a season, a stage in the day, a stage of consciousness, and above all a stage in the heroic myth. Romance parallels at once spring, sunrise, awakening, and the birth of the hero. Comedy parallels summer, midday, waking consciousness, and the triumph of the hero. Tragedy parallels

autumn, sunset, daydreaming, and the isolation of the hero. Satire parallels winter, night, sleep, and the defeat of the hero. The literary genres do not merely parallel the heroic myth but derive from it. The myth itself derives from ritual – from the version of Frazer's myth-ritualism in which divine kings are killed and replaced.

Like most other literary myth-ritualists, Frye does not reduce literature to myth. On the contrary, he, most uncompromisingly of all, insists on the autonomy of literature. Like Fergusson, he faults Murray and Cornford not for speculating about the myth-ritualist origin of tragedy (Murray) and comedy (Cornford) – a nonliterary issue – but for interpreting the meaning of both as the enactment of Frazer's scenario of regicide – the literary issue.

Yet Frye proceeds to enlist both Frazer and Jung to help extricate the meaning, not just the origin, of literature. For he takes their key works to be themselves works of literary criticism and not merely or even chiefly works of anthropology or psychology:

> the fascination which *The Golden Bough* and Jung's book on libido symbols [i.e., *Symbols of Transformation* (Jung's Collected Works, vol. 5)] have for literary critics is ... based ... on the fact that these books are primarily studies in literary criticism. . . . *The Golden Bough* isn't really about what people did in a remote and savage past; it is about what human imagination does when it tries to express itself about the greatest mysteries, the mysteries of life and death and afterlife.
>
> (Frye, 'The Archetpes of Literature', p. 17;
> 'Symbolism of the Unconscious', p. 89)

Similarly, Jung's *Psychology and Alchemy* (Jung's Collected Works, vol. 12), which Frye also singles out, 'is not a mere specious paralleling of a defunct science [i.e., alchemy] and one of several Viennese schools of psychology, but a grammar of literary symbolism which for all serious students of literature is as important as it is endlessly fascinating'.

Frye surely goes too far in characterizing Frazer and Jung as at heart mythographers rather than theorists. Both Frazer and Jung intend to be accounting for the origin and the function, not merely the meaning, of myth, and the 'grammars' they provide are intended as proofs, not as compendia of symbols. Frazer claims that ritualistic regicide really did occur, even if it later got watered down to mere drama. Jung claims that archetypes really exist in the mind and even in the world.

Because Frye brings myth and literature so closely together, even without collapsing literature into myth, his literary criticism is confusingly called 'myth criticism', of which he himself is often considered the grandest practitioner. Equally commonly, his literary criticism is called 'archetypal criticism' because in innocently calling the genres of literature 'archetypes', he is mistaken for a Jungian and, again, the grandest of practitioners. To compound the confusion, there *are* outright Jungian literary critics who are aptly called archetypal critics, beginning with Maud Bodkin in *Archetypal Patterns in Poetry*. To compound the confusion yet further, there are post-Jungians who call themselves 'archetypal psychologists' *rather than* Jungians. The most prominent are James Hillman and David Miller, both of whom write voluminously on myth.

In *Violence and the Sacred* and other works René Girard, whose theory was discussed in the previous chapter, offers the sharpest break between myth and literature. Like Fergusson and Frye, Girard faults Harrison and Murray for conflating myth and ritual with tragedy. But he faults the two even more sternly for domesticating tragedy. For Harrison and Murray, myth merely *describes* the Frazerian ritual, and tragedy merely *dramatizes* it. Worse, tragedy turns an actual event into a mere theme. For Girard, myth *covers up* the ritual, and tragedy, as in Sophocles' plays about Oedipus, *uncovers* it. Girard's criticism, however, is directed at Frazer's second myth-ritualist scenario, in which the king is outright killed. Harrison and Murray use instead Frazer's first myth-ritualist scenario, in which the king merely plays the part of

the god of vegetation. In that scenario the god dies but the king does not, and the god may die without being killed, as in Adonis' annual trek to Hades. Girard's charge that Harrison, Murray, and even in part Frazer miss the human killing that underlies all tragedy is thus embarrassingly misdirected.

Myth as story

Another aspect of myth as literature has been the focus on a common story line. Nowhere in Tylor or Frazer is there any consideration of myth as story. (I will use 'story' rather than 'narrative', the fancier term preferred today.) It is not that either Tylor or Frazer would deny that a myth is a story. It is, rather, that both deem myth a causal explanation of events that merely happens to take the form of a story. The parallel of myth to science requires the downplaying of the story form and the playing up of the explanatory content. Of course, myth for both tells the 'story' of how Helios becomes responsible for the sun and how he exercises that responsibility, but what interests Tylor and Frazer is the information itself, not the way it is conveyed. Standard literary considerations, such as characterization, time, voice, point of view, and reader response, are ignored, just as they would be in the analysis of a scientific law.

Because myth for Tylor and Frazer is intended to explain recurrent events, it could be rephrased as a law. For example: Whenever rain falls, it falls because the god of rain has decided to send it, and always for the same reason. When the sun rises, it rises because the sun god has chosen to mount his chariot, to which the sun is attached, and to drive the chariot across the sky, and again always for the same reason. Insofar as Frazer takes the gods to be symbols of natural processes, myth rephrased would be merely descriptive and not explanatory: it would simply be saying *that* rain falls (regularly or not) or *that* the sun rises (regularly) but not *why*.

For Tylor in particular, who reads myth literally, myth is anything but literature, and to approach myth as literature is to trivialize it, to

turn its explanatory truth claims into elaborate poetic descriptions. Where Frye and others argue that literature is not reducible to myth, Tylor argues that myth is not reducible to literature. In the wake of postmodernism, in which arguments in all fields, including science and law, are re-characterized as stories, Tylor's indifference to the story aspect of myth is notable.

Tylor's separation of myth from story is no less notable when seen from the standpoint of the American literacy critic Kenneth Burke (1897–1993). In, above all, *The Rhetoric of Religion* Burke argues that myth is the transformation of metaphysics into story. Myth expresses symbolically, in terms of temporal priority, what *primitives* cannot express literally: metaphysical priority. In Burke's famous phrase, myth is the 'temporizing of essence'. For example, the first creation story in Genesis puts in the form of six days what in fact is the 'classification' of things in the world into six categories:

> Thus, instead of saying 'And that completes the first broad division, or classification, of our subject matter,' we'd say: 'And the evening and the morning were the first day'.
>
> (Burke, *The Rhetoric of Religion*, p. 202)

While myth for Burke is ultimately the expression of nontemporal truths, it is still the expression of them in story form, so that even if the meaning needs to be extricated from the form, story is still what makes myth myth. Here Burke is like Lévi-Strauss, whose approach to myth as story will be considered in Chapter 7. What Burke calls 'essence', Lévi-Strauss calls 'structure'.

Mythic patterns

Myths collectively are too varied to share a plot, but common plots have been proposed for specific kinds of myths, most often for hero myths. Other categories of myths, such as creation myths, flood myths, myths of paradise, and myths of the future, have proved too disparate for all but the broadest commonalities. Tylor specifies

only that myths tell how a god decides to cause a natural event, but not what the god is like or how the god acts. Narrowing his focus to gods of vegetation, Frazer specifies only that they die and are reborn, not how either occurs.

Back in 1871 our same Tylor, surprisingly turning briefly from myths about gods to hero myths, argued that in many hero myths the subject is exposed at birth, is saved by other humans or animals, and grows up to become a national hero. Tylor sought only to establish a common pattern, not to apply to hero myths his theory of the origin, function, and subject matter of myths generally. Nevertheless, he appeals to the uniformity of the pattern to claim that whatever the origin, function, or subject matter of hero myths is, it must be the same in all hero myths to account for the similarity in plot:

> The treatment of similar myths from different regions, by arranging them in large compared groups, makes it possible to trace in mythology the operation of imaginative processes recurring with the evident regularity of mental law . . .

> (Tylor, *Primitive Culture*, I, p. 282)

Where Frye attributes myth to untethered imagination, Tylor attributes it to imagination subject to rigid cognitive constraints – a foreshadowing of present-day cognitive psychology.

In 1876 the Austrian scholar Johann Georg von Hahn used fourteen cases to argue that all 'Aryan' hero tales follow an 'exposure and return' formula more comprehensive than Tylor's. In each case the hero is born illegitimately, out of the fear of the prophecy of his future greatness is abandoned by his father, is saved by animals and raised by a lowly couple, fights wars, returns home triumphant, defeats his persecutors, frees his mother, becomes king, founds a city, and dies young. Though himself a solar mythologist, von Hahn, like Tylor, tried only to establish a pattern for hero myths. Had he proceeded to theorize about the tales, his theory would have rested on the commonality of the plot.

Similarly, in 1928 the Russian folklorist Vladimir Propp sought to demonstrate that Russian fairy tales follow a common plot, in which the hero goes off on a successful adventure and upon his return marries and gains the throne. Propp's pattern skirts both the birth and the death of the hero. While himself a Marxist, Propp here, in his earlier, formalist phase, attempted no more than Tylor and von Hahn: to establish a pattern for hero stories. But again, any theoretical salvo would have depended on the commonality of the plot.

Of the scholars who have theorized about the patterns that they have delineated in hero myths, the most important have been the Viennese psychoanalyst Otto Rank (1884–1939), the American mythographer Joseph Campbell (1904–87), and the English folklorist Lord Raglan (1885–1964). Rank later broke irreparably with Sigmund Freud, but when he wrote *The Myth of the Birth of the Hero*, he was a Freudian apostle. While Campbell was never a fully fledged Jungian, he wrote *The Hero with a Thousand Faces* as a kindred soul of C. G. Jung. Raglan wrote *The Hero* as a Frazerian. Rank's and Campbell's works will be considered in detail in the next chapter, on myth and psychology. Let us here take Raglan as an illustration of the centrality of plot.

Lord Raglan

Raglan takes Frazer's second myth-ritualist version and applies it to myths about heroes. Where Frazer identifies the king with the god of vegetation, Raglan in turn identifies the king with the hero. For Frazer, the king's willingness to die for the community may be heroic, but Raglan outright labels the king a hero. Frazer presents a simple pattern for the myth of the god: the god dies and is reborn. Raglan works out a detailed, twenty-two step pattern for the myth of the hero – a pattern he then applies to twenty-one myths. But Raglan does more: he links up the myth with the ritual. Recall that in Frazer's second version the ritual enacted is not the myth of the death and rebirth of a god but the sheer transfer of the soul

 (1) The hero's mother is a royal virgin;
 (2) His father is a king, and
 (3) Often a near relative of his mother, but
 (4) The circumstances of his conception are unusual, and
 (5) He is also reputed to be the son of a god.
 (6) At birth an attempt is made, usually by his father or his maternal grandfather, to kill him, but
 (7) He is spirited away, and
 (8) Reared by foster-parents in a far country.
 (9) We are told nothing of his childhood, but
(10) On reaching manhood he returns or goes to his future kingdom.
(11) After a victory over the king and/or a giant, dragon, or wild beast,
(12) He marries a princess, often the daughter of his predecessor, and
(13) Becomes king.
(14) For a time he reigns uneventfully, and
(15) Prescribes laws, but
(16) Later he loses favour with the gods and/or his subjects, and
(17) Is driven from the throne and city, after which
(18) He meets with a mysterious death,
(19) Often at the top of a hill.
(20) His children, if any, do not succeed him.
(21) His body is not buried, but nevertheless
(22) He has one or more holy sepulchres.

Raglan's hero myth pattern, from *The Hero*

of the god from one king to another. There is really no myth at all. Raglan, by making the heart of hero myths not the attainment of the throne but the loss of it, matches the myth of the hero with the Frazerian ritual of the removal of the king. The king in the myth who loses his throne and later his life parallels the king in the ritual who loses both at once. The myth that Raglan links to ritual is not that of a god but that of a hero – some legendary figure whose selflessness real kings are expected to emulate. Strictly, then, the myth is less the script for the ritual, as in Frazer's *first* myth-ritualist scenario, than the inspiration for the ritual.

Unlike the patterns of Tylor, Propp, or, as we shall see, either Rank or Campbell, Raglan's, like von Hahn's, covers the whole of the hero's life.

Raglan equates the hero of the myth with the god of the ritual. First, the king connects the hero to the god: heroes are kings, and kings are gods. Second, many of the events in the life of the hero are superhuman, especially points 5 and 11. True, the hero must die, but his death accomplishes a god-like feat: reviving vegetation. Third, in both the myth and the ritual the removal of the king ensures the survival of the community, which would otherwise starve. In both myth and ritual the king is a saviour.

Doubtless Raglan would never expect Adonis to fit his pattern. While points 1 through 4 seem to fit snugly, few of the others fit at all. For example, there is an attempt on the life of Adonis' mother but no attempt on Adonis' own life, at least at the outset (point 6). Perhaps Adonis can be said to have been raised by foster parents – Aphrodite and Persephone – and in a distant land (point 8), but not because he has been spirited away (point 7). Most important, Adonis never becomes king and so has no throne to lose. He does lose his life, but not while reigning as king, or even while living in a society. Of all of Raglan's chosen examples, the one that fits best is Oedipus. A biblical hero who would fit almost as well is King Saul. Unlike Frazer, Raglan is too timid to mention the case of Jesus. A modern example

9. The Duke and Duchess of Windsor on their wedding day, June 1937, after Edward's abdication

would be King Edward VIII of England, the heart of whose life was his abdication.

What matters in this chapter is the centrality of the plot to Raglan's theory. Raglan appeals to the commonality of the plot to argue that the meaning of hero myths lies in that common plot, that the heart of the common plot is the loss of the throne, and that only an accompanying ritual of regicide makes sense of the common focus in the myth on the toppling of the king. Raglan's myth-ritualism does not merely make the plot the scenario for the ritual but argues for the ritual from the plot.

Chapter 6
Myth and psychology

There are multiple theories in each discipline that have contributed to the study of myth. In psychology, two theories have almost monopolized the field: those of the Viennese physician Sigmund Freud (1856–1938) and of the Swiss psychiatrist C. G. Jung (1875–1961).

Sigmund Freud

While Freud analyses myths throughout his writings, his main discussion of his key myth, that of Oedipus, fittingly occurs in *The Interpretation of Dreams*, for he, and Jung as well, parallel myths to dreams:

> If *Oedipus Rex* moves a modern audience no less than it did the contemporary Greek one, the explanation can only be that its effect does not lie in the contrast between destiny and human [free] will, but is to be looked for in the particular nature of the material on which that contrast is exemplified. There must be something [latent] which makes a voice within us ready to recognize the compelling force of destiny in the *Oedipus*. ... His [Oedipus'] destiny moves us only because it might have been ours – because the oracle laid the same curse upon us before our birth as upon him. ... Our dreams convince us that that is so. King Oedipus, who slew his father Laïus and married his mother Jocasta, merely shows us the

fulfilment of our own childhood wishes. But, more fortunate than he, we have meanwhile succeeded, in so far as we have not become psychoneurotics, in detaching our sexual impulses from our mothers and in forgetting our jealousy of our fathers.

(Freud, *Interpretation of Dreams*, IV, pp. 262–3)

On the surface, or manifest, level, the story of Oedipus describes that figure's vain effort to elude the fate that has been imposed on him. Latently, however, Oedipus most wants to do what manifestly he least wants to do. He wants to act out his 'Oedipus Complex'. The manifest, or literal, level of the myth hides the latent, symbolic meaning. On the manifest level Oedipus is the innocent victim of Fate. On the latent level he is the culprit. Rightly understood, the myth depicts not Oedipus' failure to circumvent his ineluctable destiny but his success in fulfilling his fondest desires.

Yet the latent meaning scarcely stops here. For the myth is not ultimately about Oedipus at all. Just as the manifest level, on which

10. Sigmund Freud

Oedipus is the victim, masks a latent one, on which Oedipus is the victimizer, so that level in turn masks an even more latent one, on which the real victimizer is the myth-maker and any reader of the myth grabbed by it. Here the myth is about the fulfilment of the Oedipus Complex in the male myth-maker or reader, who identifies himself with Oedipus and through him fulfils his own Oedipus Complex. At heart, the myth is not biography but autobiography.

In whom does the Oedipus Complex lie? To a degree it lies in all adult males, none of whom has fully outgrown the desires that first arose in childhood. But the complex lies above all in neurotic adult males who are stuck, or fixated, at their Oedipal stage. For many reasons they cannot fulfil their desires directly. Their parents may no longer be alive, or, if alive, may no longer be so intimidating or so alluring. Furthermore, surely not even the most indulgent parents would readily consent. Any son who did succeed would likely get caught and punished. And the guilt felt for having killed the father whom one loved as much as hated, and for having forced oneself upon a resisting mother, would be overwhelming. But the biggest obstacle to the enactment of the complex is more fundamental. One does not know that the complex exists. It has been repressed.

Under these circumstances, myth provides the ideal kind of fulfilment. True, the outer layers of the myth hide its true meaning and thereby block fulfilment, but they simultaneously reveal that true meaning and thereby provide fulfilment. After all, on even the literal level Oedipus does kill his father and does have sex with his mother. He simply does so unintentionally. If on the next level it is Oedipus rather than the myth-maker or reader who acts intentionally, the action is still intentional. The level above therefore partly reveals, even as it partly hides, the meaning below. The true meaning always lies at the level below but is always conveyed by the level above. By identifying themselves with Oedipus, neurotic adult males secure a partial fulfilment of their own lingering Oedipal desires, but without becoming conscious of

those desires. Myth thus constitutes a compromise between the side of oneself that wants the desires satisfied outright and the side that does not even want to know they exist. For Freud, myth functions *through* its meaning: myth vents Oedipal desires by presenting a story in which, symbolically, they are enacted.

In all these ways myths parallel dreams, which, like science for Tylor and Frazer, provide the model by which Freud and Jung analyse myths. To be sure, there are differences between myths and dreams. Where dreams are private, myths are public. Where for Freud myths are limited to neurotics, dreams are universal. But for Freud and Jung alike the similarities are more significant.

Otto Rank

The classical Freudian analyses of myth are Karl Abraham's *Dreams and Myths* and Otto Rank's *The Myth of the Birth of the Hero*. Both Abraham and Rank follow the master in comparing myths with dreams – the title of Abraham's book says it all – and in deeming both the disguised, symbolic fulfilment of repressed, overwhelmingly Oedipal wishes lingering in the adult myth-maker or reader. But Rank considers more myths, analyses them in more detail, and most of all presents a common plot, or pattern, for one category of myths: those of heroes, specifically male heroes. Freudians analyse all kinds of myths, not just hero myths. Still, they often turn other kinds of myths into hero myths. Rank himself turns birth and survival into heroic feats. Even creation myths have been seen as accomplishing the feat of giving birth to the world – by males as well as by females.

For Rank, following Freud, heroism deals with what Jungians call the 'first half of life'. The first half – birth, childhood, adolescence, and young adulthood – involves the establishment of oneself as an independent person in the external world. The attainment of independence expresses itself concretely in the securing of a job and a mate. The securing of either requires both separation from one's

> The standard saga itself may be formulated according to the following outline: The hero is the child of most distinguished parents, usually the son of a king. His origin is preceded by difficulties, such as continence, or prolonged barrenness, or secret intercourse of the parents due to external prohibition or obstacles. During or before the pregnancy, there is a prophecy, in the form of a dream or oracle, cautioning against his birth, and usually threatening danger to the father (or his representative). As a rule, he is surrendered to the water, in a box. He is then saved by animals, or by lowly people (shepherds), and is suckled by a female animal or by an humble woman. After he has grown up, he finds his distinguished parents, in a highly versatile fashion. He takes his revenge on his father, on the one hand, and is acknowledged, on the other. Finally he achieves rank and honors.

Rank's hero myth pattern, from *The Myth of the Birth of the Hero*

parents and mastery of one's instincts. Independence of parents means not the rejection of them but self-sufficiency. Similarly, independence of instincts means not the denial of them but control over them. When Freud says that the test of happiness is the capacity to work and love, he is clearly referring to the goals of the first half of life, which for him hold for all of life. Freudian problems involve a lingering attachment to either parents or instincts. To depend on one's parents for the satisfaction of instincts, or to satisfy instincts in antisocial ways, is to be stuck, or fixated, at a childish level of psychological development.

Rank's pattern, which he applies to over thirty hero myths, falls within the first half of life. Roughly paralleling Johann Georg von Hahn's pattern, which was mentioned in Chapter 5 and of which he

was apparently unaware, Rank's goes from the hero's birth to his attainment of a 'career'.

Literally, or consciously, the hero is a historical or legendary figure like Oedipus. He is heroic because he rises from obscurity to, typically, the throne. Literally, he is an innocent victim of either his parents or Fate. While his parents have yearned for a child and decide to sacrifice him only to save the father, they nevertheless do decide to sacrifice him. The hero's revenge, if the parricide is even committed knowingly, is, then, understandable: who would not consider killing one's would-be killer?

Symbolically, or unconsciously, the hero is heroic not because he dares to win a throne but because he dares to kill his father. The killing is definitely intentional, and the cause is not revenge but sexual frustration. The father has refused to surrender his wife – the real object of the son's efforts:

> as a rule the deepest, generally unconscious root of the dislike of the son for the father, or of two brothers for each other, is referable to the competition for the tender devotion and love of the mother.
>
> (Rank, *The Myth of the Birth of the Hero*, p. 66)

Too horrendous to face, the true meaning of the hero myth is covered up by the concocted story, which makes the father, not the son, the culprit. The pattern is simply

> the excuse, as it were, for the hostile feelings which the child harbors against his father, and which in this fiction are projected against the father.
>
> (Rank, *The Myth of the Birth of the Hero*, p. 63)

What the hero seeks gets masked as power, not incest. Most of all, who the hero is becomes some third party – the named hero – rather than either the creator of the myth or anyone stirred by it. Identifying himself with the named hero, the

myth-maker or reader vicariously revels in the hero's triumph, which in fact is his own. *He* is the real hero of the myth.

Literally, the myth culminates in the hero's attainment of a throne. Symbolically, the hero gains a mate as well. One might, then, conclude that the myth aptly expresses the Freudian goal of the first half of life. In actuality, it expresses the opposite. The wish fulfilled is not for detachment from one's parents and from one's antisocial instincts but, on the contrary, for the most intense possible relationship to one's parents and for the most antisocial of urges: parricide and incest, even rape. Taking one's father's job and one's mother's hand does not quite spell independence of them.

The myth-maker or reader is an adult, but the wish vented by the myth is that of a child of three to five:

> Myths are, therefore, created by adults, by means of retrograde childhood fantasies, the hero being credited with the myth-maker's personal infantile history.
>
> (Rank, *The Myth of the Birth of the Hero*, p. 71)

The fantasy is the fulfilment of the Oedipal wish to kill one's father in order to gain access to one's mother. The myth fulfils a wish never outgrown by the adult who either invents or uses it. That adult is psychologically an eternal child. Having never developed an ego strong enough to master his instincts, he is neurotic:

> There is a certain class of persons, the so-called psychoneurotics, shown by the teachings of Freud to have remained children, in a sense, although otherwise appearing grown up.
>
> (Rank, *The Myth of the Birth of the Hero*, p. 58)

Since no mere child can overpower his father, the myth-maker imagines being old enough to do so. In short, the myth expresses not the Freudian goal of the first half of life but the fixated childhood goal that keeps one from accomplishing it.

To be sure, the fulfilment of the Oedipal wish is symbolic rather than literal, disguised rather than overt, unconscious rather than conscious, mental rather than physical, and vicarious rather than direct. By identifying himself with the named hero, the creator or reader of the myth acts out in his mind deeds that he would never dare act out in the world. Even the Oedipal deeds of the *named* hero are disguised, for the heroic pattern operates at or near the manifest, not the latent, level. Still, the myth does provide fulfilment of a kind and, in light of the conflict between the neurotic's impulses and the neurotic's morals, provides the best possible fulfilment. Rank contrasts the neurotic, who has repressed his impulses and so needs an indirect outlet for them, to the 'pervert', who acts out his impulses and so presumably has no need of any halfway measure like myth.

Jacob Arlow

Mainstream psychoanalysis has changed considerably since Rank's *Myth of the Birth of the Hero*. Led by the development of ego psychology, which has expanded the scope of psychoanalysis from abnormal to normal personality, contemporary psychoanalysts like the American Jacob Arlow (b. 1912) see myth as contributing to normal development rather than to the perpetuation of neurosis. For them, myth helps one to grow up rather than, like Peter Pan, to remain a child. Myth abets adjustment to the social and the physical worlds rather than childish flight from them. Myth may still serve to fulfil wishes of the id (the part of the mind from which instinctual impulses arise), but it serves far more the functions of the ego – defence and adaptation – and of the superego – renunciation. Furthermore, myth for contemporary Freudians serves everyone, not merely neurotics. Put summarily, contemporary Freudians take myth positively rather than, like classical ones, negatively. To quote Arlow:

> Psychoanalysis has a greater contribution to make to the study of mythology than [merely] demonstrating, in myths, wishes often

encountered in the unconscious thinking of patients. The myth is a particular kind of communal experience. It is a special form of shared fantasy, and it serves to bring the individual into relationship with members of his cultural group on the basis of certain common needs. Accordingly, the myth can be studied from the point of view of its function in psychic integration – how it plays a role in warding off feelings of guilt and anxiety, how it constitutes a form of adaptation to reality and to the group in which the individual lives, and how it influences the crystallization of the individual identity and the formation of the superego.

(Arlow, 'Ego Psychology and the Study of Mythology', p. 375)

Where for classical Freudians myths are like dreams, for contemporary Freudians myths are unlike them. Dreams still serve to satisfy wishes, but myths serve either to deny or to sublimate them. For classical Freudians, myths are simply public dreams. For contemporary Freudians, myths, *because* public, serve to socialize.

Bruno Bettelheim

In his bestselling book *The Uses of Enchantment* the well-known Freudian analyst Bruno Bettelheim (1903–90), Viennese-born and eventually American-resident, says much the same as Arlow but says it of fairy tales *rather than* of myths, which he quirkily pits against fairy tales and interprets in a classically Freudian way. Classical Freudians tend to see myths and fairy tales as akin, just as they do myths and dreams. It is contemporary Freudians who contrast myths to fairy tales, but usually they favour myths over fairy tales, seeing myths as serving the ego or the superego and seeing fairy tales as serving the id. (The key exception among classical Freudians to the paralleling of myths to fairy tales was the Hungarian anthropologist Géza Róheim [1891–1953], who contrasts myths to fairy tales, or folk tales, in a fashion that presciently anticipates Arlow.)

Bettelheim does the reverse of Arlow. To be sure, he does not consider myths to be wish fulfilments. Echoing Arlow, he maintains that

> Myths typically involve superego demands in conflict with id-motivated action, and with the self-preserving desires of the ego.
>
> (Bettelheim, *The Uses of Enchantment*, p. 37)

But for Bettelheim, in contrast to Arlow, the mythic superego is so unbending that the maturation it espouses is unattainable. Fairy tales no less than myths preach maturation, but they do so more gently and thereby succeed where myths fail. In myths the heroes, who are often gods, succeed only because they are exceptional. In fairy tales the heroes are ordinary persons, whose success inspires emulation. In short, myths for Bettelheim wind up hindering psychological growth, where fairy tales foster it.

Alan Dundes

Not all present-day Freudians have spurned the classical approach to myth. The pre-eminent American folklorist Alan Dundes (b. 1934) is defiantly old fashioned. For him, myth fulfils rather than renounces or sublimates repressed wishes. Declares Dundes:

> The content of folklore ... is largely unconscious. Hence it represents id, not ego, for the most part. From this perspective, ego psychology cannot possibly illuminate much of the content of folklore.
>
> (Dundes, *Parsing through Customs*, p. xii)

Dundes delights in demonstrating the hidden, antisocial wishes vented by myths – wishes that are as often anal as Oedipal, as often homosexual as heterosexual, and at times completely nonsexual.

Post-Freudian Rank

While Freud was prepared to grant that 'the act of birth is the first experience of anxiety, and thus the source and prototype of the affect of anxiety', he was never prepared to make birth the main, let alone the sole, source of anxiety and neurosis. He refused to subordinate the Oedipus Complex, which centres on the father, to the trauma of birth, which necessarily centres on the mother. For Rank, who broke with Freud over this issue, the infant's anxiety at birth is the source of all subsequent anxiety. Conflict with the father remains, but because he blocks the son's yearning to return to the mother's womb rather than because he blocks the son's Oedipal yearning. Fear of the father is a displacement of fear of the mother, who, moreover, has abandoned, not castrated, her son. Sexual desire for the mother is likewise a means of returning to the womb, not of securing Oedipal satisfaction.

Rank's *The Myth of the Birth of the Hero* already evinces the hiatus between his subsequent, post-Freudian focus on the hero's birth and his original, Freudian focus on the hero's deeds. While the title obviously singles out the hero's birth, the pattern subordinates the birth to the deeds: the birth is decisive not because of the hero's separation from his mother but because of the parents' attempt to fend off at birth the prophesied parricidal consequences. Rank does observe that the son's birth thereby constitutes defiance of the parents, but it is the parents who oppose the son's birth, not the son who opposes his own birth.

The real shift comes with Rank's *The Trauma of Birth*, in which he systematically interprets all of human life to fit the birth trauma. Rank continues to see myth as wish fulfilment, but the wish now fulfilled is, like that in the rest of culture, either to undo birth or to create a second womb. Where in *Myth of the Birth of the Hero* the father is the culprit for *opposing* birth, in *The Trauma of Birth* the mother is the culprit for *giving* birth. Oedipus' blinding of himself

upon discovering that he has committed incest represents not guilt for his Oedipal deeds but

> a return into the darkness of the mother's womb, and his final disappearance through a cleft rock into the Underworld expresses once again the same wish tendency to return into the mother earth.
>
> (Rank, *The Trauma of Birth*, p. 43)

Surely the myth of Adonis would fall here as a case of pre-Oedipal, not Oedipal, attachment to the mother. Yet Adonis' case is more extreme: he does not even realize that he has been born and has been thrust into the world. He assumes that he still lives in a womb-like world. Not his birth but his death proves his undoing, and it provides no return to the womb.

C. G. Jung

Where for Freud and Rank heroism is limited to the first half of life, for C. G. Jung it involves the second half even more. For Freud and Rank, heroism involves relations with parents and instincts. For Jung, heroism involves, in addition, relations with the unconscious. In the first half of life heroism means separation not only from parents and antisocial instincts but even more from the unconscious: every child's managing to forge consciousness is for Jung a supremely heroic feat. Like Freudians, Jungians at once analyse all kinds of myths, not just hero myths, and interpret other kinds heroically. Creation myths, for example, symbolize the creation of consciousness out of the unconscious.

For Freud, the unconscious is the product of the repression of instincts. For Jung, it is inherited rather than created and includes far more than repressed instincts. Independence of the Jungian unconscious therefore means more than independence of instincts. It means the formation of consciousness, the object of which in the first half of life is the external world.

11. C. G. Jung

The goal of the uniquely Jungian second half of life is likewise
consciousness, but now consciousness of the Jungian unconscious
rather than of the external world. One must return to the
unconscious, from which one has invariably become severed. But
the aim is not thereby to sever one's ties to the external world. On
the contrary, the aim is still to return to the external world. The
ideal is a balance between consciousness of the external world and
consciousness of the unconscious. The aim of the second half of
life is to supplement, not abandon, the achievements of the
first half.

Just as classically Freudian problems involve the failure to establish
oneself externally, so distinctively Jungian problems involve the
failure to re-establish oneself internally. Freudian problems stem
from excessive attachment to the world of childhood. Jungian
problems stem from excessive attachment to the world one enters
upon breaking free of the childhood world: the external world. To
be severed from the internal world is to feel empty and lost.

Joseph Campbell

Jung himself allows for heroism in both halves of life, but Joseph Campbell, whose *Hero with a Thousand Faces* provides the classically Jungian counterpart to Rank's *Myth of the Birth of the Hero*, does not. Just as Rank confines heroism to the first half of life, so Campbell restricts it to the second half.

Rank's scheme begins with the hero's birth; Campbell's, with his adventure. Where Rank's scheme ends, Campbell's begins: with the adult hero ensconced at home. Rank's hero must be young enough

The standard path of the mythological adventure of the hero is a magnification of the formula represented in the rites of passage: *separation–initiation–return:* which might be named the nuclear unit of the monomyth.

A hero ventures forth from the world of common day into a region of supernatural wonder: fabulous forces are there encountered and a decisive victory is won: the hero comes back from this mysterious adventure with the power to bestow boons on his fellow man.

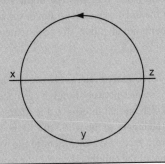

Campbell's hero myth pattern, from *The Hero with a Thousand Faces*

for his father and in some cases even his grandfather still to be reigning. Campbell does not specify the age of his hero, but the hero must be no younger than the age at which Rank's hero myth ends: young adulthood. He must, again, be in the second half of life. Campbell does acknowledge heroism in the first half of life and even cites Rank's *Myth of the Birth of the Hero*, but he demotes this youthful heroism to mere preparation for adult heroism. Antithetically to Jung, he dismisses birth itself as unheroic because it is not done consciously!

Rank's hero must be the son of royal or at least distinguished parents. Campbell's can be of any class. Campbell cites at least as many female heroes as male ones, even though stage two of his pattern – initiation – necessitates male heroes! Likewise some of his heroes are young, even though his pattern requires adult heroes! Finally, Campbell's pattern commits him to human heroes, even though some of his heroes are divine! Rank's pattern, by contrast, allows for divine as well as human heroes.

Where Rank's hero returns to his birthplace, Campbell's marches forth to a strange, new world, which he has never visited or even known existed:

> destiny has summoned the hero and transferred his spiritual center of gravity from within the pale of his society to a zone unknown. This fateful region of both treasure and danger may be variously represented: as a distant land, a forest, a kingdom underground, beneath the waves, or above the sky, a secret island, lofty mountaintop, or profound dream state.
>
> (Campbell, *The Hero with a Thousand Faces*, p. 58)

This extraordinary world is the world of the gods, and the hero must hail from the human world precisely for the worlds to stand in contrast.

In this exotic, supernatural world the hero encounters above all a

supreme female god and a supreme male god. The maternal goddess is loving and caring:

> She is the paragon of all paragons of beauty, the reply to all desire,
> the bliss-bestowing goal of every hero's earthly and unearthly quest.
> (Campbell, *The Hero with a Thousand Faces*, pp. 110–11)

By contrast, the male god is tyrannical and merciless – an 'ogre'. The hero has sex with the goddess and marries her. He fights the god, either before or after his encounter with the goddess. Yet with both, not just the goddess, he becomes mystically one and thereby becomes divine himself.

Where Rank's hero *returns* home to encounter his father and mother, Campbell's hero *leaves* home to encounter a male and a female god, who are father- and mother-like but are not his parents. Yet the two heroes' encounters are remarkably akin: just as Rank's hero kills his father and, if usually only latently, marries his mother, so Campbell's hero, even if often in reverse order, marries the goddess and fights, even if not kills, the god.

The differences, however, are even more significant. Because the goddess is not the hero's mother, sex with her does not constitute incest. Moreover, the two not only marry but also become mystically one. And despite appearances, the hero's relationship to the male god is for Campbell no less positive. The hero is really seeking from the father god the same love that he has just won or will soon win from the goddess. He seeks reconciliation, or 'atonement'.

When Campbell writes that the myths accompanying initiation rituals 'reveal the benign self-giving aspect of the *archetypal* father', he is using the term in its Jungian sense. For Freudians, gods symbolize parents. For Jungians, parents symbolize gods, who in turn symbolize father and mother archetypes, which are components of the hero's personality. The hero's relationship to these gods symbolizes not, as for Freud and Rank, a son's

relationship to other persons – his parents – but the relationship of one side of a male's personality – his ego – to another side – his unconscious. The father and the mother are but two of the archetypes of which the Jungian, or 'collective', unconscious is composed. Archetypes are unconscious not because they have been repressed but because they have never been made conscious. For Jung and Campbell, myth originates and functions not, as for Freud and Rank, to satisfy neurotic urges that cannot be manifested openly but to express normal sides of the personality that have just not had a chance at realization.

By identifying himself with the hero of a myth, Rank's male myth-maker or reader vicariously lives out in his mind an adventure that, if ever directly fulfilled, would be acted out on his parents themselves. By contrast, Campbell's male or female myth-maker or reader vicariously lives out mentally an adventure that even when directly fulfilled would still be taking place in the mind. For parts of the mind are what the hero is really encountering. In drug lingo, Campbell's heroic adventure amounts to 'tripping'.

Having managed to break free of the secure, everyday world and go off to a dangerous new one, Campbell's hero, to complete the journey, must in turn break free of the new world, in which the hero has by now become ensconced, and return to the everyday one. So enticing is the new world that leaving it proves harder than leaving home was. Circe, Calypso, the Sirens, and the Lotus Eaters thus tempt Odysseus with a carefree, immortal life.

Though often misconstrued, Jung no less than Freud opposes a state of sheer unconsciousness. Both strive to make the unconscious conscious. The ideal for both remains consciousness. Jung opposes the rejection of ordinary, or ego, consciousness for unconsciousness as vigorously as he opposes the rejection of unconsciousness for ego consciousness. He seeks a balance between ego consciousness and the unconscious, between consciousness of the external world and consciousness of the

unconscious. For Jung, the hero's failure to return to the everyday world would spell failure to resist the allure of the unconscious.

By contrast to Jung, Campbell seeks pure unconsciousness. Campbell's hero never returns to the everyday world. He surrenders to the unconscious. Yet Campbell himself demands the hero's return to the everyday world. How, then, can his hero really be rejecting it? The answer is that the world to which Campbell's hero returns is the strange, new world, which turns out to pervade the everyday one. No separate everyday world exists. The everyday world and the new world are really one:

> The two worlds, the divine [i.e., new] and the human [i.e., everyday], can be pictured only as distinct from each other – different as life and death, as day and night. . . . Nevertheless . . . the two kingdoms are actually one.
>
> (Campbell, *The Hero with a Thousand Faces*, p. 217)

Like Dorothy in 'The Wizard of Oz', the hero need never have left home after all. Where Jung espouses balance between ego consciousness and the unconscious, Campbell espouses fusion. Combining a philosophical interpretation of hero myths with a psychological one, he takes all hero myths to be preaching mystical oneness.

Adonis

While Jung himself mentions Adonis only in passing, he does mention him as an instance of the archetype of the eternal child, or *puer aeternus*. That archetype Jung also discusses only in passing, though he does devote many pages to an allied archetype, the Great Mother. Marie-Louise von Franz, one of Jung's closest disciples, wrote a book on the *puer* archetype, though she deals largely with cases other than that of Adonis.

From a Jungian point of view, the myth of Adonis functions not

merely to present the archetype of the *puer* but also to assess it. The myth serves as a warning to those who identify themselves with the archetype. To live as a *puer*, the way Adonis does, is to live as a psychological infant and, ultimately, as a foetus. The life of a *puer* in myth invariably ends in premature death, which psychologically means the death of the ego and a return to the womb-like unconscious – but not, as for post-Freudian Rank, to the actual womb.

As an archetype, the *puer* constitutes a side of one's personality, which, as a side, must be accepted. A *puer* personality is one who simply goes too far: he makes the *puer* the whole of his personality. Unable to resist its spell, he surrenders himself to it, thereby abandoning his ego and reverting to sheer unconsciousness.

The reason a *puer* personality cannot resist the *puer* archetype is that he remains under the spell of the archetype of the Great Mother, who initially is identical with the unconscious as a whole. Unable to free himself from her, he never forges a strong, independent ego, without which he cannot in turn resist any smothering female he meets. His surrender to the *puer* archetype means his surrender to the Great Mother, to whom he yearns only to return. A *puer* 'only lives on and through the mother and can strike no roots, so that he finds himself in a state of permanent incest'. Jung even calls him a mere 'dream of the mother', who eventually draws him back into herself.

Biologically, a *puer* can range in age from adolescence, the period of most dramatic expression, to middle or even old age. Psychologically, however, a *puer* is an infant. Where for Freud a person in the grip of an Oedipus Complex is psychologically fixated at three to five years of age, for Jung a *puer* is fixated at birth. Where an Oedipus Complex presupposes an independent ego 'egotistically' seeking to possess the mother for itself, a *puer* involves a tenuous ego seeking to surrender itself to the mother. A *puer* seeks not domination but absorption – and thereby reversion to the state prior even to birth.

For Freud and for Rank, Freudian and post-Freudian alike, attachment to the mother at any stage means attachment to one's actual mother or mother substitute. For Jung, attachment to the mother means attachment to the mother archetype, of which one's actual mother or mother substitute is only a manifestation. Where for Freud a boy should free himself of his yearning, infantile or Oedipal, for his own mother, for Jung a boy should free himself of his inclination to identify himself with the mother archetype. For Freud, the failure to free oneself means eternal attachment to one's own mother. For Jung, it means the restriction of one's personality to the mother archetype within. Where for Freud the struggle for freedom is between one person and another – son and mother – for Jung it is between one part of a person and another – ego and unconscious, which, again, the mother archetype first symbolizes.

Because an archetype expresses itself only through symbols, never directly, the aspects of the mother archetype which a boy knows are only those filtered through his actual mother or mother substitute. A mother who refuses to let her son go limits him to only the smothering, negative side of the mother archetype. A mother who, however reluctantly, finally lets her child go opens him to the nurturing, positive side of the archetype. Initially, any child is reluctant to leave. A smothering mother, by revealing only the smothering side of the mother archetype, tempts him to stay. A nurturing mother, by revealing the nurturing side of the archetype as well, prods him to resist the temptation. In all its aspects the mother archetype, as an archetype, is inherited. One's experience of mother figures determines only which aspects of the archetype are elicited. A boy who never experiences a nourishing mother figure will never develop that dimension of the archetype latent in him.

A *puer* may be either conscious or unconscious of his character. To be sure, even a conscious *puer* experiences alluring females as epiphanies of the Great Mother, but at least he recognizes that other males experience women differently – as possible mates. He simply takes for granted that mystical union alone is right for him. He is

both aware and proud of his unconventionality. The best-known case of a conscious *puer* is Casanova.

An unconscious *puer*, by contrast, assumes that everyone else is like him. He assumes that all other males seek unity with women, for no other possible relationship exists. A spectacular example is Elvis Presley, a quintessential mamma's boy who lived his last twenty years as a recluse in a womb-like, infantile world in which all of his wishes were immediately satisfied, yet who deemed himself entirely normal, in fact 'all-American'.

A *puer* can thus be either an actual person or a symbol. Some famous historical *pueri* even become symbols themselves. While a historical *puer* is biologically an adult, a symbolic one may never grow up, and can thereby exemplify exactly the eternally young life that actual *puer* personalities strive to emulate. The most celebrated symbolic *pueri* are Peter Pan and the Little Prince.

Just as a *puer* may be conscious or unconscious, so he may outwardly be adjusted or maladjusted. Outwardly, he may be settled in a marriage and a job, but he finds no satisfaction in them. Or he may be unsettled even outwardly, as in the cases of Don Juan and the eternal student.

The opposite of the *puer* archetype is that of the hero. The hero succeeds where the *puer* fails. In the first half of life an ego is heroic in managing to liberate itself from the unconscious and to establish itself in society. A hero manages to secure a fulfilling job and a mate. A *puer* fails to do either. In the second half of life a now independent ego is heroic in managing to break with society and to return to the unconscious without thereby falling back into it. Where a hero in the first half of life establishes himself in the conventions of society, a hero in the second half defies those conventions. But a hero is consciously defiant. A *puer* is only unconsciously so. Where a hero risks everything for whatever he has committed himself to, a *puer*

Myth and psychology (side margin)

has committed himself to nothing and so risks nothing. Where a real hero is like Daedalus, a *puer* is like his son Icarus. Because a *puer* is a failed hero in the first half of life, he is necessarily a failed hero in the second half as well. Indeed, for him there is no second half.

Adonis is a quintessential *puer* because he never marries, never works, and dies young. He simply never grows up. He must first break out of a tree in order to be born. In Ovid's version his mother, transformed into the tree, is reluctant to let him out. Like any other mother, she may be overjoyed at his conception, but unlike normal mothers, she wants to hoard him. Adonis himself has to find an exit.

No sooner does Adonis emerge from the tree than, in Apollodorus' version, Aphrodite thrusts him back – not, to be sure, into the tree but into a chest. She thereby undoes the birth that had proved so arduous. When Persephone, to whom Aphrodite has entrusted the chest without revealing its contents, opens it, she likewise falls in love with Adonis and refuses to return him. Each goddess, just like his mother, wants to possess him exclusively. Though Zeus' decision leaves Adonis free for a third of the year, Adonis readily cedes his third to Aphrodite. Never, then, is he outside the custody of these archetypal mother figures.

Adonis is unable to resist the goddesses, but not because they arouse him sexually. He sees them not as irresistibly beautiful females but as his mother, with whom he seeks not intercourse but absorption. Between him and the goddesses there exists the primordial state of mystical oneness that Lucien Lévy-Bruhl, whom Jung often cites, calls *participation mystique* (see Chapter 1). Psychologically, Adonis is at exactly that stage of humanity which Lévy-Bruhl and, following him, Jung consider primitive. Oblivious to the difference between his life and anyone else's, he is the most extreme kind of *puer* – an unconscious as well as outward one. Where Campbell would laud Adonis' identification with the world as mystical, Jung condemns it as infantile.

Chapter 7
Myth and structure

Claude Lévi-Strauss

Claude Lévi-Strauss' contribution to the study of myth, first considered in Chapter 1, was not only the revival of a Tylorian view of myth as proto-scientific but, even more, the invention of a 'structuralist' approach to myth. Recall that for Lévi-Strauss myth is an instance of thinking per se, modern or primitive, because it classifies phenomena. Humans, argues Lévi-Strauss, think in the form of classifications, specifically pairs of oppositions, and project them onto the world. Not only myth and science, which Lévi-Strauss treats as taxonomies, but cooking, music, art, literature, dress, etiquette, marriage, and economics also evince humanity's pairing impulse.

For Lévi-Strauss, the distinctiveness of myth among these phenomena is threefold. First, myth is seemingly the least orderly of them: 'It would seem that in the course of a myth anything is likely to happen. There is [seemingly] no logic, no continuity.' To be able to organize even myths into sets of oppositions would be to prove irrefutably that order is inherent in all cultural phenomena and that the mind must therefore underlie it. As Lévi-Strauss declares at the outset of *Introduction to a Science of Mythology*, his four-volume tome on Native American mythology:

The experiment I am now embarking on with mythology will consequently be more decisive. . . . [I]f it were possible to prove in this instance, too, that the apparent arbitrariness of the mind, its supposedly spontaneous flow of inspiration, and its seemingly uncontrolled inventiveness imply the existence of laws operating at a deeper level, we would inevitably be forced to conclude that when the mind is left to commune with itself and no longer has to come to terms with objects, it is in a sense reduced to imitating itself as object . . . [I]f the human mind appears determined even in the realm of mythology, *a fortiori* it must also be determined in all its spheres of activity.

(Lévi-Strauss, *The Raw and the Cooked*, p. 10)

Like Tylor, Lévi-Strauss appeals to the orderliness of the mind to prove that it stems from the scientific-like processes of observation and hypothesis rather than from unbounded imagination.

Second, myth, together with totemism, is the only exclusively primitive phenomenon among the ones that Lévi-Strauss considers. To prove that it is orderly would prove that its creator is orderly, hence logical and intellectual, as well.

Third and most important, myth alone not only expresses oppositions, which are equivalent to contradictions, but also resolves them: 'the purpose of myth is to provide a logical model capable of overcoming a contradiction'. Myth resolves or, more precisely, tempers a contradiction 'dialectically', by providing either a mediating middle term or an analogous, but more easily resolved, contradiction.

Like the contradictions expressed in other phenomena, those expressed in myth are of innumerable kinds. All, however, are apparently reducible to instances of the fundamental contradiction between 'nature' and 'culture', a contradiction which stems from the conflict that humans experience between themselves as animals,

12. Claude Lévi-Strauss

and so a part of nature, and themselves as human beings, and so a part of culture. That conflict is the projection onto the world of the oppositional character of the human mind. Humans not only think 'oppositionally' but consequently experience the world 'oppositionally' as well. It might, then, seem as if Lévi-Strauss, like Freud and Jung, makes the subject matter of myth the mind rather than the world. But in fact he does not. He is not, like them, seeking to identify projections in order to withdraw them. He is seeking simply to trace the source of them. (At the same time Lévi-Strauss maintains that the world is itself organized 'oppositionally', so that human projections, while remaining projections, match the nature of the world. Jung says the same in his doctrine of synchronicity.) Once Lévi-Strauss does trace the source of projections, he proceeds to deal with them as experiences of the world, so that the subject matter of myth for him, as for Bultmann, Jonas, and Camus, is the encounter with the world – but with the world experienced as contradictory, not as alien.

The clearest examples of the conflict between nature and culture are the recurrent oppositions that Lévi-Strauss finds between raw and cooked food, wild and tame animals, and incest and exogamy. It is much less clear how other oppositions that he finds – such as those between sun and moon, earth and sky, hot and cold, high and low, left and right, male and female, and life and death – symbolize the split between nature and culture rather than a split within nature. Similarly, it is far from clear how oppositions like those of sister versus wife and of matrilocal and patrilocal kinship symbolize other than a split within society and therefore within culture.

According to Lévi-Strauss, the Oedipus myth tempers an instance of the clash between nature and culture by noting that humans are able to tolerate a parallel case of the clash:

> Although the problem [i.e., the opposition] obviously cannot be solved [i.e., resolved], the Oedipus myth provides a kind of logical tool which, to phrase it coarsely, replaces the original problem. . . . By a correlation of this type [i.e., of the original opposition with an analogous one], the overrating of blood relations is to the underrating of blood relations [i.e., the more easily tolerated opposition] as the attempt to escape autochthony is to the impossibility to succeed in it [i.e., the opposition needing resolution].
>
> (Lévi-Strauss, 'The Structural Study of Myth', p. 82)

Arranging the elements of the myth not in the chronological order of the plot but in the recurrent order of two sets of opposing pairs, Lévi-Strauss argues that the myth is ameliorating the tension within one pair by juxtaposing it with a comparable pair that is already accepted. The already accepted opposition is that between the 'overrating' and the 'underrating' of 'blood relations'. Overrating refers to either the commission of incest (Oedipus' marrying his mother) or the violation of a prohibition in the name of family (Antigone's burying her brother Polynices). 'Underrating' refers to either fratricide (Eteocles' killing his brother Polynices) or patricide

(Oedipus' killing his father). Overrating represents nature, for it is instinctual. Underrating represents culture, for it is unnatural. In taking on the myth of Oedipus, and in focusing on familial sex and killing, Lévi-Strauss might appear to be following Freud, but in fact he dismisses Freud's analysis as just one more version of the myth itself rather than as even an inferior analysis of it.

In the myth of Oedipus the opposition requiring acceptance is that between the 'denial' and the 'affirmation' of 'autochthonous origin'. Denial refers to the killing of earthborn monsters which either prevent the birth of humans (Kadmos' killing the dragon, from the extracted teeth of which humans are born) or threaten the survival of humans (Oedipus' killing the Sphinx, which is starving Thebes). Affirmation refers to the common mythological association of humans born from the earth with difficulty in walking (Oedipus' name meaning 'swollen footed'). To kill earthborn monsters is to deny the connection of humans to the earth; to name humans on basis of difficulty in walking is to affirm the connection of humans to the earth. Denial represents nature, for humans are in fact born from human parents rather than from the earth. Affirmation represents culture, for mythology maintains that humans are born from the earth. How ancient Greeks were able to tolerate the one set of oppositions more easily than the other, Lévi-Strauss never discloses.

Yet other myths fail to overcome oppositions to even this extent. They show instead that any alternative arrangement would be worse. The Tsimshian Native American myth of Asdiwal, for example, serves,

> to justify the shortcomings [i.e., the contradictions] of reality, since the extreme [i.e., alternative] positions are only imagined in order to show that they are untenable.
>
> (Lévi-Strauss, 'The Study of Asdiwal', p. 30)

Rather than resolving the contradiction between death and life, a myth makes death superior to immortality, or eternal life:

The Indians of North America explain this by saying that if death did not exist, the earth would become overpopulated and there would not be room for everyone.

(Lévi-Strauss, in André Akoun et al., 'A Conversation
with Claude Lévi-Strauss', p. 74)

Because myth concerns the human experience of the world, not to say the deepest anxieties experienced in the world, it would seemingly have existential import, as myth does for Bultmann, Jonas, and Camus. Yet Lévi-Strauss, like Tylor, treats myth as a coldly intellectual phenomenon: the oppositions expressed in myth constitute logical puzzles rather than existential predicaments. Myth involves thinking, not feeling. At the same time myth involves more the process than the content of thinking. Here Lévi-Strauss anticipates the focus of contemporary cognitive psychologists.

In calling his approach to myth 'structuralist', Lévi-Strauss intends to distinguish it from 'narrative' interpretations, or those that adhere to the plot of myth. All other theories discussed here do so. Whether their meaning is literal or symbolic, they deem myth a story, progressing from beginning to end. Not all these theorists, to be sure, are equally interested in the plot. Lévy-Bruhl, for example, is concerned with the world view underlying it, but he still attributes a plot to myth. For Tylor, by contrast, the plot is central: myth presents the process by which the world was created or operates.

Lévi-Strauss alone dispenses with the plot, or 'diachronic dimension', of myth and locates the meaning of myth in the structure, or 'synchronic dimension'. Where the plot of a myth is that event A leads to event B, which leads to event C, which leads to event D, the structure, which is identical with the expression and resolution of contradictions, is either that events A and B constitute an opposition mediated by event C, or that events A and B, which constitute the same opposition, are to each other as events C and D, an analogous opposition, are to each other.

Every myth contains a series of oppositional sets, each composed of a pair of oppositions resolved one way or the other. The relationship among the sets matches that among the elements within each set. Rather than set one's leading to set two, which leads to set three, which leads to set four, either set three mediates the opposition between set one and set two, or set one is to set two as set three is to set four.

The structural meaning of a myth is both noncumulative and interlocking. It is noncumulative because the myth contains a series of resolutions of the oppositions it expresses rather than a single, gradual resolution. Every three or four sets provide a resolution, and in either of the fashions described, but the myth as a whole does not. Its meaning is thus cyclical rather than linear, recurrent rather than progressive. Each cycle of three or four sets, like each cycle of the three or four elements within a set, represents not the consequence but only the 'transformation', or variant expression, of its predecessor.

The structural meaning of a myth is interlocking because the meaning of any element within a set lies not in itself but in its 'dialectical' relationship to other elements in the set. Similarly, the meaning of any set lies not in itself but in its 'dialectical' relationship to other sets. By itself, an element or a set has no meaning, literal or symbolic.

A myth has the same interlocking and noncumulative relationship to other myths as its parts have to one another. Its meaning lies not in itself but in its 'dialectical' relationship to other myths, and the set composed of these myths represents the 'transformation' rather than the consequence of its predecessor. Finally, myths collectively have the same relationship to other human phenomena, including rituals, as individual myths have to one another. In Lévi-Strauss' unique brand of myth-ritualism, myths and rituals operate together, but as structural opposites rather than, as for other myth-ritualists, parallels.

Vladimir Propp, Georges Dumézil, and the Gernet School

Lévi-Strauss is not the only or even the earliest theorist of myth labelled a structuralist. Notably, the Russian folklorist Vladimir Propp (1895–1970) and the French Indo-Europeanist Georges Dumézil (1898–1986) wrote both before Lévi-Strauss and independently of him. The common plot that, as summarized in the chapter on myth and literature, Propp deciphers in Russian fairy tales is his structure. Unlike that of Lévi-Strauss, who disdains his effort for this reason, Propp's structure remains on the narrative level and is therefore no different from the kind of 'structure' found by Otto Rank, Joseph Campbell, and Lord Raglan. By contrast, the structure that Dumézil unravels lies no less beneath the surface level than Lévi-Strauss', but it reflects the order of society rather than, as for Lévi-Strauss, the order of the mind, and is three-part rather than two-part.

A group of French classicists inspired by Louis Gernet and headed by Jean-Pierre Vernant (b. 1914) have proved the most faithful followers of Lévi-Strauss' brand of structuralism, though even they have adapted it. Lévi-Strauss has regularly been lambasted for isolating myth from its various contexts – social, cultural, political, economic, even sexual. In his essay on Asdiwal he does provide a detailed ethnographic analysis of a myth, examining and integrating geographical, economic, sociological, and cosmological factors. But he does so almost nowhere else. Vernant and his fellow classicists – notably, Marcel Detienne, Pierre Vidal-Naquet, and Nicole Loraux – have taken the analysis of Asdiwal as their model. As the heirs of Lévi-Strauss, these classicists have sought to decipher underlying, often latent patterns in myths, but they have then sought to link those patterns to ones in the culture at large.

Marcel Detienne on Adonis

The French classicist Marcel Detienne (b. 1936), at the time a staunch disciple of Lévi-Strauss, devoted a whole book to the myth

of Adonis: *The Gardens of Adonis*. Where for Frazer Adonis is an impersonal force rather than a god, for Detienne Adonis is a human being rather than a god. Where for Frazer Adonis symbolizes vegetation, for Detienne one form of vegetation symbolizes – better, parallels – Adonis. Where for Frazer Adonis, like vegetation, annually dies and revives, for Detienne Adonis, like the vegetation associated with him, grows up quickly and then just as quickly dies, once and for all. Above all, where for Frazer the meaning of the myth lies in the plot – the birth, adolescence, death, and rebirth of Adonis – for Detienne the meaning lies in the dialectical relationship among the elements of the plot – characters, places, times, and events.

For Detienne, following Lévi-Strauss, this dialectical relationship exists on a host of levels: dietary, botanical, astronomical, seasonal, religious, and social. At each level a middle ground lies between extremes. The levels parallel, not symbolize, one another. The relationship among the elements at, say, the dietary level is similar to that at the botanical. Still, the dietary level – with cereals and cooked meat lying between spices at one extreme and lettuce and raw meat at the other – most tightly links the others.

Detienne first associates spices with the gods, cereals and cooked meat with humans, and lettuce and raw meat with animals. Spices are burned during sacrifices to the gods. The smell ascends to the gods, who inhale it as the equivalent of food. Because the meat is cooked rather than burned, it goes to humans, who also cultivate cereals. Just as burned meat goes to the gods in the form of fumes, so raw meat goes to animals, with which Detienne also somehow links lettuce. Spices are further associated with the gods because of their relationship to the sun and so, as the place atop earth in the Greek imagination, to Olympus. Spices not only are burned by the sun but also grow where and when the sun is nearest: in the hottest places and on the hottest days of summer. By contrast, lettuce is cold and is therefore connected with the coldest places and times:

the world below earth – the seas and the Underworld – and winter. To eat meat raw is to eat it 'cold'.

Cereals and cooked meat lie between spices on the one hand and lettuce and raw meat on the other. Just as, for humans, meat must be cooked rather than either burned or eaten raw, so cereals, to grow, need some sun but not too much: 'In the middle range, situated at a fair distance from the fire of the sun, are the edible plants, . . . the cereals and the fruits.' Cereals are therefore grown neither above ground nor below it but in it. Where spices are gathered during the summer and lettuce somehow during the winter, crops are harvested in the autumn in between.

Spices are tied to the gods for other reasons. Less cultivated than gathered, they require no work and thereby befit the lives of the gods. Conversely, animals, eating only what they find, do not work for their supper either. But the gods eat what they want. Animals eat only what they find. The gods, then, do not have to work to eat better than humans. Animals, by not working, eat worse than humans. Humans again fall in between. They must work to eat, but when they work, they have enough, if barely enough, to eat. In the Greek poet Hesiod's Golden Age, humans were like the gods precisely because they had plenty without working. In the future they will be like animals, refusing to work, and so presumably going hungry.

Spices are associated not only with gods but also with promiscuity. Rather than making promiscuity a divine prerogative, Detienne deems Zeus and Hera the perfect couple, even in the face of Zeus' escapades: 'the Zeus-Hera couple stresses the ritual consecration that sanctions the unity of husband and wife'. Not gods but spices, with their fragrant, hence seductive, aroma, are connected to promiscuity: 'In the form of ointments, perfumes and other cosmetic products they [spices] also have an erotic function.' Not coincidentally, spices pervaded the Adonia festival, which was celebrated during the hottest days and which was notorious for its

promiscuity. Conversely, Detienne links not animals but lettuce and raw meat to sterility and celibacy. For the foul smell of at least rotten, if not raw, meat – Detienne somehow equates the two – repels rather than attracts and thereby fends off sex. Not coincidentally, the women of Lemnos were spurned by men because of their stench.

Between promiscuity on the one hand and sterility or celibacy on the other stands marriage, with which, notes Detienne, the Thesmophoria festival was connected. Though barred to men, the festival, which was celebrated annually at Athens for three days, really celebrated marriage. If its celebrants were all female, they were also all married. Falling between the fragrance of the Adonia and the stench of Lemnos, the mildly foul smell of the festival served to fend off men during only the festival.

Detienne connects all of these levels with the life of Adonis and with the ritualistic gardens dedicated to him. At every level, argues Detienne, Adonis falls in either extreme rather than in the middle. Indeed, Adonis jumps from one extreme to the other, bypassing the middle. Adonis' fate represents that of any human who dares to act like a god: he is reduced to an animal. Daring to be promiscuous, he proves impotent.

For Detienne, as a structuralist, the extremes on each level *parallel*, not *symbolize*, the life of Adonis. At each level the extremes are to the middle as Adonis is to normal humans. Where for Frazer the myth uses humans to symbolize impersonal forces of nature, for Detienne the myth uses impersonal forces of nature as analogues to human behaviour.

The gardens of Adonis, planted during the Adonia festival, involve little work. The plants shoot up immediately. Tending them parallels the toilless lives of the gods. In fact, the gardens are like the spices of the gods. The plants are merely gathered, not cultivated, and grow in the hottest places and times. They are carried to the

roofs of houses at the height of summer. Where regular crops take eight months to grow, the plants take only eight days. Where regular crops demand the strength of men, the gardens are tended by women. Unlike the spices, however, the gardens die as quickly as they sprout; and unlike regular crops, they die without yielding food. Having begun above the earth, they end up below it – cast into the sea. In short, the gardens are a futile 'get rich quick' scheme to get food without work. Gods need not work, but humans must. When they seek 'fast food' instead of regular fare, they get no food at all.

Adonis himself is related to spices through his mother, Myrrha, who becomes a myrrh tree. Adonis' gestation takes place in the tree, and his birth requires his breaking out of it. In Ovid's version wood nymphs even bathe the infant in the myrrh formed from his mother's tears. More important, Adonis is tied to spices through promiscuity. Unable to control her desire, Adonis' mother commits incest with her father. Unable to control their desire, Aphrodite and Persephone, according to Apollodorus, fight for custody of the infant Adonis. Adonis himself, for Detienne, is less an innocent victim of divine seduction than a seducer of divinities.

Adonis is a precocious seducer. Like the gardens, he grows up quickly. But like the gardens as well, he dies quickly. Just as the gardens die too early to yield any food, so Adonis dies too young to marry and have children. Having begun promiscuous, he ends up sterile. Conversely, his mother, who began sterile or at least abstinent – she had spurned all males – becomes promiscuous at the least. Jumping from one extreme to the other, mother and son alike reject and, more, threaten the middle ground of marriage.

Adonis' sterility takes the form of not only childlessness but also effeminacy. His death from the boar shows his unfitness for the masculine hunt. Instead of the hunter, he becomes the hunted: 'The perfect antithesis of a warrior hero such as Herakles', Adonis 'is nothing more than a victim as weak as he is pitiable'. Adonis' effeminacy signifies insufficient distance between male and female. His mother's

initial rejection of all males signifies the opposite. The ideal lies, again, in between: males and females should be related but distinct.

Just as Detienne links Adonis' promiscuity with spices, so he links Adonis' sterility and death with lettuce, in which, in several variants of the myth, Adonis tries vainly to hide from the boar. Just as myrrh 'has the power to arouse the desires of an old man', so lettuce 'can extinguish the ardour of young lovers'. Lettuce 'brings impotence, which is equivalent to death'.

Put summarily, Adonis does not know his place. He does not know that he is neither god nor animal but human and that what is distinctively human is marriage. In dying before marrying, he fails to fulfil his human nature.

If the *meaning* of the myth for Detienne is the presentation of an almost endless series of levels, the *function* of the myth is social. It advocates marriage as the middle ground between promiscuity on the one hand and sterility or celibacy on the other. In the next chapter I will be arguing that the myth advocates marriage as a bulwark of the *polis*.

Chapter 8
Myth and society

Bronislaw Malinowski

Where for Tylor and Frazer myth deals exclusively, or nearly exclusively, with physical phenomena – flooding, disease, death – for Bronislaw Malinowski myth deals even more with social phenomena – marriage, taxes, and, as already considered in Chapter 4, ritual. Myth still serves to reconcile humans to the unpleasantries of life, but now to unpleasantries that, far from unalterable, *can* be cast off. Here, too, myths spur resigned acceptance by tracing these unpleasantries – or at least impositions – back to a hoary past, thereby conferring on them the clout of tradition:

> The myth comes into play when rite, ceremony, or a social or moral
> rule demands justification, warrant of antiquity, reality, and sanctity.
> (Malinowski, 'Myth in Primitive Psychology', p. 107)

Myth persuades denizens to defer to, say, ranks in society by pronouncing those ranks long-standing and in that sense deserved. A myth about the British monarchy would make the institution as ancient as possible, so that to tamper with it would be to tamper with tradition. In England today fox hunting is defended on the grounds that it has long been part of country life. Social myths say, 'Do this because this has always been done.' In the case of physical

13. Bronislaw Malinowski, *c*.1935

phenomena the beneficiary of myth is the individual. In the case of social phenomena the beneficiary is society itself.

To say that myth traces back the origin of phenomena is equivalent to saying that myth explains those phenomena. When, then, Malinowski, railing against Tylor, declares that primitives 'do not want to "explain," to make "intelligible" anything which happens in their myths', he is really asserting that myths are not, as for Tylor, explanations for their own sake. Yet explanations they must still be, for only by explaining phenomena do they serve their conciliatory function.

Malinowski never makes clear whether moderns as well as primitives have myths. As modern science provides far more control over the physical world than primitive science does, there are surely fewer modern myths of physical phenomena. If there are none, there can still be modern myths of social phenomena. If not even these remain, their place has been taken by ideology.

Georges Sorel

The view of myth as itself ideology is to be found classically in
Reflections on Violence, by the French syndicalist Georges Sorel
(1847–1922). For Sorel, myth is eternal, not merely primitive, and,
antithetically to Malinowski, serves not to bolster society but to
topple it. Sorel asserts that the only way to establish the socialist
ideal is through revolution, which requires both violence and myth.
By 'violence' he means forceful action but not mere bloodshed.
The key 'violent' action is a strike by all workers. By 'myth' he means
a guiding ideology, one that preaches an imminent end to present
society, advocates a fight to the death with the ruling class, makes
rebels heroes, declares the certainty of victory, and espouses a moral
standard for the future society:

> In the course of this study one thing has always been present in my
> mind ... – that men who are participating in a great social
> movement always picture their coming action as a battle in which
> their cause is certain to triumph. These constructions . . . I propose
> to call myths; the syndicalist 'general strike' and Marx's catastrophic
> revolution are such myths. . . . Catholics have never been discouraged
> even in the hardest trials, because they have always pictured the
> history of the Church as a series of battles between Satan and the
> hierarchy supported by Christ; every new difficulty which arises is
> only an episode in a war which must finally end in the victory of
> Catholicism.

> (Sorel, *Reflections on Violence*, pp. 41–2)

Oliver Cromwell's vowed determination to remove King Charles I of
England would typify myth for Sorel.

Sorel asserts that both violence and myth are indispensable for
revolution and are therefore justified. He spurns any neutral,
scientific analysis of myth, including a Marxist one. He turns
Marxism itself into a myth, for commitment to it goads followers to
revolution. Sorel is like Malinowski in his indifference to the truth

of myth. For both, what matters is that myth works when believed to be true. And for Sorel, the ultimate truth of myth – the success of a revolution – is unknowable in advance anyway.

For Malinowski, myth is like ideology in justifying submission to society. For Sorel, myth *is* ideology in justifying rejection of society. Sorel's theory is wholly inapplicable to the case of Adonis, who acts alone, is more passive victim than active agent, and is hardly motivated by any ideology. Sorel's theory clearly fits today's terrorists, whose myth justifies 9/11 as the first stage in the defeat of the reigning international power, the demonized America. Yet how much Sorel's theory actually illuminates any myth beyond labelling it as such, it is not easy to see.

René Girard

René Girard, whose take on Frazer's myth-ritualism was considered in Chapter 5, transforms not merely the relationship between myth and ritual but also the origin and function of both. The two arise to secure not food but peace. The scapegoat, whether king or commoner, is sacrificed to end not winter but violence, which is the *problem* rather than, as for Sorel, the *solution*. Myth and ritual are ways of coping not with nature but with human nature – with human aggression.

In *Violence and the Sacred* Girard, like Raglan and Rank, cites Oedipus as the best example of his theory. Far from causing the plague besetting Thebes during his reign as king, Oedipus, according to Girard, is in fact an innocent victim. Either there never was a plague, or the plague was not the cause of the upheaval. Or the plague is a metaphor for violence, which has spread across society like a contagion. The violence among Thebans is evinced in the tension among the principals of Sophocles' play: Oedipus, Creon, and Teiresias. The only way to end the violence and thereby preserve society is by making a scapegoat of a vulnerable member of society. Even though the king, Oedipus is doubly stigmatized

and thereby doubly vulnerable. He is an outsider: he is not yet known to be a Theban and has won the throne not by heredity but by the toppling of the Sphinx. And he is a cripple – the result of the piercing of his tendons at birth. The myth, concocted only after Oedipus' downfall, serves to absolve the community by blaming him: he has killed his father and married his mother, and it is for his parricide and his incest that Thebes now endures plague. Or so argues Sophocles' Teiresias:

> If we take Tiresias's reply literally, the terrible charges of patricide and incest that he has just leveled at Oedipus did not stem from any supernatural source of information [and so do not represent the 'truth']. The accusation is simply an act of reprisal arising from the hostile exchange of a tragic debate. Oedipus unintentionally initiates the process by forcing Tiresias to speak. He accuses Tiresias of having had a part in the murder of [Oedipus' father] Laius; he prods Tiresias into reprisal, into hurling the accusation back at him. . . . [For each] to accuse the other of Laius' murder is to attribute to him sole responsibility for the sacrificial crisis; but as we have seen, everybody shares equal responsibility, because everybody participates in the destruction of a cultural order.
>
> (Girard, *Violence and the Sacred*, p. 71)

In actuality, according to Girard, Thebans simply decide to accept Teiresias' and Creon's opinions rather than Oedipus' over who is responsible for the breakdown in society. Only the subsequent myth turns the victors' opinions into the truth:

> The Thebans – religious believers – sought a cure for their ills in a formal acceptance of the myth, in making it the indisputable version of the events that had recently convulsed the city and in making it the charter for a new cultural order – by convincing themselves, in short, that all their miseries were due exclusively to the plague. Such an attitude requires absolute faith in the guilt of the surrogate victim.
>
> (Girard, *Violence and the Sacred*, p. 83)

That collective violence rather than the individual Oedipus is the real cause of the problem is borne out by events thereafter. True, the plague ends, but it is soon followed by a fight for the throne among Creon; Oedipus' son Polynices; and his other son, Eteocles. According to Girard, Sophocles challenges the myth, but never explicitly, so that the play has regularly has been taken, by Harrison and Murray included, as the dramatized *version* of the myth rather than as, for the more perceptive Girard, a *challenge* to the myth.

But the myth, which continues with *Oedipus at Colonus*, does more than blame Oedipus for Theban woes. It proceeds to turn him into a hero. Even as king, Oedipus is heroic in deeming it his duty to end the plague that has befallen his subjects, in vowing to discover who the culprit is, and in insisting on being banished once he discovers that he himself is the culprit. Yet for Girard the real hero is not the fallen, self-sacrificing Oedipus, as for Raglan, but the elevated one. Even as culprit, Oedipus has the power to save Thebes: just as his presence caused the plague, so his departure ends it. He is a hero even while a criminal. He already has the god-like power both to bring plague and to end it.

But by the time of *Oedipus at Colonus* Oedipus' stature has grown. Having arrived, after years of wandering, at Colonus, near Athens, he is now beckoned to return to Thebes. Just as the welfare of Thebes once depended on Oedipus' exile, so now it depends on his return. Oedipus refuses, for we learn that he had wanted to remain at Thebes following the events in *Oedipus the King* but had eventually been forcibly exiled by Creon and others. Now Creon is prepared to seize him and bring him back to Thebes. King Theseus offers Oedipus asylum. In return, Oedipus declares that his burial spot in Athens will protect Athens against Thebes. In short, Oedipus, having in *Oedipus as King* begun as a divine-like King of Thebes, in *Oedipus at Colonus* ends as a divine-like benefactor of Athens.

Adonis

Ancient Greeks linked psychological immaturity to political immaturity: Adonis' failure to become an adult would have meant his failure to become a citizen. Adonis would have been suited for precisely that form of government which involves no responsibility and assumes political infancy: tyranny. Adonis' submission to mother-like gods fits a matriarchal society. Having experienced only smothering females, he projects those qualities onto all females and thereby submits unquestioningly to them.

The family constitutes the link between personality and the *polis*, the city-state run by male citizens. The opposition that Herodotus draws between the *polis* of Greece, in which even the ruler is subject to the law, and the tyranny of the East, in which the ruler is above the law, holds for family life as well.

To demonstrate the tyranny of Eastern potentates, Herodotus catalogues their violations of familial mores. King Candaules of Sardis orders Gyges, his bodyguard, to look secretly at the Queen as she disrobes. She then forces Gyges to kill her husband (Herodotus 1.8–13). Solon tells King Croesus of Lydia that the happiest man he has known was an obscure Athenian who had fine sons and lived to see them raise children in turn. Croesus himself has two sons, one deaf and dumb, the other killed – like Adonis, while hunting boar – by a friend who had accidentally killed his brother and been banished by his father for it (Herodotus 1.29–33). King Astyages of Media orders Cyrus, his grandson, to be killed at birth to prevent his usurpation of the throne. In revenge for Harpagus' failure to carry out the deed, Astyages serves him up his son. Cyrus subsequently does topple, though not kill, his grandfather (Herodotus 1.117–19). King Cambyses of Persia, Cyrus' son and successor, marries two of his sisters, murders one of them, and murders his brother as well. He goes insane and dies childless (Herodotus 3.31–32). And so on through, worst of all, King Xerxes of Persia.

132

As for the domestic lives of Greek tyrants, whom Herodotus acknowledges but deems aberrations, Periandros of Corinth murders his wife, deposes his father-in-law, and dispossesses his one talented son (Herodotus 3.50.3–3.52.6). Peisistratos of Athens refuses to have 'normal' sex with his second wife because he fears a curse upon her family (Herodotus 1.61.1).

Adonis is incapable of citizenship because he, like the tyrants, is incapable of family life. On the one hand he fosters no family: he never marries, has no children, and dies young. On the other hand he is born into no family: he is the child of incest, not marriage, and his father tries to kill his mother. He is thus barred doubly from citizenship: he lacks not only maturity but also a pedigree, itself the result of the immaturity of his mother. If Herodotus testifies to the political necessity of siring a family, the Aristotelian *Constitution of the Athenians* testifies to the political necessity of descending from one: 'the right of citizenship belongs to those whose parents have been citizens'.

Until Cleisthenes in 507 BC changed the basis of Athenian citizenship from kinship to locale, membership in a phratry, or kinship group, was prerequisite. Even after the deme, which was a matter of locale, replaced the phratry as the prime political unit, the phratry remained important. Though a fourth-century Athenian, for example, could be a citizen without belonging to a phratry, his position would be both 'uncomfortable and questionable'. Moreover, membership in the deme was itself hereditary. Consequently, citizenship remained a matter of birth, as the *Constitution of the Athenians*, referring to the time after Cleisthenes, states.

The Greeks linked immaturity not only to politics but also to hunting. Adonis' haplessness at hunting would have symbolized his haplessness at adulthood. He becomes the hunted instead of the hunter. He has no conception of hunting and of its dangers. Either he thinks the world maternal, or he thinks himself protected from it

by maternal goddesses. To Venus' warnings that dangerous animals respect neither youth nor beauty, he is deaf.

The tie between human and hunter becomes a metaphor for the tie between human and citizen. Pierre Vidal-Naquet (b. 1930) suggests that hunting was a key aspect of the two-year military stint that, according to the *Constitution of the Athenians*, Athenian youths were required to undergo before citizenship. Vidal-Naquet argues that those years were a rite of passage and therefore involved a break with the life that the youths, or *ephebes*, both had known until now and would know afterwards. The *ephebes* thus spent their years at the frontier rather than in the city and spent them with one another rather than with their families.

Above all, claims Vidal-Naquet, the adolescent *ephebes* engaged in a brand of hunting that was the opposite of the brand that, as adult *hoplites*, they would soon be undertaking. As *ephebes*, they hunted individually, in the mountains, at night, and armed only with nets – thereby relying on trickery to capture their prey. As *hoplites*, they would be hunting in a group, on the plain, during the day, and armed with spears – thus relying on courage and skill to kill their prey. The contrast between the hunting of *ephebes* and the hunting of *hoplites* served to inculcate hoplite values in the *ephebes*.

Vidal-Naquet's evidence for the link of the *ephebeia* with hunting is twofold. He appeals, first, to the myth associated with the Apatouria, the festival at which Athenian fathers registered their sixteen-year-old sons as at once citizens, members of phratries, and *ephebes* for two years. Vidal-Naquet asserts that the subject of the myth, the Athenian Melanthos, or 'Black One', is a negative model for the *ephebes*: he is an *ephebe* who never becomes a *hoplite*. Even as an adult, he resorts to deceit rather than courage or skill to defeat his opponent, the Boeotian King Xanthos (the 'Blond One').

Vidal-Naquet appeals, second, to the figure of Melanion, the Black Hunter, as described by Aristophanes:

> I wish to tell you a story I once heard
> when I was still a boy:
> how there was once a youth, by the name of Melanion,
> who, eschewing marriage, went away to live in the mountains.
> He spent the time hunting hares,
> for which he set snares,
> and he had a dog,
> and he hated women so much that he never went home again.
> Melanion loathed women, and so, no less than he,
> do we, the wise.
>
> (Aristophanes, *Lysistrata*, 781–96)

The connection between Melanion and the *ephebeia* is both that Melanion, as a fellow black character, has all of the dark associations of Melanthos, and that Melanion is an *ephebe*-like hunter who never marries.

If one extrapolates from Melanthos as fighter to him as hunter, both he and Melanion succeed at hunting of only an adolescent variety. But Adonis is worse: he fails at hunting of any kind. He is thus not, like Melanthos and Melanion, merely an adolescent who never advances to adulthood but an infant who never even advances to childhood. The severity of his failure as a hunter signifies the severity of his failure as a citizen. The myth preaches citizenship, just by a conspicuously negative example.

Conclusion: The future of the study of myth

Nineteenth-century theories of myth, if one can generalize from the cases of Tylor and Frazer, saw myth as entirely about the physical world. Myth was assumed to be part of religion, which was assumed to be the primitive counterpart to science, which in turn was assumed to be wholly modern. In the twentieth century Tylor's and Frazer's theories have been spurned exactly for pitting myth against science and thereby precluding traditional myths, for subsuming myth under religion and thereby precluding secular myths, for deeming the subject matter of myth the physical world, for deeming the function of myth explanatory, and for deeming myth false.

The overarching twentieth-century rejoinder to Tylor and Frazer has been the denial that myth must go when science comes. Twentieth-century theories have defiantly sought to preserve myth in the face of science. Yet they have not done so by challenging science as the reigning explanation of the physical world. They have not taken any of the easy routes: 'relativizing' science, 'sociologizing' science, or 'mythicizing' science. Rather, they have re-characterized *myth*. Either myth, while still about the world, is not an explanation, in which case its function differs from that of science (Malinowski, Eliade), or myth, read symbolically, is not even about the physical world (Bultmann, Jonas, Camus). Or both (Freud, Rank, Jung, Campbell). In the twentieth century myth has been

reconciled with science by the reconfiguration of myth, not by any reconfiguration of science. Only at the end of the century, with the emergence of postmodernism, has the deference to science been questioned.

In so far as twentieth-century theories have not challenged the supremacy of science, why bother trying to reconcile myth with science? Why not simply accept the nineteenth-century view and dispense with myth in favour of science? The twentieth-century answer has been that the restriction of myth to either a literal explanation (Tylor) or a symbolic description (Frazer) of physical events fails to account for the array of other *functions* and *meanings* that myth harbours. The tell-tale evidence of these other functions and meanings is that myth is still around. If Tylor and Frazer were right, myth would by now be long dead.

D. W. Winnicott

In the twenty-first century the question is whether myth can be brought back to the external world – without facilely dismissing the authority of science. As a way of doing so, I propose applying to myth the analysis of play by the English child psychiatrist and psychoanalyst D. W. Winnicott (1896–1971).

For Winnicott, play is *acknowledged* as other than reality: children grant that they are just playing. Play grants itself the right to treat a spoon as a train, and a parent is barred from asking whether the spoon really is a train. But once play is over, the train is again a mere spoon. Still, play is more than fantasy or escapism. It is the construction of a reality with personal meaning. It takes something from the everyday world – a spoon – and transforms it into something more – a train.

As adult extensions of play, Winnicott, in stereotypically English fashion, names gardening and cooking, in both of which one creates a world with personal meaning out of elements from the external

world. Winnicott also names art and religion, in both of which one constructs a world with a far deeper meaning:

> It is assumed here that the task of reality-acceptance is never completed, that no human being is free from the strain of relating inner and outer reality, and that relief from this strain is provided by an intermediate area of experience which is not challenged (arts, religion, etc.). This intermediate area is in direct continuity with the play area of the small child who is 'lost' in play.
>
> (Winnicott, 'Transitional Objects and Transitional Phenomena', p. 13)

In Winnicott's terms, play is a 'transitional' activity. It provides a transition from childhood to adulthood, from the inner world of fantasy to outer reality, and from the known outer world to the unknown one. Just as a child clings to a physical object – a teddy bear – to create a safe world that then enables the child to explore with confidence the outside world, so an adult clings to an internalized object – a hobby, an interest, a value, or, I suggest, a myth – that then enables the adult to deal with a much wider world. Just as the child knows that the teddy bear is not Mummy yet clings to it as if it were, so the adult recognizes that the myth is not reality yet adheres to it as if it were. Myth is 'make-believe'.

Doubtless not all myths are treated as make-believe. Some myths can likely be taken only as unassailable truths – for example, myths about the impending end of the world. Other myths can surely be taken either way – for example, the belief in progress, ideologies, and world views like Marxism. Taken as make-believe, these kinds of myths serve as *guides* to the world rather than as *depictions* of the world.

The 'rags to riches' myth would fall here – if, that is, a mere credo dare qualify as a myth. The credo can certainly be held as a dogma, as ironically it is held at least as effusively around the world as in America itself, and can lead to frustration and recrimination

when it does not pan out. But the myth can also be held as 'make-believe' – not as a false characterization of American life but as a hoped-for one. Here America is seen *as if* it were a haven of opportunity. The present-day epitome of this myth is Anthony Robbins, salesman par excellence for success. His myth is a story – his story of his own rise from loser to winner. What, according to Robbins, keeps others from succeeding? Not trying.

Admittedly, Robbins' myth is still about the social world and not about the physical one. Better, then, are the biographies of those credited with divine-like powers – namely, celebrities. It is they who lead campaigns not merely to eradicate poverty, racism, and other social ills but also to end pollution, curb global warming, and save species. They can get things done that whole nations, even the United Nations, have failed to achieve.

The most elevated of celebrities are Hollywood stars. Like the popular conception of god found in Homer and even the Hebrew Bible, Hollywood stars are rarely seen in person and, when beheld on the screen, are gargantuan in size, can do anything, take on disguises, and are immortalized in their films. They have qualities so hyped as to be superhuman: not mere bravery but fearlessness, not mere kindliness but saintliness, not mere strength but omnipotence, not mere wisdom but omniscience.

A sceptic might protest that where gods are gods in private as well as in public, film stars are stars only on screen and are mere mortals off screen. But surely most fans make no distinction. The on-screen qualities are expected to be the off-screen ones as well. In fact, film stars are assumed to be playing themselves on screen, simply 'acting' as they themselves would in the situations in which they are placed. Fans are dismayed to learn that in 'real life' their favourite actors fall short of their roles – literally so in the case of the not very tall Mel Gibson. Robert Mitchum had to caution his fans not to expect military strategy from him. Greta Garbo had to become a recluse to preserve her youthful image. Gay Hollywood actors

dare not come out, lest they no longer be cast in straight roles. Tom Cruise is professionally obliged to sue anyone who calls him gay.

It might be said that where gods are born, film stars are made. And it is well known how capricious becoming a film star can be. But surely most fans believe that film stars are born, not made. When Lana Turner was spotted innocently drinking a milkshake at Schwab's drug store on Hollywood Boulevard, she was discovered, not invented.

It might be said that film stars cannot, like gods, do as they please. But surely most fans assume that stars are immune to the laws to which the rest of us are bound. Thus it shocks fans for their favourites to be subjected to arrest for drug taking (Robert Downey, Jr), shoplifting (Winona Ryder), or even paedophilia (Michael Jackson).

It is a cliché that contemporary film stars are drawn from a far wider array of types and that they are as much antiheroes as heroes. But the biggest box office draws, male and female alike, still look the part on screen, and it is looks, not acting ability, that put them there.

The terms used of fans' admiration say it all: stars are 'idolized' and 'worshipped'. And the greatest are called 'gods'. As 'stars', they shine brightly in a heaven far above us. Fans are 'star struck'.

Against my argument that film stars are modern gods, it might sensibly be argued that these days nobody believes the hype. No one believes that Hollywood stars are really different from you and me. They may have a bigger disposable income, but they face the same obstacles and tribulations as the rest of us. What sells better than an 'unauthorized' biography of a star – a biography that brings a star down to earth? If nothing else, the revelation of the disparity, put mildly, between the on-screen Rock Hudson, the quintessential heterosexual hunk, and the off-screen Rock Hudson, withering

away from AIDS, surely drove home the difference between on-screen persona and off-screen reality.

But this hard-nosed view of present-day fans is the naive one. Fans continue to 'idolize' and 'worship' stars, not in ignorance of their flaws but in defiance of them. The flaws are either denied or discounted. It is not that fans don't know. It is that they don't want to know, or else don't care. But their devotion is not mindless. It is done knowingly. It is, following Winnicott, make-believe, not credulity. It requires the refusal to let contrary evidence get in the way.

Cinema-going abets the deification of film stars. The cinema blocks out the outside world and substitutes a world of its own. The more effective the film, the more the audience forget where they are and imagine themselves in the time and place on the screen. Things are permitted in films that never happen in the proverbial 'real world'. In films, as in heaven, anything is possible. The phrase 'only in the movies' is telling. To go to the cinema is to suspend disbelief. It is to agree to '*play* along'. The ultimate payoff of cinema-going is encountering the actors themselves, even if only on the screen. Going to the cinema is like going to church – to a set-off, self-contained place where God is likeliest to be found. Cinema-going combines myth with ritual and brings gods, hence myths, back to the world – and does so without spurning science.

References

References are presented in the order in which they appear in each chapter.

Introduction

On the antiquity of theories of myth, see, for example, Richard Chase, *Quest for Myth* (Baton Rouge: Louisiana State University Press, 1949), chapter 1; Jan de Vries, *Forschungsgeschichte der Mythologie* (Freiburg: Alber, 1961), chapter 1.

On parallels between earlier theories and social scientific ones, see Burton Feldman and Robert D. Richardson, *The Rise of Modern Mythology, 1680-1860* (Bloomington: Indiana University Press, 1972), pp. xxii–xxiii.

John Beattie, *Other Cultures* (New York: Free Press, 1964).

For a standard folkloristic classification of stories, see William Bascom, 'The Forms of Folklore: Prose Narratives', *Journal of American Folklore*, 78 (1965): 3–20. On the blurriness of these distinctions, see Stith Thompson, *The Folktale* (Berkeley: University of California Press, 1977 [1946]), p. 303.

William D. Rubinstein, *The Myth of Rescue: Why the Democracies Could Not Have Saved More Jews from the Nazis* (London and New York: Routledge, 1987).

Apollodorus, *Gods and Heroes of the Greeks: The 'Library' of Apollodorus*, tr. Michael Simpson (Amherst: University of Massachusetts Press, 1976); Ovid, *Metamorphoses*, tr. Rolfe Humphries (Bloomington: Indiana University Press, 1955).

For scepticism over the universality of theories, see Stith Thompson, 'Myths and Folktales', *Journal of American Folklore*, 68 (1955): 482–8; G. S. Kirk, *Myth* (Berkeley: University of California Press, 1970), p. 7.

Chapter 1

On the history of creationism, see Ronald L. Numbers, *The Creationists* (Berkeley: University of California Press, 1992).

On scientific reinterpretation of the Noah myth, see, for example, William Ryan and Walter Pitman, *Noah's Flood* (London: Simon and Schuster, 1999). For a superb collection of the array of ways that flood stories worldwide have been approached, see Alan Dundes (ed.), *The Flood Myth* (Berkeley: University of California Press, 1988).

In the passage on the plagues of Egypt, the reference is to Herbert G. May and Bruce M. Metzger (eds.), *The New Oxford Annotated Bible with the Apocrypha*, Revised Standard Version (New York: Oxford University Press, 1977 [1962]). Quotations are taken from p. 75. For a comparable attempt to 'naturalize' myth from outside of the Bible, see Samuel Noah Kramer, *Sumerian Mythology*, rev. edn. (New York: Harper & Row, 1961 [1st edn. 1944]).

The classic attempt not to replace but to reconcile a theological account of the plagues with a scientific account is that of the Jewish existentialist philosopher Martin Buber, for whom the believer, on the basis of faith, attributes to divine intervention what the believer acknowledges can be fully accounted for scientifically. See Buber, *Moses* (New York: Harper Torchbooks, 1958 [1946]), especially pp. 60–8, 74–9. Buber is the Jewish counterpart to Rudolf Bultmann, considered in Chapter 2.

The classic work on finding science in myth is Giorgi de Santillana and Hertha von Dechend, *Hamlet's Mill* (Boston: Gambit, 1969).

The work cited is Andrew Dixon White, *A History of the Warfare of Science with Theology in Christendom* (1986), abridged by Bruce Mazlish (New York: Free Press, 1965). For a balanced corrective, see John Hedley Brooke, *Science and Religion* (Cambridge: Cambridge University Press, 1991).

The classic work by Edward Burnett Tylor is *Primitive Culture*, 2 vols, 1st edn. (London: Murray, 1871). Citations are from the reprint of the 5th (1913) edition (New York: Harper Torchbooks, 1958). The work by Stephen Jay Gould quoted is *Rocks of Ages* (London: Vintage, 2002 [1999]). On possible ways of distinguishing myth from science, see my *Theorizing about Myth* (Amherst: University of Massachusetts Press, 1999), pp. 7–9.

For a refreshingly sensible postmodern approach to myth, see Laurence Coupe, *Myth* (London and New York: Routledge, 1997).

For a modern Tylorian perspective, see David Bidney, *Theoretical Anthropology*, 2nd edn. (New York: Schocken, 1967 [1st edn. 1953]), chapter 10; 'Myth, Symbolism, and Truth', *Journal of American Folklore*, 68 (1955): 379–92.

On the term 'euhemerist', see Joseph Fontenrose, *The Ritual Theory of Myth* (Berkeley: University of California Press, 1966), pp. 20–3.

Friedrich Max Müller, 'Comparative Mythology' (1856), in his *Chips from a German Workshop* (London: Longmans, Green, 1867), pp. 1–141.

A theologian who assumes that Genesis 1 is anything but an account of creation is Langdon Gilkey. See his *Maker of Heaven and Earth* (Lanham, MD: University Press of America, 1985 [1959]), especially pp. 25–9, 148–55.

J. G. Frazer, *The Golden Bough*, 1st edn., 2 vols (London: Macmillan, 1890); 2nd edn., 3 vols (London: Macmillan, 1900); 3rd edn., 12 vols (London: Macmillan, 1911–15); one-vol. abridgment (London: Macmillan, 1922).

Hans Blumenberg, *Work on Myth*, tr. Robert M. Wallace (Cambridge, MA: MIT Press, 1985).

Lucien Lévy-Bruhl, *How Natives Think*, tr. Lilian A. Clare (New York: Washington Square Press, 1966 [1926]).

Bronislaw Malinowski, 'Magic, Science and Religion' [1925] and 'Myth in Primitive Psychology' [1926], in his *Magic, Science and Religion and Other Essays*, ed. Robert Redfield (Garden City, NY: Doubleday Anchor Books, 1954 [1948]), pp. 17–92 and 93–148.

Claude Lévi-Strauss, *The Savage Mind*, tr. not given (Chicago: University of Chicago Press, 1966); *Myth and Meaning* (Toronto: University of Toronto Press, 1978); André Akoun et al., 'A Conversation with Claude Lévi-Strauss', *Psychology Today*, 5 (May 1972): 36–9, 74–82.

Robin Horton, 'African Traditional Thought and Western Science', *Africa*, 37 (1967): 50–71 (part I), 155–87 (part II).

Stewart Guthrie, *Faces in the Clouds* (New York and Oxford: Oxford University Press, 1993).

Karl Popper, *Conjectures and Refutations*, 5th edn. (London: Routledge & Kegan Paul, 1974 [1st edn. 1962]); *The World of Parmenides*, ed. Arne F. Peterson and Jorgen Mejer (London: Routledge, 1998).

F. M. Cornford, *From Religion to Philosophy* (London: Arnold, 1912); *Principium Sapientiae*, ed. W. K. C. Guthrie (Cambridge: Cambridge University Press, 1952), chapters 1–11.

Chapter 2

Paul Radin, *Primitive Man as Philosopher*, 2nd edn. (New York: Dover, 1957 [1st edn. 1927]); *The World of Primitive Man* (New York: Dutton, 1971), chapter 3.

Ernst Cassirer, *The Philosophy of Symbolic Forms*, tr. Ralph Manheim, II (New Haven, CT: Yale University Press, 1955); *The Myth of the State* (New Haven, CT: Yale University Press, 1946). On political myths, see also Cassirer, *Symbol, Myth, and Culture*, ed. Donald Phillip Verene (New Haven: Yale University Press, 1979), pp. 219–67.

Henri Frankfort and H. A. Frankfort, John A. Wilson, Thorkild Jacobsen, and William A. Irwin, *The Intellectual Adventure of Ancient Man: An Essay on Speculative Thought in the Ancient Near East* (Chicago: University of Chicago Press, 1946 [reprinted Phoenix Books, 1997]); paperback retitled *Before Philosophy: The Intellectual Adventure of Ancient Man: An Essay on Speculative Thought in the Ancient Near East* (Harmondsworth: Pelican Books, 1949).

Rudolf Bultmann, 'New Testament and Mythology' (1941), in *Kerygma and Myth*, ed. Hans-Werner Bartsch, tr. Reginald H. Fuller, I (London: SPCK, 1953), pp. 1–44; *Jesus Christ and Mythology* (New York: Scribner's, 1958); Hans Jonas, *Gnosis und spätantiker Geist*, 2 vols, 1st edn. (Göttingen: Vandenhoeck und Ruprecht, 1934 [vol. I] and 1954 [vol. II, part 1]); *The Gnostic Religion*, 2nd edn. (Boston: Beacon Press, 1963 [1958]), Epilogue.

For the myth of Sisyphus, see Albert Camus, *The Myth of Sisyphus and Other Essays*, tr. Justin O'Brien (New York: Vintage Books, 1960 [1955]), pp. 88–91; Homer, *The Odyssey*, tr. Richmond Lattimore (New York: Harper Torchbooks, 1968 [1965]), p. 183.

Chapter 3

Bultmann, 'New Testament and Mythology' and *Jesus Christ and Mythology*.

Jonas, *The Gnostic Religion.*

Jonas is not the only philosopher to 'update' Gnosticism. The political philosopher Eric Voegelin seeks to show how modern movements like positivism, Marxism, Communism, Fascism, and psychoanalysis evince what he calls 'the Gnostic attitude'. See his *Science, Politics and Gnosticism* (Chicago: Regnery Gateway Editions, 1968) and *The New Science of Politics* (Chicago: University of Chicago Press, 1952).

On Norman Schwarzkopf, see Jack Anderson and Dale Van Atta, *Stormin' Norman: An American Hero* (New York: Zebra Books, 1971).

Mircea Eliade, *Myth and Reality*, tr. Willard R. Trask (New York: Harper Torchbooks, 1968 [1963]); *The Sacred and the Profane*, tr. Willard R. Trask (New York: Harvest Books, 1968 [1959]).

On John F. Kennedy, Jr, see, for example, Wendy Leigh, *Prince Charming* (New York: New American Library, 2000); Christopher Anderson, *The Day John Died* (New York: William Morrow, 2000); Richard Blow, *American Son* (New York: Henry Holt, 2002).

On George Washington, see Barry Schwartz, *George Washington* (New York: Free Press; London: Collier Macmillan, 1987). From the bestselling hagiographical biography by Mason Weems comes the story that the scrupulously honest young George could not lie when asked who had cut down his father's cherry tree. See Weems, *The Life of Washington*, 9th edn., ed. Peter S. Onuf (Armonk, NY: Sharpe, 1996 [1st edn. 1800; 9th edn. 1809]), pp. 9–10.

Chapter 4
William Robertson Smith, *Lectures on the Religion of the Semites*, First Series, 1st edn. (Edinburgh: Black, 1889), Lecture 1.

Tylor, *Primitive Culture*, 5th edn., II, chapter 18.

Frazer, *The Golden Bough*, abridged edn., especially chapters 29–33 (first myth-ritualist scenario); 6–8, 24 (second myth-ritualist scenario).

Jane Ellen Harrison, *Themis*, 1st edn. (Cambridge: Cambridge University Press, 1912); *Alpha and Omega* (London: Sidgwick & Jackson, 1915), chapter 6; *Epilegomena to the Study of Greek Religion* (Cambridge: Cambridge University Press, 1921); on myth and art, *Ancient Art and Ritual* (New York: Holt; London: Williams and Norgate, 1913).

S. H. Hooke, 'The Myth and Ritual Pattern of the Ancient East', in *Myth and Ritual*, ed. Hooke (London: Oxford University Press, 1933), chapter 1; Introduction to *The Labyrinth*, ed. Hooke (London: SPCK; New York: Macmillan, 1935), pp. v–x; *The Origins of Early Semitic Ritual* (London: Oxford University Press, 1938); 'Myth and Ritual: Past and Present', in *Myth, Ritual, and Kingship*, ed. Hooke (Oxford: Clarendon Press, 1958), chapter 1.

Gregory Nagy, 'Can Myth Be Saved?', in *Myth*, ed. Gregory Schrempp and William Hansen (Bloomington: Indiana University Press, 2002), chapter 15. See also Edmund Leach, *Political Systems of Highland Burma* (Boston: Beacon, 1965 [1954]); 'Ritualization in Man', *Philosophical Transactions of the Royal Society*, Series B, no. 772, vol. 251 (1966): 403–8.

Gilbert Murray, 'Excursis on the Ritual Forms Preserved in Greek Tragedy', in Harrison, *Themis*, pp. 341–63; *Euripides and His Age*, 1st edn. (New York: Holt; London: Williams and Norgate, 1913), pp. 60–8; *Aeschylus* (Oxford: Clarendon Press, 1940); 'Dis Geniti', *Journal of Hellenic Studies*, 71 (1951): 120–8; on myth and literature, 'Hamlet and Orestes: A Study in Traditional Types', *Proceedings of the British Academy*, 6 (1913–14): 389–412.

F. M. Cornford, 'The Origin of the Olympic Games', in Harrison, *Themis*, chapter 7; *The Origin of Attic Comedy* (London: Arnold, 1914); 'A Ritual

Basis for Hesiod's *Theogony*' (1941), in his *The Unwritten Philosophy and Other Essays*, ed. W. K. C. Guthrie (Cambridge: Cambridge University Press, 1950), pp. 95–116; *Principium Sapientiae*, ed. W. K. C. Guthrie (Cambridge: Cambridge University Press, 1952), pp. 191–256.

A. B. Cook, *Zeus*, 3 vols in 5 (Cambridge: Cambridge University Press, 1914–40).

Ivan Engnell, *Studies in Divine Kingship in the Ancient Near East*, 1st edn. (Uppsala: Almqvist & Wiksells, 1943); *A Rigid Scrutiny*, ed. and tr. John T. Willis (Nashville: Vanderbilt University Press, 1969) (retitled *Critical Essays on the Old Testament* [London: SPCK, 1970]).

Aubrey R. Johnson, 'The Role of the King in the Jerusalem Cults', in *The Labyrinth*, ed. Hooke, pp. 73–111; 'Hebrew Conceptions of Kingship', in *Myth, Ritual, and Kingship*, ed. Hooke, pp. 204–35; *Sacral Kingship in Ancient Israel*, 1st edn. (Cardiff: University of Wales Press, 1955).

Sigmund Mowinckel, *The Psalms in Israel's Worship*, tr. D. R. Ap-Thomas, 2 vols (New York: Abingdon, 1962); *He That Cometh*, tr. G. W. Anderson (Nashville: Abingdon, 1954), chapter 3.

Malinowski, 'Myth in Primitive Psychology'; 'Magic, Science and Religion', especially pp. 83–4; 'The Role of Myth in Life', *Psyche*, 6 (1926): 29–39; *Malinowski and the Work of Myth*, ed. Ivan Strenski (Princeton, NJ: Princeton University Press, 1992).

Eliade, *The Sacred and the Profane*, chapter 2; *Myth and Reality*.

Applications of the theory of myth to literature: Jessie L. Weston, *From Ritual to Romance* (Cambridge: Cambridge University Press, 1920); E. M. Butler, *The Myth of the Magus* (Cambridge: Cambridge University Press; New York: Macmillan, 1948); C. L. Barber, *Shakespeare's*

Festive Comedy (Princeton, NJ: Princeton University Press, 1959);
Herbert Weisinger, *Tragedy and the Paradox of the Fortunate
Fall* (London: Routledge & Kegan Paul; East Lansing: Michigan
State College Press, 1953); Francis Fergusson, *The Idea of a Theater*
(Princeton, NJ: Princeton University Press, 1949); Lord Raglan,
'Myth and Ritual', *Journal of American Folklore*, 68 (1955):
454–61; Northrop Frye, *Anatomy of Criticism* (Princeton, NJ:
Princeton University Press, 1957), pp. 131–239; Stanley Edgar
Hyman, 'Myth, Ritual, and Nonsense', *Kenyon Review*, 11
(1949): 455–75.

René Girard, *Violence and the Sacred*, tr. Patrick Gregory (London:
Athlone Press; Baltimore: Johns Hopkins University Press, 1977); *'To
Double Business Bound'* (London: Athlone Press; Baltimore: Johns
Hopkins University Press, 1978); *The Scapegoat*, tr. Yvonne Freccero
(London: Athlone Press; Baltimore: Johns Hopkins University Press,
1986); *Things Hidden since the Foundation of the World*, tr. Stephen
Bann and Michael Metteer (London: Athlone Press; Stanford: Stanford
University Press, 1987); *Job, the Victim of his People*, tr. Yvonne Freccero
(London: Athlone Press; Stanford: Stanford University Press, 1987);
'Generative Scapegoating', in *Violent Origins*, ed. Robert G. Hamerton-
Kelly (Stanford: Stanford University Press, 1987), pp. 73–105. Against
Frazer, see *Violence and the Sacred*, pp. 28–30, 96, 121–3, 316–18;
The Scapegoat, p. 120.

Clyde Kluckhohn, 'Myths and Rituals: A General Theory', *Harvard
Theological Review*, 35 (1942): 45–79.

Walter Burkert, *Structure and History in Greek Mythology and Ritual*
(Berkeley: University of California Press, 1979), especially pp. 56–8,
99–101; *Homo Necans*, tr. Peter Bing (Berkeley: University of California
Press, 1983), especially pp. 29–34; *Ancient Mystery Cults* (Cambridge,
MA: Harvard University Press, 1987), pp. 73–8; 'The Problem of Ritual
Killing', in *Violent Origins*, ed. Hamerton-Kelly, pp. 149–76; *Creation
of the Sacred* (Cambridge, MA: Harvard University Press, 1996),
chapters 2–3.

References

Chapter 5

On the preservation of classical mythology, see, for example, Douglas Bush, *Mythology and the Renaissance Tradition in English Poetry* (Minneapolis: University of Minnesota Press, 1932); *Mythology and the Romantic Tradition in English Poetry* (Cambridge, MA: Harvard University Press, 1937); Gilbert Highet, *The Classical Tradition* (New York: Oxford University Press, 1939): Jean Seznec, *The Survival of the Pagan Gods* (New York: Pantheon Books, 1953 [1940]). For a useful sourcebook on three classical myths, see Geoffrey Miles (ed.), *Classical Mythology in English Literature* (London: Routledge, 1999).

Jessie L. Weston, *From Ritual to Romance* (Cambridge: Cambridge University Press, 1920).

Francis Fergusson, *The Idea of a Theater* (Princeton, NJ: Princeton University Press, 1949); '"Myth" and the Literary Scruple', *Sewanee Review*, 64 (1956): 171–85.

Northrop Frye, 'The Archetypes of Literature' (1951) and 'Myth, Fiction, and Displacement' (1961), in his *Fables of Identity* (New York: Harcourt, Brace, 1963), pp. 7–20 and 21–38; *Anatomy of Criticism* (Princeton, NJ: Princeton University Press, 1957), pp. 131–239; 'Literature and Myth,' in *Relations of Literary Study*, ed. James Thorpe (New York: Modern Language Association, 1967), pp. 27–55; 'Symbolism of the Unconscious' (1959) and 'Forming Fours' (1954), in *Northrop Frye on Culture and Literature*, ed. Robert D. Denham (Chicago: University of Chicago Press, 1978), pp. 84–94 and 117–29; 'Myth', *Antaeus* 43 (1981): 64–84.

See, as classical Jungians, Maud Bodkin, *Archetypal Patterns in Literature* (London: Oxford University Press, 1934); Bettina L. Knapp, *A Jungian Approach to Literature* (Carbondale: Southern Illinois University Press, 1984).

See, as archetypal psychologists, James Hillman, *Re-Visioning*

Psychology (New York: Harper & Row, 1975); David L. Miller, *The New Polytheism* (Dallas: Spring Publications, 1981).

Girard, *Violence and the Sacred*.

On the distinction between story and narrative, see Shlomith Rimmon-Kenan, *Narrative Fiction*, 2nd edn. (London and New York: Routledge, 2002 [1st edn. 1983]), p. 3. On the yet further distinction among story, narrative, and plot – all of which I innocently use interchangeably – see Paul Cobley, *Narrative* (London and New York: Routledge, 2001), pp. 4–7.

Kenneth Burke, *The Rhetoric of Religion* (Boston: Beacon Press, 1961); *A Grammar of Motives* (New York: Prentice-Hall, 1945), pp. 430–40; 'Myth, Poetry and Philosophy', *Journal of American Folklore*, 73 (1960): pp. 283–306.

Tylor, *Primitive Culture*, 5th edn., I, pp. 281–2. Hero myths are a surprising category for someone for whom all myths are seemingly about physical events.

On the application of cognitive psychology to religion, under which would fall myth, see Pascal Boyer, *The Naturalness of Religious Ideas* (Berkeley: University of California Press, 1994).

Johann Georg von Hahn, *Sagwissenschaftliche Studien* (Jena: Mauke, 1876), p. 340; tr. Henry Wilson in John C. Dunlop, *History of Prose Fiction*, rev. Wilson (London: Bell, 1888), in an unnumbered attachment to the last page of vol. I.

Vladimir Propp, *Morphology of the Folktale*, tr. Laurence Scott, 2nd edn., rev. and ed. Louis A. Wagner (Austin: University of Texas Press, 1968 [1958]).

Otto Rank, *The Myth of the Birth of the Hero*, 1st edn., tr. F. Robbins and Smith Ely Jelliffe (New York: Journal of Nervous and Mental Disease Publishing, 1914).

Joseph Campbell, *The Hero with a Thousand Faces*, 1st edn. (New York: Pantheon Books, 1949).

Lord Raglan, *The Hero* (London: Methuen, 1936). Citations are from the reprint of Part 2, which is on myth, in Otto Rank et al., *In Quest of the Hero* (Princeton, NJ: Princeton University Press, 1990), pp. 89–175.

Chapter 6

Sigmund Freud, *The Interpretation of Dreams*, vols IV–V, *Standard Edition of the Complete Psychological Works of Sigmund Freud*, ed. and tr. James Strachey et al. (London: Hogarth Press and Institute of Psycho-Analysis 1953 [1913]).

Karl Abraham, *Dreams and Myths*, tr. William A. White (New York: Journal of Nervous and Mental Disease Publishing, 1913).

Rank, *The Myth of the Birth of the Hero*, 1st edn. Citations are from the reprint in Rank et al., *In Quest of the Hero* pp. 3–86. See also Rank's even more Oedipal *The Incest Theme in Literature and Language*, 1st edn., tr. Gregory Richter (Baltimore: Johns Hopkins University Press, 1992). See also Rank and Hanns Sachs, *The Significance of Psychoanalysis for the Mental Sciences*, tr. Charles R. Payne (New York: Nervous and Mental Disease Publishing, 1913). For post-Freudian Rank, see *The Trauma of Birth*, tr. not given (London: Kegan Paul; New York: Harcourt Brace, 1929).

On male creation myths, see Alan Dundes, 'Earth-Driver: Creation of the Mythopoeic Male', *American Anthropologist*, 64 (1962): 1032–51.

Jacob A. Arlow, 'Ego Psychology and the Study of Mythology', *Journal of the American Psychoanalytic Association*, 9 (1961): 371–93.

Bruno Bettelheim, *The Uses of Enchantment* (New York: Vintage Books, 1977 [1976]).

Géza Róheim, 'Psycho-Analysis and the Folk-Tale', *International Journal of Psycho-Analysis*, 3 (1922): 180–6; 'Myth and Folk-Tale', *American Imago*, 2 (1941): 266–79; *The Riddle of the Sphinx*, tr. R. Money-Kyrle (New York: Harper Torchbooks, 1974 [1934]); *Fire in the Dragon and Other Psychoanalytic Essays on Folklore*, ed. Alan Dundes (Princeton, NJ: Princeton University Press, 1992).

Alan Dundes, *Analytic Essays in Folklore* (The Hague: Mouton, 1975); *Interpreting Folklore* (Bloomington: Indiana University Press, 1980); *Parsing through Customs* (Madison: University of Wisconsin Press, 1987); *Folklore Matters* (Knoxville: University of Tennessee Press, 1989).

On creation myths, see Erich Neumann, *The Origins and History of Consciousness*, tr. R. F. C. Hull (Princeton, NJ: Princeton University Press, 1970 [1954]); Marie-Louise von Franz, *Creation Myths*, rev. edn. (Boston: Shambhala, 1995 [1st edn. (entitled *Patterns of Creativity Mirrored in Creation Myths*) 1972]).

Campbell, *The Hero with a Thousand Faces*. Citations are from the second edition (Princeton, NJ: Princeton University Press, 1968).

On Adonis, see especially C. G. Jung, *Symbols of Transformation*, *Collected Works of C. G. Jung*, ed. Sir Herbert Read et al., tr. R. F. C. Hull et al., V, 2nd edn. (Princeton, NJ: Princeton University Press, 1967 [1956]), pp. 219, 223 n. 32, 258–9, 343 n. 79.

On the archetype of the *puer aeternus*, see especially Jung, *Symbols of Transformation*, pp. 257–9, 340; 'Psychological Aspects of the Mother Archetype', in *The Archetypes and the Collective Unconscious*, *Collected Works*, IX, Part 1, 2nd edn. (Princeton, NJ: Princeton University Press, 1968 [1959]), p. 106; Marie-Louise von Franz, *Puer aeternus*, 2nd edn. (Santa Monica, CA: Sigo, 1981 [1970]).

On the archetype of the Great Mother, see especially Jung, 'Psychological Aspects of the Mother Archetype', pp. 75–110; *Symbols of Transformation*, pp. 207–444.

Chapter 7

Claude Lévi-Strauss, 'The Structural Study of Myth', *Journal of American Folklore*, 68 (1955): 428–44, reprinted in *Myth: A Symposium*, ed. Thomas A. Sebeok (Bloomington: Indiana University Press, 1958), paperback (1965); also reprinted, slightly revised, in Lévi-Strauss, *Structural Anthropology*, tr. Claire Jacobsen and Brooke Grundfest Schoepf (New York: Basic Books, 1961), chapter 11. Citations are from the Sebeok paperback. *Introduction to a Science of Mythology*, tr. John and Doreen Weightman, 4 vols (New York: Harper & Row, 1969–81), paperback (New York: Harper Torchbooks, 1970–82). Citations are from the paperback. The volumes are individually named: *The Raw and the Cooked*, *From Honey to Ashes*, *The Origin of Table Manners*, and *The Naked Man*. 'The Study of Asdiwal', tr. Nicholas Mann, in *The Structural Study of Myth and Totemism*, ed. Edmund Leach (London: Tavistock, 1967), pp. 1–47. André Akoun et al., 'A Conversation with Claude Lévi-Strauss'.

On Lévi-Strauss' myth-ritualism, see 'The Structural Study of Myth'; 'Structure and Dialectics', in his *Structural Anthropology*, chapter 12; 'Comparative Religions of Nonliterate Peoples', in his *Structural Anthropology*, II, tr. Monique Layton (New York: Basic Books, 1976), chapter 5.

Vladimir Propp, *Morphology of the Folktale*, tr. Laurence Scott, 2nd edn., rev. and ed. Louis A. Wagner (Austin: University of Texas Press, 1968 [1958]); Georges Dumézil, *Archaic Roman Religion*, tr. Philip Krapp, 2 vols (Chicago: University of Chicago Press, 1970).

Jean-Pierre Vernant, *Myth and Thought among the Greeks*. tr. not given (London and Boston: Routledge & Kegan Paul, 1983); Vernant and Pierre Vidal-Naquet, *Myth and Tragedy in Ancient Greece*, tr. Janet

Lloyd (Brighton: Harvester Press, 1981); Nicole Loraux, *The Invention of Athens*, tr. Alan Sheridan (Cambridge, MA: Harvard University Press, 1987).

Marcel Detienne, *The Gardens of Adonis*, tr. Janet Lloyd (Hassock: Harvester Press; Atlantic Highlands, NJ: Humanities Press, 1977).

Chapter 8

Malinowski, 'Myth in Primitive Psychology'.

Georges A. Sorel, *Reflections on Violence*, tr. T. E. Hulme and J. Roth (New York: Collier Books; London: Collier-Macmillan, 1961 [1950]).

On myth and ideology, see Ben Halpern, '"Myth" and "Ideology" in Modern Usage', *History and Theory*, 1 (1961): 129–49; Christopher G. Flood, *Political Myth* (New York: Routledge, 2001 [1996]).

Girard, *Violence and the Sacred*.

On matriarchy in Greece and elsewhere, see, classically, J. J. Bachofen, *Myth, Religion, and Mother Right*, tr. Ralph Manheim (Princeton, NJ: Princeton University Press, 1967).

Herodotus, *The Histories*, tr. Aubrey de Sélincourt, rev. and ed. A. R. Burn (Harmondsworth: Penguin, 1972 [1954]).

Aristotle, *Constitution of Athens and Related Texts*, tr. Kurt von Fritz and Ernst Kapp (New York: Hafner Press, 1974 [1950]).

Antony Andrewes, *The Greeks* (New York: Knopf, 1967).

Pierre Vidal-Naquet, 'The Black Hunter and the Origin of the Athenian Ephebeia', in R. L. Gordon (ed.), *Myth, Religion and Society* (Cambridge: Cambridge University Press, 1981), pp. 147–62.

Aristophanes, *Lysistrata*, tr. Benjamin Bickley Rogers, Loeb Classical Library (London: Heinemann; New York: Harvard University Press, 1924).

Conclusion

D. W. Winnicott, 'Transitional Objects and Transitional Phenomena' (1951), in his *Through Paediatrics to Psychoanalysis* (London: Karnac Books, 1992 [1958]), chapter 18. Slightly revised version in his *Playing and Reality* (London and New York: Routledge, 1982 [1971]), chapter 1. The citation is from the revised version.

Index

N

O

P

R

Myth

VERY SHORT
INTRODUCTIONS

es

n

➤ **Contact** the editors

➤ **Order** other **VSIs** on-line

List of illustrations

Contents

In memory of Skip, a beloved cat

OXFORD
UNIVERSITY PRESS

Great Clarendon Street, Oxford OX2 6DP

Oxford University Press is a department of the University of Oxford.
It furthers the University's objective of excellence in research, scholarship,
and education by publishing worldwide in

Oxford   New York

Auckland Bangkok Buenos Aires Cape Town Chennai
Dar es Salaam Delhi Hong Kong Istanbul Karachi Kolkata
Kuala Lumpur Madrid Melbourne Mexico City Mumbai Nairobi
São Paulo Shanghai Taipei Tokyo Toronto

Oxford is a registered trade mark of Oxford University Press
in the UK and in certain other countries

Published in the United States
by Oxford University Press Inc., New York

British Library Cataloguing in Publication Data

Data available

Library of Congress Cataloging in Publication Data

Data available

ISBN: 978-0-19-280347-4

5 7 9 10 8 6

Typeset by RefineCatch Ltd, Bungay, Suffolk
Printed in Great Britain by
Ashford Colour Press Ltd, Gosport, Hampshire

Robert A. Segal

MYTH

A Very Short Introduction

OXFORD
UNIVERSITY PRESS

Available soon:

For more information visit our web site

www.oup.co.uk/vsi

VERY SHORT INTRODUCTIONS are for anyone wanting a stimulating and accessible way in to a new subject. They are written by experts, and have been published in more than 25 languages worldwide.

The series began in 1995, and now represents a wide variety of topics in history, philosophy, religion, science, and the humanities. Over the next few years it will grow to a library of around 200 volumes – a Very Short Introduction to everything from ancient Egypt and Indian philosophy to conceptual art and cosmology.

Very Short Introductions available now:

Myth: A Very Short Introduction

This book by Robert A. Segal is a concise, elegant, erudite overview of the major nineteenth and twentieth century theories of myth, using the Adonis narrative as a litmus test case for various approaches.
Alan Dundes, Professor of Anthropology and Folklore,
University of California, Berkeley

A delightfully clear, engagingly organized, and remarkably comprehensive treatment of theories of myth.
Ivan Strenski, Holstein Family and Community Professor, Department of Religious Studies, University of California at Riverside

This is the most helpful orientation to the field of mythological studies that I have ever encountered.
John Beebe, M.D., Past President, The C.G. Jung Institute of San Francisco

Segal writes to be understood and to instruct . . . One learns from the book much that will encourage and ease further reading.
William M. Calder III, William Abbott Oldfather Professor of the Classics, University of Illinois at Urbana/Champaign

This remarkably clear book is probably the widest-ranging presentation ever written of the various contemporary approaches to myth.
Antoine Faivre, Professor Emeritus at the Ecole Pratique des Hautes Etudes, Religious Studies, Sorbonne

The whole discussion is a profound exploration of a subject that touches on human experience, hopes, and expectations in religion, philosophy, drama, literature, and psychology.
John Rogerson, Professor Emeritus of Biblical Studies, University of Sheffield

'Problem,' she agreed, barely able to squeeze that single word out.

'Not an impossible one, *cara*,' Santino assured her in his wicked dark drawl, his intense bronzed eyes signalling pure enticement and sensual promise. 'I can think of several very interesting pursuits that I can talk through.'

The atmosphere sizzled. His smile flashed out once more and she just ached so much for contact again that she sat up, grabbed his shoulder to steady herself and found his passionate mouth again for herself. A low moan of response was wrenched from her as he suckled at her lips and then parted them to invade her mouth again.

'Thought I had to talk,' Santino teased as he lowered her back to the sofa and unbuttoned the rest of his shirt.

'No…' Her mouth ran dry as she stared up at him. He looked so big and powerful. A haze of short dark curls delineated his broad, muscular chest and his skin was the vibrant colour of bronze. Her body tensed, wild heat snaking up inside her again.

'Last time I was on a sofa with a female, I was sixteen,' Santino confided with dancing amusement in his dark golden gaze.

He lifted her up to him with easy strength and curved her round him. Cool air hit her taut spine as he unzipped her dress. He brushed down the delicate straps on her slim shoulders and released his breath in a slow, sexy hiss of appreciation as he bared her lush, pouting breasts.

'Superb…every inch of you is a work of art, *cara mia*,' Santino swore with husky fervour as a tide of shy pink washed up into her cheeks. 'Without a doubt you are the perfect reward at the end of a lousy day.'

Then he touched her and she was immediately lost in the passion again. All control was wrested from her by the seductive delight of his skilled fingers on her tender flesh and the even more intense excitement of his knowing mouth caressing the almost painfully sensitive rosy peaks. With a whimper of tormented response, she surrendered to that world of wild sensation…

CHAPTER FIVE

SANTINO wakened to the buzz of his mobile phone.

Disorientated in a way that was far from being the norm for him, he sat up, realised that he was still in the office and dug into his jacket for his phone. It was a very apologetic security guard calling up from the ground floor to ask if he was still upstairs working. *Working?* Santino stole a lingering glance at Poppy where she lay fast asleep beneath the suit jacket in which he had rifled for his phone. Shame and discomfiture gripped him.

'Yes, I'm here. I'll be a while, Willis.' Discarding his mobile again, he checked the illuminated dial on his watch. It was after four on Saturday morning. His teeth gritted as he attempted to come up with a viable plan that would enable him to smuggle an admittedly very small redhead past the security guards down in the foyer. Otherwise, Poppy's reputation was likely to be in tatters by Monday.

Santino swore under his breath. How much alcohol had he consumed yesterday? There had been the pre-dinner drinks with the Delsens, the wine over the meal he had barely touched and then several brandies in succession. That kind of boozing was not a habit of his. All right, he had not been drunk, but he had not been quite sober either. Alcohol had certainly released all inhibitions and slaughtered his ethics, he conceded grimly.

He looked at Poppy again. Her gorgeous hair was a wild tumble spilling across the leather, one pale bare shoulder and his jacket. She looked adorable, totally at peace and innocent. Only, as he now had very good cause to know, she was no longer *quite* the innocent she had been *before* he laid his womanising hands on her. In the midst of examining his conscience, Santino was appalled to register a powerful temptation just to grab her back into his arms again and kiss her awake. Drink was supposed to be death to the average male libido. *Dio mio*, so much for that old chestnut!

Raking angry hands through his tousled black hair, Santino suppressed a groan. He was furious with himself. How could he have taken advantage of Poppy like that? He struggled to work out how it had happened. They had almost had an argument. He had thrown that vicious comment. She had been leaving when he'd apologised. At that instant, it had somehow seemed unbelievably important to him that she did *not* walk out through that door. Then she had said that about her mother not answering her letters and...?

Ebony brows pleated, Santino gave up on that confusing angle to concentrate on the logical facts that he was more comfortable with. She *worked* for him. Affairs between staff were officially frowned on in Aragone Systems. And guess which smartass had laid down that ground rule for the greater good of interpersonal office relationships and morale? He grimaced. She had been a virgin. He hadn't taken a single precaution. It dawned on him that the last time he had been on a sofa with a woman he might only have been a teenager, but he had exercised a lot more caution then than he had demonstrated the night before. He had screwed up, royally screwed up. In the midst of that lowering acknowledgement, which sat not at all well with his pride, he wondered whether there were still any valentine cards for sale. Finding himself wondering something so inane and out of character unsettled him even more. He breathed in very deep.

Poppy wakened to the sound of a shower running somewhere and her sleepy eyes opened only to widen in dismay when the first thing she saw was her dress lying in a heap on the carpet. A split second later, she realised that she was actually lying under…Santino's jacket! Her heart skipped a beat as she finally appreciated that she had spent most of the night in his office. In *his* arms. As the events that had led up to that staggering development unreeled in her blitzed brain like a very shocking film, she leapt off the sofa like a scalded cat. Praying that Santino would stay in the shower next door long enough for her to make an escape, she dressed at excessive speed.

Tiptoeing to the door, her shoes gripped in one trembling hand, she crept out and then raced for the lift. How could she have behaved like that with Santino? She hadn't even been out on a date with him! Sick with shame and embarrassment, she emerged from the lift and slunk out past the two men chatting at the security desk and mercifully behaving as if she were invisible. The buzzer went, though, to unlock the door and let her out, and her face was as red as a beetroot by the time she reached the street.

'She's a right little looker,' Santino's chauffeur remarked to Willis, the head security guard. A long night of playing poker together had formed an easy camaraderie between the two older men.

'She's a nice friendly kid. That's the first time she's walked out of here without saying goodnight,' Willis said. 'I suppose I can recall the rest of my team now—'

'They'll be getting suspicious if you don't. I'd better get out to the limo and look like I've been dozing. Still, at least you got them shifted before the cleaners come on. Like I said, the boss doesn't usually carry on like this.'

Minutes later, Santino strode from the lift out of breath, black hair still wet from the shower, stormy golden eyes sweeping the foyer in search of Poppy. He couldn't believe she had walked out on him without a word. As if he were some sleazebag of a one-night stand she didn't want to face in daylight! He was outraged. That kind of treatment had never come his way before. Indeed, the clinging habits of certain previous lovers had driven him near to distraction. He had never had one who'd evaporated like scotch mist the first chance she'd got.

He had had hardly any sleep…he was going home, he was going to bed and he'd call on her in the afternoon, he decided. She'd be glad to see him then. She'd appreciate him by then. He hoped she spent the whole lousy morning miserable because that was what she deserved and, in that self-righteous and ripping mood, Santino strode out of the building.

Late that afternoon, Poppy sat on the train watching the countryside fly by with eyes that were blank and faraway. In her mind all she could truly see was a lean, dark, handsome face.

It was amazing how little time it had taken to pack up her belongings and give notice on her bedsit. Everything she possessed fitted into two suitcases. But then she never had been one for gathering clutter, and money to spend on non-essential items had always been in short supply. A fresh start was the best thing, she reminded herself painfully. She could not go back to work at Aragone Systems again. Yes, she could have steeled herself to live down the gossip about that stupid card and her own silliness, but *no*, she could not put herself through the agony of seeing Santino again. She imagined he would be relieved when word of her letter of resignation finally filtered through to him.

Well, she had surely taught herself one good, hard lesson about what happened when a woman flung herself at a man. After all, wasn't that exactly what she had done? Humiliation and guilt engulfed her, for she blamed herself entirely: that childish card telling him that she loved him.

Once Santino had known who the sender was, he wouldn't have been human if that hadn't made him curious. Craig's malice, Santino's concern and her own distress had led to a physical intimacy that would never have developed in normal circumstances. There they had been all alone in the enervating quiet of his office. No doubt even the admiring way she had looked at him had been a provocative encouragement and invitation on male terms. And she might not have much experience with men but every magazine she read warned her that, while nature had programmed women to seek a relationship, men were programmed to seek something an awful lot more basic.

While the train was speeding Poppy towards Wales where her father's aunt, Tilly, lived, Santino was having a very trying dialogue with one of Poppy's former neighbours.

'Nah…haven't seen her for weeks,' the guy with an obvious heavy hangover groused, yawning in Santino's face. 'Maybe she's in there and just doesn't want to answer the door. I had a woman who did that to me. Do you mind if I go back to bed now?'

'Not in the slightest,' Santino breathed grittily.

Santino was now in what was totally unknown territory for him. Maybe Poppy didn't want anything further to do with him. Maybe she *was* in her bedsit not answering the door and praying that he would take the hint and leave her alone. It wasn't exactly a mature response, but a woman who had retained her virtue to the age of twenty-one might well hate his guts for having slept with her when she'd been in such a vulnerable state. If she was so keen to avoid him, and her flight from his office had already brought that message home once, did he have the right to crowd her? Or was he more likely to make a difficult situation worse by pushing too hard too soon? At the end of that logical internal discussion with himself, Santino was still fighting an almost irresistible urge just to smash the door down!

Three weeks later, Poppy was shouting at Tilly's pet geese for lurking behind a gate in an effort to spring a surprise attack on the postman. But the older man was even wilier than the web-footed watchdogs and he leapt into his van unscathed, honked the horn in cheerful one-upmanship and drove off.

Poppy went back into her great-aunt's cottage, clutching the post and the newspaper. Tilly, a small, spry woman with short grey curly hair, well into her seventies but very fit and able, set her book down in favour of the paper.

'Have you got some answers to that ad you placed?' Tilly asked.

'By the looks of it, several,' Poppy answered with determined cheer. 'With a little luck, you'll be shot of your uninvited house guest within a few weeks!'

'You know I *love* having you here,' Tilly scolded.

But her great-aunt's cottage was tiny, perfect for one, crowded for two. Furthermore, Tilly Edwards was one of those rare individuals who actually enjoyed her own company. She had her beloved books and her own set little routine and Poppy did not want to encroach for too long on her hospitality. Within days of her arrival at Tilly's rather isolated home, she had placed an advertisement in a popular magazine seeking employment again as a nanny.

She would take anything—short-term, long-term, whatever came up. The sooner she was working again and too busy to sit feeling sorry for herself, the happier she would be. In the minuscule kitchen, she made a pot of tea for herself and coffee for Tilly. Of recent, she herself had gone off coffee. But then she had pretty much gone off food, too, she conceded wryly, thinking of the irritating bouts of queasiness she had suffered in recent days. Obviously a broken heart led not just to sleepless nights, but poor appetite and indigestion as well. So out of misery might come skinniness. She couldn't even smile at the idea.

She was grateful that she had had enough pride and sense to leave Aragone Systems, but the pain of that sudden severance from all that was familiar and the knowledge that she would never see Santino again was unimaginable and far worse than she had expected. But then it was short, sharp shock treatment, exactly what she had deserved and most needed, she told herself.

'Poppy…' Tilly said from the sitting room.

Poppy moved a few feet back to the doorway. Her great-aunt held up her newspaper. 'Isn't that the man you used to work for?'

Poppy focused on the small black and white photo. Initially the only face she saw was Santino's and then right beside him, beaming like a megawatt light bulb she recognised Jenna Delsen. 'What about him?' she prompted as evenly as she could manage, for one glance even from a distance at Santino in newsprint upset her.

'Seems he's got engaged…an attractive woman, isn't she? Would you like to read it for yourself?' Tilly immediately extended the paper.

'No, thanks. I'll take a look at it later.' Poppy retreated back into the kitchen again and knew that the glimpse she had already had of that damning photo was more than sufficient. She felt incredibly dizzy and assumed that that was the effect of shock. Bracing unsteady hands on the sink unit, she snatched in a stricken breath and shut her anguished eyes tight. *Engaged?* To Jenna Delsen only weeks after he had referred to the beautiful blonde as 'just an old friend'?

Later she went out for a long walk. The strain of trying to behave normally around Tilly had been immense. So, the man you love isn't perfect, after all, she told herself heavily. Shouldn't that make it much easier to get over him? His engagement put a very different complexion on their night together. Santino had *lied* to her. He had lied without hesitation. He was a two-timing louse, who had simply used her for a casual sexual encounter. Clearly he had already been involved in a relationship with Jenna Delsen that went way beyond the boundaries of platonic friendship.

Three days later, Santino arrived in Wales. Finding out where Poppy's only relative lived had been a long and stony road, which had entailed ditching quite a lot of cool and calling Australia several times before eventually contriving to talk to Poppy's sister-in-law, the doctor. And if Karrie Bishop ever got tired of medicine, secret police forces everywhere would vie for her services. Santino had not appreciated the interrogation he had received, and even less did he appreciate getting lost three times in succession in his efforts to find a remote cottage that he had even begun suspecting Dr Bishop might have only dreamt up out of a desire to punish him!

But there the cottage was, a minute building hiding behind an overgrown hedge, the sort of home loved by those who loathed unexpected visitors, Santino reflected with gritty black humour. His tension was at an all-time high now that he had arrived and he had to think about what he was going to say to Poppy. Oddly enough, Santino had not considered that contentious issue prior to his actual arrival. *Finding* Poppy had been his objective. What he might do with her when he found her was not a problem for his imagination in any way, but what he could reasonably say was something more of a challenge. He missed her at the office? He couldn't get that night out of his mind?

Very unsettled by that absence of cutting-edge inspiration, but too impatient to waste time reflecting on it, Santino climbed out of his sleek car in the teeming rain. When a pair of manic honking geese surged out of nowhere in vicious attack, Santino could happily have wrung their long, scrawny necks, built a bonfire on the spot and cooked them for dinner. The confident conviction that the cottage might lie round every next corner had prevented him from stopping off for lunch and he was in a very aggressive mood.

Hearing the noisy clamour of the geese announcing a rare visitor, Poppy hurried to the front door to yank it open. The car was a startling vivid splash of scarlet against the winter-bare garden. But it was Santino, sleek and immaculate in a charcoal-grey business suit, who knocked most of the air in her lungs clean out of her body.

In the act of holding his feathered opponents at bay with his car door, Santino caught sight of Poppy lurking in the doorway and stilled. The pink sweater made her look cuddly and the floral skirt with the pattern that made him blink was *cheering* on a dull day, he decided, rain dripping down his bronzed features. He just wanted to drag her into the car and drive off with her.

Shock having made Poppy momentarily impervious to his battle with the geese, she stared back at Santino, only dimly wondering why he was standing in heavy rain and getting drenched. What on earth was he doing in Wales? How could he possibly have found out where she was? She met his beautiful eyes, dark as ebony and shameless in their steady appraisal, and she knew she ought to slam the door closed in his face. Seeing him in the flesh again hurt. It only served to refresh painful memories of how much that one night, which had meant so little to him, had meant to her. For just a few hours she had been happier than she had ever hoped to be, but her happiness had flourished in a silly dream world, not in reality, and punishment had not been long in coming.

'Are you planning to call the geese off?' Santino enquired gently. 'Or is this supposed to be a test that picks out the men from the boys?'

Forcing herself free of her nervous paralysis, Poppy lifted the broom by the door and shooed the geese back to allow Santino a free passage indoors.

'Grazie, cara,' Santino drawled, smooth as silk.

Her soft mouth wobbled. With an inner quiver, she recalled the liquid flow of Italian words she hadn't understood in the hot, dark pleasure of that night. She turned her burning face away, but not before he had seen the shuttered look in her once trusting and open gaze. She was ashamed of her own weakness. She knew she ought to tell him to go away, but she just didn't have the strength to do that and then never know why he had called in the first place. At least Tilly was out, she thought guiltily, and she wouldn't find herself having to make awkward explanations for his visit.

As Poppy led him into the sitting room Santino bent his dark glossy head to avoid colliding with the low lintel. The room was packed to the gills with furniture and so short of floor space he was reluctant to move in case he knocked something over.

She could not look away from him. Her entire attention was welded to every hard, masculine angle of his bold profile, noting the tension etched there but secretly revelling in the bittersweet pleasure of seeing him again. He turned with measured care to look at her, curling black lashes screening his keen gaze to a sliver of bright, glittering gold.

The atmosphere hummed with undercurrents. Her restive hands clenched together, longing leaping through her in a wildfire wicked surge. Lips parted and moist, in a stillness broken only by the crackling of the fire in the brass grate, she gazed back at him and leant almost imperceptibly forward. Santino needed no further encouragement. Body language like that his male instincts read for him. Without a second of hesitation, he reached for her. Tugging her slight body to him, he meshed one possessive hand into a coil of her Titian red curls and tasted her lush mouth with a slow, smouldering heat that demanded her response.

She was in shaken turmoil at that sensual assault, and a muffled gasp escaped Poppy. His tongue delved with explicit hunger into the tender interior of her mouth. The liquid fire of need ignited in her quivering body faster than the speed of light. She was imprisoned in intimate, rousing contact with his big, powerful length, and her spread fingers travelled from his shoulder up into his luxuriant black hair to hold him to her.

And Santino? In the course of that single kiss, Santino went from wary defensiveness to the very zenith of blazing confidence that he was welcome. Indeed, he was totally convinced that everything was one hundred and one per cent fine. He would have her back in London by midnight. Mission accomplished. Simple, straightforward—why had he ever imagined otherwise?

Then, without the smallest warning, Poppy brought her hands down hard on his arms to break his hold. She wrenched herself free of him with angry tears of self-loathing brimming in her eyes. A wave of dizziness assailed her and she had to push her hands down on the dining table to steady herself and breathe in slow and deep. There was just no excuse for her having let him kiss her when he belonged to another woman. As for him, he was even more of a rat than she had believed he was. He was a hopeless womaniser!

'What's wrong?' Santino breathed in a tone of audible mystification and indeed annoyance.

Her back turned to him, Poppy finally managed to swallow the tears clogging up her vocal cords and she stared with wooden fixity out the window at his car. 'What are you doing in Wales?'

'I had a business meeting in Cardiff earlier.' Santino had decided to play it cool. He was a step ahead of her, he believed and he was already thinking of how to present his having phoned Australia as the ultimate in casual gestures.

But Poppy took the wind right out of his sails by saying, 'I suppose my landlady gave you my forwarding address.'

Infuriatingly, so simple a means of establishing her whereabouts had not even occurred to Santino, but, ignoring that angle, he cut to the chase. 'I wanted to see you.'

He had some nerve. Did he really believe that she was still that naive? In the area on business and at a loose end on a Friday afternoon, he had decided to look her up. Why? Well, she had been free with her favours before and why shouldn't he assume that she would be again? No man could think much of a woman who let him make love to her on his office sofa for a cheap, easy thrill. Poppy felt horribly humiliated.

'I would've thought that most men in these circumstances would've been glad *not* to see me again,' Poppy countered painfully in a small voice.

Santino wondered why it was that, when she had run to the other side of the country to avoid *him*, he was being accused of not wanting to see *her*. Suddenly he too was asking himself what he was doing in Wales. Suddenly he suspected that he could well be within an ace of making a total ass of himself.

'Why would you assume that?' Santino enquired.

'Well, if you don't know that for yourself, I'm certainly not going to be the one to remind you!' Poppy condemned chokily, for she refused to lower herself to the level of mentioning Jenna Delsen's name. She refused to give him that much satisfaction. No doubt his ego would relish the belief that she was heart-broken at the news of his engagement. Or maybe he imagined that she was still in blissful ignorance of the true nature of his relationship with the beautiful blonde.

Unable to work out exactly where the unproductive dialogue was going, Santino decided that it was time to be blunt. 'Why did you send me a card telling me that you loved me?'

If the window had been open at that moment, Poppy would have scrambled through it and fled without hesitation. Aghast at that loaded question, she went rigid.

'I don't think that's an unreasonable question,' Santino continued, tension flattening his accented drawl into the command tone he used at work. 'And I'm tired of talking to your back.'

Seething discomfiture flamed hot colour into Poppy's cheeks, but pride came to her rescue. Flipping round on taut legs, she encountered brilliant dark-as-midnight eyes and forced a dismissive shrug. 'For goodness sake...the valentine card was a joke!'

The silence that fell seemed to last for ever.

Santino had gone very still, his strong bone structure clench-ing hard. 'A joke...?' A flame of raw derision flared in his gaze as he absorbed that demeaning explanation. The most obvious explanation, yet one that for some reason he had never consid-ered. 'What are you...fourteen years old or something?'

'Or something...' Her nails were digging purple welts into her damp palms while she struggled to control the wobble that had developed in her knee joints. 'It was just a stupid joke...and then Craig got hold of it and blew it up into something else and I ended up looking like an idiot!'

'I hope you don't also end up pregnant,' Santino framed with a ragged edge to his dark, deep drawl, wide, sensual mouth compressed, the pallor of anger lightening the bronzed skin round his hard jawline. 'I doubt very much that that would strike even you as a joke.'

Poppy gazed back at him in appalled silence, her tongue cleaving to the roof of her mouth, for not once since that night had she even considered that there might be consequences. She had, without ever really thinking about it, simply assumed that he had taken care of that risk for her.

'You mean, you *didn't*…?' she began shakily.

'I'm afraid not.' Brooding dark eyes acknowledging the level of her dismay and disconcertion, Santino released his breath in a slow speaking hiss of regret. 'But I do accept that, whatever happens, the responsibility is mine.'

CHAPTER SIX

AT THAT moment, Poppy wanted to curl up in a ball like a toddler and cry her heart out, for what Santino had just revealed shed a very different light on what had motivated his visit.

Since when had she got so vain that she believed Santino Aragone was so bereft of females willing to share his bed that he had sought her out in Wales? The idea was laughable, *ridiculous*! Now she was remembering his tension when he'd first arrived. Had she precipitated that kiss? Had that been her fault once again? Or just one of those crazy mishaps that occurred when people were all wound up and not really knowing how to react or what to say?

Well, it scarcely mattered now, Poppy conceded painfully. Santino had come to find her and speak to her for a very good reason, and indeed the fact that he had made the effort told her much more about his strength of character than anything else. He had been worried that he might have got her pregnant. That was the only reason he had taken the trouble to seek her out again. Most men, particularly one who had just asked or had been about to ask another woman to marry him, would have done nothing and just hoped for the best. But Santino had *not* taken the easy way out.

'The night of the party…' Santino caught and held her swift upward glance '…we had both been drinking. I have never been so reckless, but then I don't have a history of that kind of behaviour and I know that you had no history at all.'

Feverish colour flared in Poppy's tense face. She was still in shock at her own naivety, her own foolish, pitiful assumptions about why he had come to see her. It took enormous willpower for her to confront the more serious issue. Might she have conceived that night? A belated rethink on what might have caused her recent bouts of nauseous disinterest in food froze Poppy to the spot. And what about the little dizzy turns she had written off as being the results of not eating or sleeping well? *Was* it possible that she was pregnant? She had never bothered to keep track of her own cycle. How long had it been since the party? A couple of weeks, *more*? Her brain was in turmoil, refusing to function. When had she last…? She couldn't remember. It seemed like a long time ago. Santino had just delivered what had to be the ultimate male put-down. He had come to tell *her* she might be pregnant!

Poppy shifted her head in a dazed motion. 'I really don't know yet if I'm…you know…I don't know…er…either way.'

Santino took a slight step forward. She looked so much like a terrified teenager. She couldn't even find the words to talk about conception. He wanted to close his arms round her, drive out the panic and uncertainty clouding her eyes, tell her that she had nothing to worry about and that he would look after her. And then he stiffened, sudden bitter anger flaring through him, making him suppress his own natural instincts. The valentine card had been a joke, a childish, stupid joke with no sense that he could see, but then someone might have dared her to do it for a laugh. How did he know? He didn't feel as if he knew anything any more about Poppy.

In fact, the more Santino thought of how she had behaved, the more alienated he felt. She wasn't in love with him, never had been in love with him. Even a little dose of infatuation would have lasted longer than a couple of weeks. Maybe she had slept with him because she had decided it was time she acquired some experience. Whatever, her behaviour ever since had spoken for her: she didn't want to see him and preferred to forget about that night. In fact, she could not have made her feelings clearer. She had jacked in her job, left London. Exactly why had he gone to such extraordinary lengths to locate her? Had he become such an arrogant jerk that he couldn't accept a woman's rejection?

'Presumably you'll know whether or not you're pregnant very soon,' Santino drawled without any expression at all. 'If you are, please get in touch with me immediately and we'll deal with it together. Obviously I will give you my support. You know how to reach me.'

His beautiful dark eyes were still level but his detachment was noticeable and complete. Poppy could feel that change like a wall he had thrown up between them. He wanted to leave. She could feel that, too. But then why not? It hadn't been a very pleasant visit for him to have to make, she recognised miserably. It had been a waste of time too when she had been unable to tell him that he had nothing to worry about. Naturally he would be praying that there would be no repercussions from that night and that awareness prevented her from sharing her own misgivings. Why say anything when she might well be fretting about nothing?

Santino strode towards his car and then swung back for one last look at her. 'Look after yourself,' he offered gruffly.

Feeling as if she were dying inside, Poppy stood like a statue watching the car reverse out. She had the most terrible urge to run after it and tell him that, even though she ought to hate him, she still loved him. But what would he want to know that for? He *had* to be in love with Jenna.

A couple of miles down the road, Santino brought the car to a halt, buzzed down the window and drank in a great lungful of the fresh, rain-wet air. *Mission accomplished?* A raw-edged laugh, empty of all humour, broke from him. Why was he chickening out of confronting the obvious: his success scores before the sofa, and on the sofa, had been nil. Everything that had struck him as fantastic and very special had left her distinctly underwhelmed. She hadn't even offered him a cup of coffee. All the way to Wales for the privilege of being shot down in flames in the space of ten minutes!

Thinking of the stupid, naff valentine card he had bought for her, a violent miasma of emotion lanced through Santino. He just wanted to smash something. He didn't want to think about her. In fact he was determined not to think about her. Of course, she wasn't going to be pregnant! Off the top of his head, he could have named three young, healthy married couples tying themselves in knots in a desperate effort to conceive a child. The chances of his having fathered a baby in one night were slim and surely she would have known by now? He would check into a hotel, get something to eat…only he wasn't hungry any more.

So he would check into a hotel and have a lost weekend. Why? He just felt like it! He wanted to drink himself into a stupor. He was off women, really, really *seriously* off women.

Three days later, Poppy learned that she was indeed pregnant.

During the weekend, she had had to content herself with purchasing a pregnancy test kit. When the test had come up positive, she'd barely slept for the following two nights. Unsure of how reliable a home test was, she'd made an appointment at her local surgery. When the doctor gave her the same confirmation and discussed options with her, she already knew that she didn't want a termination. She loved children, had always hoped that some day she would have some of her own, but that prospect had until then existed in some dim, distant future. Now that a baby, Santino's baby, was a much more immediate reality, she also knew she had some hard thinking to do about how she intended to manage.

At first, she believed that she could steel herself to phone Santino to tell him that she was carrying his child, but when it came to the point she couldn't face it. Santino was engaged to Jenna. Like it or not, what she had to tell him was very bad news on his terms. She had her pride too and she didn't want to risk getting all weepy and apologetic on the phone, did she? As she wasn't prepared to consider a termination, she decided that it would be less painful all round if she wrote a letter spelling out her intentions.

So, Poppy sat in Tilly's narrow little guest-room bed and tried to write a letter. But she kept on sitting there and trying to write it and failing and scrunching up her every attempt and ended up in floods of miserable tears.

Finally, she stopped trying to save face and just let her own honest feelings speak for her in what she wrote. After all, did she really want Santino to go on thinking now that the valentine card had just been a cheap, silly joke? That their baby had been conceived as a result of such a joke? Poppy cringed at that image. Some day, she would want to tell their child that she had loved his father and that truth was surely more important than her own pride.

When it dawned on Poppy that she would have to send the letter to Aragone Systems because she *still* didn't know Santino's home address and he wasn't in the phone book either, she was careful to print 'Private and Confidential' in block capitals on one corner of the envelope. Once it was in the post, she tried not to think about it. The ball was in his court now. She would just have to wait and see what happened.

During the following week she was offered interviews with two families in search of a nanny, in fact *desperate* for a nanny. Qualified nannies, it seemed, were in even shorter supply than they had been when she had first emerged from her training. But did she admit she was pregnant or not? She decided that she would be happier being honest from the outset as she would need time off to attend pre-natal hospital appointments, and then of course she would have a baby in tow. At the same time, on every occasion that Tilly's phone rang, her heart would start banging like a drum and she would think that it was Santino calling her. But Santino *didn't* call and watching the post proved to be no more productive.

But then, had she but known it, Santino never received her letter. He was in Italy when it arrived and Craig Belston was working his last day at Aragone Systems. An astute operator, Craig had recognised that his promotion prospects were slim if he stayed; Santino had been cold with him ever since the night of that party. Although Craig had found lucrative employment elsewhere, his resentment at what a little teasing of Poppy Bishop had cost him still rankled. He examined the letter, his mouth twisting at the 'P. Bishop' and return address printed on the back of the envelope. Walking over to the tall drinks cabinet, which had of recent contained nothing stronger than soft drinks and mineral water, he dropped the letter down between it and the wall and he smiled.

Within a month Poppy had left Wales and started work as a nanny again. Initially shocked that Santino had not responded to her letter, she grew more cynical as time passed. After all, his silence was in itself an answer, wasn't it? Confronted with the worst-case scenario, Santino had decided that he didn't want to know about the baby. Why had she swallowed all that impressive guff about him being willing to take responsibility? Why once again had she begun thinking of him as an essentially decent guy?

After all, Santino had lied that night about Jenna to get her onto that sofa, so, why shouldn't he have lied again? She was on her own in *every* way and, for the sake of the child she was expecting, she reckoned that she had better get used to the idea.

CHAPTER SEVEN

'YES, that uniform looks the thing, all right. Turn round,' Daphne Brewett urged Poppy, her be-ringed hands clasped together, an approving smile blooming on her plump, attractive face. 'You look like a *proper* nanny now, luv. No chance of folk mistaking you for one of those au pair girls, who work for pocket change! What do you think, Harold?'

Her balding husband, Harold, removed his admiring gaze with reluctance from Poppy's slim black nylon-clad ankles. 'Does anyone but the Royals put their nannies in uniform these days?' he enquired in his refined public school accent, his tone apologetic.

Daphne stuck her hands on her ample hips and skewered him with one warning glance. 'Poppy's wearing a uniform…OK?' she rapped out loudly.

Harold nodded in submission and picked up his newspaper. Poppy, who had been toying with the idea of mentioning that she was afraid that the fussy white apron and the frilly little hat were *definitely* over the top, thought better of it. Daphne had a terrible temper and Harold might be a very astute and respected business tycoon, but he was terrified of his wife and knew when to keep quiet. Poppy reminded herself that she was earning an enormous salary. If pleasing Daphne meant dressing like a cross between a French maid and a Victorian nurse, she would just have to put up with it. After all, Daphne had been broad-minded enough to hire a nanny who came with a very young child of her own in tow. Indeed, Daphne had been warmly accepting of what had struck other potential employers as a serious drawback.

'Right…' Having vanquished Harold, Daphne turned her attention on Poppy again. 'You have the kiddies packed and ready for two this afternoon. We're off to Torrisbrooke Priory for the weekend. That'll be a treat for you. You can look forward to seeing some real landed gentry there,' she said with unhidden satisfaction.

Poppy walked out of the drawing room. Three children were seated on the stairs: Tristram, aged ten, Emily Jane, aged eight, Rollo, aged five, all blond and blue-eyed and very unspoilt and pleasant children. Daphne Brewett might be a very domineering personality but beggars could not be choosers, Poppy reminded herself squarely, determined to make the best of her recent employment with the family.

'Well, did you tell Ma how dumb you looked?' Tris asked with rich cynicism.

Poppy shook her head in wincing apology.

'I'm not going to be seen dead with you in that daft get-up!' Tris warned her.

'It's very uncool,' Emily Jane pronounced in a pained tone.

'You look funny!' Rollo giggled. 'I like your silly hat.'

With a rueful grin, Poppy went over to the pram parked below the stairs. Florenza was wide awake, big blue eyes sparkling beneath her soft mop of tiny black curls. Poppy reached in and scooped her daughter out to take her back upstairs again. Florenza was three months old, cute as a button, and the undeniable centre of her adoring mother's world.

'Who lives at Torisbrooke Priory?' Poppy asked Tris on the way upstairs.

'Dunno. But Ma thinks the invitation's really great, so it's probably somebody posh with a title. I wish she'd just leave us at home,' he grumbled. 'She's really embarrassing in other people's houses.'

'Don't talk about your mother like that,' Poppy reproved.

'I don't like people laughing at her,' Tris said defensively.

Ignoring that, for to deny that Daphne could be both vulgar and comical in her desire to impress all with the conspicuous extent of the Brewett wealth, was impossible.

At four that afternoon, the Brewett cavalcade of limousines drove at a stately pace up the long, wooded, winding drive to Torrisbrooke Priory. A vast and ancient building appeared round the final bend. It was built of weathered Tudor brick, winter sunshine glittering over the many mullioned windows, and Poppy gazed out at it with interest. Half a dozen big cars were already parked on the gravel frontage.

A venerable butler stood at the gothic arched front door in readiness. Daphne and Harold descended from the first limo. Florenza clasped in her arms and wearing the gabardine raincoat that went with her uniform, Poppy climbed out of the second limo in the wake of the children. The third limo was just for the luggage: Daphne did not travel light.

When a very tall, dark male strolled down the steps to greet her employers, Poppy's steps faltered. It couldn't be, it couldn't possibly be! But as her shattered eyes focused on the lean, devastatingly handsome dark features that still haunted her dreams on a shamefully regular basis, she saw that it truly was…it *was* Santino Aragone! Sheer, disbelieving panic afflicted her. Was he their host? Why else would he be shaking hands with Harold? Did that mean that the priory belonged to Santino?

Daphne summoned her children to her side to introduce them. In the background, Poppy hovered. There was no place to go, no place to hide. At the exact moment that Santino registered her presence, Poppy froze, heart thumping so hard she felt sick, her taut face pale as milk. His brilliant dark eyes welded to her and just stayed there, his surprise unconcealed.

'And this is our nanny, Poppy,' Daphne trilled in full swing. 'And little Flo.'

Her blue eyes achingly vulnerable, Poppy's chin nonetheless came up in a sudden defiant tilt. What did she have to be embarrassed about? Santino was the one who ought to be embarrassed! She noted that as his piercing gaze suddenly veiled, he did not succumb to the temptation of stealing so much as a glance at his own daughter.

'Poppy and I have met before. She used to work in Aragone Systems,' Santino remarked without any apparent discomfiture. 'Let's go inside. It's cold.'

While Daphne chattered cheerfully about what a small world it was, Santino was in shock but refusing to acknowledge it. A coincidence and life was full of them, he told himself. Poppy was the Brewetts' nanny and she would be busy with their children all weekend. It was almost a year to the day *since...* No, no way was he revisiting that memory lane. A baby wailed. As Santino hadn't noticed a baby in the party, he turned his head in bewilderment, following the sound right back to source: the small bundle cradled in Poppy's arms.

'I didn't realise you had a new baby,' he said to Daphne, struggling to act the part of interested host, endeavouring to force a relaxed smile to his taut features.

'Oh, the baby's not ours.' Daphne loosed a girlish giggle, flattered by Santino's misapprehension because she was pushing fifty. 'Three was quite enough for me! Flo is Poppy's kiddy.'

At the foot of the glorious oak carved staircase where the butler was waiting to show her upstairs, Poppy stared at Santino with very wide blue eyes. What on earth was he playing at? When his startled gaze zeroed in on her with sudden questioning force, she was at a complete loss. Why was he acting so surprised? Hadn't he appreciated that pregnancies most often led to births and little babies?

'Her name's Florenza,' Tris piped up. 'Flo's just what Ma calls her.'

'Florenza...' Santino repeated, ebony brows pleating.

'It's I-talian,' Daphne told him helpfully.

Santino angled a charged scrutiny at the little squirming

bundle. He was suffering from information overload. Was Florenza his child? What age was the little girl? She was wrapped in a shawl and, the way she was being held, the shawl was all he could see. She might be a newborn baby, she might be some other man's child. She *couldn't* be his daughter! Poppy would have told him, wouldn't she?

Fabulous cheekbones prominent below his bronzed skin, Santino dredged his attention from the mystery bundle, encountered a speculative look from Daphne Brewett's keen gaze and hastened to show his guests into the drawing room.

Poppy climbed the stairs in a daze, beneath which a growing turmoil of emotions seethed. Santino had been astounded when Daphne had informed him that the baby was her nanny's. He had stared at Florenza much as though she were a Pandora's box ready to fly open and cause a storm of catastrophe. A tremor ran through Poppy and her arms tightened round her tiny daughter. Why was she shrinking from facing the obvious explanation for Santino's incredulity? Evidently, Santino had assumed that without his support she would *not* continue her pregnancy. Well, how else could she interpret his shocked reaction to Florenza's existence?

Was Jenna waiting in that drawing room downstairs? Jenna in her gracious role of hostess as Santino's wife? Had they got married during the last year? At that awful thought, a cold, clammy chill slid down Poppy's spine and her sensitive tummy clenched in protest. For the first time, she regretted not having allowed herself to check out whether or not that wedding had taken place as yet. But refusing to allow herself to seek any information whatsoever about Santino Aragone's life had been a necessary defence mechanism. She had brought down a curtain on the past and disciplined herself to live only in the present.

'Is this Mr Aragone's home?' she enquired of the elderly butler, Jenkins, whose steps were slowing with each step up the stairs.

'Yes, madam,' he wheezed and, as he was so clearly in no fit state to answer any further questions, Poppy had to content herself with that.

Three hours later, having supervised a late and riotous tea with the children that had been served in a small dining room on the ground floor, Poppy set up Florenza's bright and cosy travel cot in the nursery and tucked her up for the night. Poppy was tired. Her days started at six when Florenza wakened and she was grateful that it was her night off. Although impressing that necessity on Daphne had been a challenge, she conceded ruefully. But she was painfully aware that live-in nannies had to define boundaries or she would soon find herself on call twenty-four hours a day.

The priory was a simply huge house. Poppy reflected that she might well contrive to stay the weekend without seeing Santino again. Unhappily, she was conscious of a dangerous craving to nonetheless throw herself in his path for a showdown. He *deserved* to be told what a rat he was! Removing her elaborate uniform with a grimace of relief, she ran a bath for herself in the bathroom beside the nursery and got in to have a soak.

In the library downstairs, undercover of having announced the necessity of making an urgent call, Santino was delving in frustration through a very old book on babies. All he needed to know was what weight the average baby was when it was born. Armed with that knowledge, he might then take a subtle peek at Poppy's baby and work out whether it was within the realms of possibility that Florenza was *his* baby, too. Why not just ask Poppy? That would entail a serious loss of face that Santino was unwilling to consider.

Convinced that Poppy would be down in the basement swimming pool supervising the Brewett children, Santino strolled into the nursery on the top floor. The grand Edwardian cot was unoccupied but the lurid plastic and mesh contraption set beside it contained his quarry. Breathing in deep, Santino advanced as quietly as he could to steal a glance over the padded rim. The first thing he saw was a downy fluff of black curls and then a pair of soft blue unblinking eyes focused on him. His first startled thought was that, for a baby, Florenza was remarkably pretty.

But it was hard to say which of them was the most surprised. Santino, who had paid only the most fleeting attention to friends' babies, fully believed that infants only operated on two modes: screeching or sleeping. He had *expected* Florenza to be asleep. Aghast, he watched Florenza's big eyes flash like an intruder-tracking device, her tiny nose screwing up as her little rosebud mouth began to open.

Santino backed off fast. But even though he was bracing himself, the threatened screech never came. Instead, Florenza turned her little head to peer at him through the mesh. When he dared to inch forward again, Florenza's tiny face tensed in warning. It dawned on him that lifting the baby to gauge her weight was not a viable option. She was a really sharp, on-the-ball baby, ready to shriek like a fire alarm at the first sign of a stranger getting too close, and he didn't want to frighten her.

Wrapped in a bath towel and barefoot, Poppy glanced into the nursery just to check on Florenza before she went to get dressed and could not credit what she was seeing. Her lips parted on a demand to know what Santino thought he was doing, but the manner in which her tiny daughter was holding him at bay was actually very funny. However, she only found it funny for about the space of ten seconds. For as she studied Santino's bold, masculine profile and switched her strained gaze to Florenza's matching dark eyes a wealth of powerful emotion overwhelmed Poppy without warning. Father and daughter didn't even know each other and never would in the normal way. Curiosity might have brought Santino to the nursery, but that did not mean he had suffered a sudden sea change in conscience.

As an odd choky little gasp sounded behind him, Santino swung round and caught only the merest glimpse of Poppy's convulsed face as she spun away and raced into the bedroom across the corridor, slamming the door in her wake.

Sobs catching in her throat, she sank down at the foot of the bed and buried her head in her arms. She hated him, she *really* hated him! She was thinking of every bad experience she had had in the months since that night they had shared, not least having been the only woman in the maternity ward without a single visitor. In addition, her parents' initially shocked and censorious reaction to the revelation of a grandchild born out of wedlock had increased Poppy's distress. Although relations had since been smoothed over and gifts had been sent, Poppy remained painfully aware that once again she had disappointed her family.

When the door opened and Santino strode in, Poppy was astonished for she had not expected him to risk forcing a confrontation in his own home. But there he stood, six feet three inches of lean, powerful masculinity, apparently so impervious to remorse that he could face her with his arrogant head high, his stubborn jaw at an angle and without any shade of discomfiture. For a timeless few seconds, she drank her fill of looking at him. He was still absolutely gorgeous, she noted resentfully, and she was ashamed to feel the quickened beat of her own heart, the licking tension of excitement and the taunting curl of heat slivering through her. In despair at her own weakness, she veiled her gaze.

'I only have one question...' Santino breathed in the taut silence. 'Is Florenza mine?'

'Are you out of your mind?' Poppy gasped.

What was he trying to do? Portray her as some loose woman, who might not know the paternity of her own child? How much lower could a guy sink than to insinuate that?

Taut as a high-voltage wire, Santino was endeavouring to make sense of the incomprehensible while resisting what had become a predictable instinct when Poppy was upset: a need to haul her into his arms that was so strong only fierce will power kept him at the other side of the room. He was also working very hard at not allowing his attention to roam one inch below her collar bone, where an expanse of smooth, creamy cleavage took over before vanishing beneath the tightly wrapped towel.

'You know very well that Florenza's yours,' Poppy splintered back at him, her bright tousled head coming up, her blue eyes angry. 'So don't you *dare* ask me a question like that!'

Knocked back by that accusing confirmation that Florenza was his child, momentarily blind to even the allurement of Poppy's exquisite shape in a towel, Santino could not immediately come up with a response. He was a father. He had a daughter. His mother was a grandparent. He was an unmarried father with a baby sleeping in a plastic playpen. His baby's mother hated him *so* much she hadn't even been able to persuade herself to accept his support, financially or in any other way…

Poppy collided with his stunning dark-as-midnight gaze and tensed at the sight of the pain and regret that he couldn't hide. 'You don't even know what to say to me, do you?'

'No…' Santino acknowledged hoarsely, lean hands coiling into fists and uncoiling only slowly again.

'I've turned up like a bad penny in the wrong place.' Poppy said what she assumed he was thinking. 'Is Jenna downstairs?'

'Jenna?' Santino echoed with a frown. 'Jenna who?'

Poppy flew upright and threw the first thing that came to her hand. A shoe thumped Santino in the chest. The second shoe caught him quite a painful clip on the ear. Poppy blazed back at him in a passion that shook him even more, 'Jenna…*who*? Jenna Delsen, your fiancée, whom you described as *just* an old friend when it suited you! You lying louse, Santino Aragone!'

Santino cast aside the second shoe, brilliant eyes narrowed in astonishment. 'I'm not engaged to Jenna. She *is* an old friend and I was a guest at her wedding last summer.'

In wordless incredulity, Poppy stared back at him, but a hollow, sick sensation was already spreading through her trembling body. He had been a guest at Jenna's wedding? Such a statement had a serious ring of truth.

Lean, strong face taut, Santino moved expressive hands in a gesture of bewilderment. 'Where on earth did you get the idea that I had got engaged to Jenna?'

Poppy snatched in a stark, quivering breath. 'It was in a newspaper…a picture of you and Jenna. It said you were engaged…er…but I never looked at it that closely.'

Santino stilled then, black brows drawing together. 'An old friend did phone me to congratulate me on my supposed engagement last year,' he recalled with an obvious effort, his frown deepening. 'The newspaper he mentioned had used an old picture of Jenna and I together and he'd misread the couple of lines below about her engagement party. Her fiancé, David, *was* named but he hadn't picked up on it.'

Silence fell like a smothering blanket of snow.

Poppy was appalled at the explanation that Santino had just proffered. Tilly had only glanced at the item because she had recognised Santino and Tilly only ever skimmed through newspapers. When her great niece had failed to display any interest in the seeming fact that her former employer had got engaged, Tilly would, in all probability, not have bothered to look back at it again. And Poppy had been far too cut up, far too much of a coward, to pick up that newspaper and read exactly what it had said for herself.

'Tell me,' Santino asked very drily, 'exactly when did you see that newspaper and decide that I was an outright liar?'

Her breath snarled up in her throat. It had been too much to hope that he would not immediately put together what she had believed him capable of doing. Squirming with guilty unease and embarrassment and a whole host of other, much more confused emotions, Poppy admitted shakily, 'Before you came to Wales…'

A harsh laugh that was no laugh at all was dredged from Santino, bitter comprehension stamped in his brooding features as he turned sizzling dark golden eyes back on her in her proud and angry challenge. '*Per meraviglia*…you had some opinion of me! You decided I'd been cheating on another woman with you. No wonder you were so surprised to see me in Wales, but you didn't have the decency to face me with your convictions, did you?'

Poppy gulped. 'I—'

'I didn't have a clue what I was walking into that day,' Santino framed in a low-pitched raw undertone, treating her to another searing appraisal that shamed her even more. 'But all the time that I was trying to make sense of your bewildering behaviour, you were thinking I was a two-timing liar with no principles and no conscience!'

'Santino…I'm *sorry*!' Poppy gasped.

His lean powerful face stayed hard and unimpressed. 'You tell our daughter you're sorry. Don't waste your breath on me!'

'No…you tell her you're sorry,' Poppy dared hoarsely. 'You're the one who decided you didn't want anything to do with her.'

'I didn't even know she *existed*!' Santino's temper finally broke free of all restraint. 'How the blazes could I have had anything to do with a child I wasn't aware had even been born?'

'But I wrote to you telling you I was pregnant,' Poppy protested.

'I didn't get a letter and why would you write anyway? Why trust an important and private communication of that nature to the vagaries of the post? Why not just phone?' Santino demanded, immediately dubious of her claim that there had ever been a letter.

Poppy closed her eyes and swallowed hard in an effort to pull herself together. It was obvious that her letter must have gone astray. Only then did she recall once reading that thousands of letters went missing in the mail every year. But why that one desperately important letter? Why *her* letter? She could have wept.

'Look, I have thirty-odd people waiting dinner for me downstairs,' Santino admitted curtly. 'I don't have time to handle this right now.'

'There *was* a letter,' Poppy repeated unsteadily.

Before he shut the door, Santino dealt her a derisive look. 'So what if there was?' he derided, turning the tables on her afresh. 'What kind of a woman lets her child's whole future rest on one miserable letter?'

CHAPTER EIGHT

STRIVING to look as though she had not passed a sleepless night waiting for the phone by her bed to ring or even the sound of a masculine footstep, Poppy knocked on her employer's bedroom door and entered. 'Tris said you wanted to see me.'

Still lying in bed, clad in an elaborate satin bed jacket, Daphne treated her to a rather glum appraisal. 'Yes. It's a shame about that uniform, though. I bet you it won't fit the next nanny.'

Poppy stilled. 'I'm sorry…er…what next nanny?'

With a sigh, Daphne settled rueful eyes on Poppy. 'Santino had a little chat with me last night. Didn't he mention it?'

Her colour rising, Poppy stiffened. 'No.'

'You just can't work for us any more, luv. Once Santino told me that little Flo is his, I saw where he was coming from all right,' Daphne continued with a speaking grimace. 'Naturally he doesn't want you running about fetching and carrying for my kids!'

'Doesn't he, indeed?' Her face burning fierily at Santino's most unexpected lack of discretion, Poppy was scarcely able to credit her own hearing.

'It wouldn't suit us either.' Daphne gave her an apologetic look. 'The point is, Harold and Santino do business together. You're the mother of Santino's kid and you working for us, well, it just wouldn't look or feel right now.'

It was obvious that the older woman had already made up her mind on that score.

'You don't even want me to work my notice?'

'No. Santino's arranged for an agency nanny for what's left of the weekend. He's a decent bloke, Poppy…' Daphne told her bluntly. 'I don't see why you should be angry with him for wanting to do what's right by you and take care of you and that little baby.'

A minute later, Poppy stalked down the corridor and then down flight after flight of stairs until she was literally giddy with speed and fury. She arrived in a breathless whirl in the main hall. Santino appeared in a doorway. He ran his lethally eloquent dark eyes from the crown of the frilly hat perched at a lopsided angle in her thick, rebellious hair to the starched apron that topped the shadow-striped dress beneath.

'Good morning, Mary Poppins,' he murmured lazily. 'Remind me to buy you more black stockings, but you can ditch the rest of the outfit.'

'Yes, I can, can't I?' Poppy hissed. 'Especially when you've just had me thrown out of my job!'

Striding forward, Santino closed a hand over hers and pressed her into the room he had emerged from. 'We don't need an audience for this dialogue, *cara*.'

'I'm surprised you care! You had no trouble last night baring my deepest secrets to Daphne Brewett!' Poppy condemned.

'Why should Florenza be a secret? I'm proud to be her father and I have no intention of concealing our relationship,' Santino stated with an amount of conviction that shook her. 'And please don't tell me that you're breaking your heart at the prospect of taking off that ludicrous uniform!'

Poppy refused to back down. 'It was a good job, well paid and with considerate employers—'

'Yet the rumour is that the Brewetts still can't keep domestic staff. Do you know why?' Santino enquired sardonically. '*Daphne.* She's wonderfully kind and friendly most of the time. But she can't control her temper and she becomes much more abusive than the average employee is willing to tolerate these days. Haven't you crossed her yet? It doesn't take much to annoy her.'

Poppy paled, reluctant to recall the older woman's worryingly sharp reproof the previous afternoon when she had been five minutes late getting the children downstairs with all their luggage.

'But then you've only been working for them for a few weeks and she'll still be wary, but I do assure you that if you had stayed much longer, you would have felt the rough edge of Daphne's tongue. She's famous for it.'

'Well, I still don't think that that gave you the right to interfere,' Poppy retorted curtly. 'I can look after myself.'

'But unfortunately, you're not the only person involved here. I want what's best for all *three* of us.' Santino surveyed her with level dark golden eyes, willing her to listen to him. 'I don't see the point in a further exchange of recriminations. Life's too short. I also want to share in Florenza's life. For that reason, I'm willing to ask you to marry me…'

Shock held Poppy still, but the way he had framed that statement also lacerated her pride. He was 'willing' to ask her to marry him? Big deal! Her first marriage proposal and he shot it at her when she was seething with angry turmoil at the manner in which he had attempted to take control of her life. Now it seemed that he had taken away her security so that he could offer her another kind of security. That of being a wife. *His wife.* Her lips trembled and she sealed them.

'Possibly I messed up the delivery of that,' Santino conceded as the tense silence stretched to breaking-point. 'I *do* want to marry you.'

Poppy spun away to gaze out the window at the rolling parkland and mature trees that gave the priory such a beautiful setting. Of course, he didn't *want* to marry her! In Daphne's parlance, Santino was offering to do 'the right thing' by her. He had got her pregnant and he saw marriage as the most responsible means of making amends. He was really lucky that she wasn't the sort of female who would snatch at his offer just because he was rich, successful and gorgeous. Or even because she still loved him, she conceded painfully.

Poppy flipped round to meet Santino's intense dark scrutiny, her face tight with strain. 'Our relationship has only been an ongoing catastrophe,' she framed unevenly.

His jawline clenched. 'That's not how I would describe it—'

'When you called on me at Tilly's, you said pretty much the same thing,' Poppy reminded him. 'I ended up on that sofa because you had had too much to drink and you regretted it. That's no basis for a marriage and, anyway, I don't want to be married to some guy who thinks it's his *duty* to put a ring on my finger!'

'Duty doesn't come into this.' Santino groaned in sudden exasperation. 'We made love because I couldn't keep my distance from you, because I couldn't help myself, *cara*—'

'Yes, but—'

'Just looking at you burns me up. Always did...*still* does,' Santino intoned, striding forward to close his lean hands round hers. 'That's not a catastrophe, that's fierce attraction. If you hadn't worked for me, we would have got together a lot sooner.'

'I can't believe that...' But even so, it was an assurance that Poppy longed to believe.

Santino reached up and whisked the frilly hat from her hair and tossed it aside.

'What are you doing?' she whispered.

The sudden slashing smile that she had feared she might never see again flashed out, lightening his lean, dark features and yanking at every fibre of her resistance. He undid the apron, removed it with careful hands and put it aside, too. Then he unbuttoned the high collar of her dress.

'You want me to prove how much you excite me?' Santino enquired with husky mesmeric intensity, molten golden eyes scanning her with anticipation. 'Ready and willing, *cara mia*.'

A little quiver of sensual response rippled through Poppy's taut frame. 'Don't...'

'Don't what?' Santino asked, flicking back the collar to press his lips to the base of her slender throat, sending such a shock wave of instantaneous response leaping through her that she let her head tip back heavily on her neck, her untouched mouth tingling, literally aching for the hungry heat of his. 'Don't do *this*…?'

He discovered a pulse point just below her ear and lingered there. She trembled, heard herself moan and she grabbed his jacket for support, feeling herself drowning in the melting pleasure she had worked so hard to forget. Then, he framed the feverish flush on her cheekbones with spread fingers and kissed her just once, hard and fast, demanding and urgent, leaving her wanting so much more.

'Now do you believe I really want you?' Santino breathed raggedly.

Poppy stumbled back from him, lips still throbbing and body still thrumming from that little demonstration against which she had discovered she was without defence. He could turn her into a shameless hussy with incredible ease, but he didn't *love* her. 'It wouldn't work…us, I mean.'

'Why not?'

'Don't you know how to take no for an answer?' Poppy muttered shakily from the door.

'I took it the last time. It gained me a daughter of three months old whom I have still to meet.' As Santino made that raw retaliation Poppy's discomfited gaze slewed from his and she left the room and was relieved when he didn't follow her, for he had given her a lot to think about.

Getting changed into jeans and a sweater, Poppy put Florenza in her buggy and went out for a walk. She was starting to see that all she had ever done with Santino was think the worst of his motivations and run away as fast as her legs could carry her. Twelve months ago, she had still had a lot of growing up left to do. So many misunderstandings might have been avoided had she not performed a vanishing act after the staff party. She had reacted like an embarrassed little girl, afraid to face reality after the fantasy of the night. Scared of getting hurt, she had ended up just as hurt anyway. She had assumed that everything that had happened between them had somehow been *her* fault and had denied them both the chance to explore their feelings.

Poppy sat down on a fallen log below the trees. In the same way she had just accepted that Santino was engaged to Jenna Delsen and had hidden behind her pride rather than confront him. But what she could forgive herself for least was the conviction that Santino was a liar and a cheat when he had never been anything but honest and straight with her.

How much could she still blame Santino for effectively getting her the sack? She understood all too well his angry impatience and his need to take control when she herself seemed to have made such a hash of things. He had made it clear that if she conceived his child, he would stand by her. What good had it been for her to talk about a letter that he had never received? Had he got the chance, he would have been a part of Florenza's life from the start. And that was why he was asking her to marry him. Her wretched pride had made her too quick to refuse that option. After all, she loved Santino, could not imagine *ever* loving anyone else...

Fifty feet away, Santino came to a halt to study Poppy on her log and Florenza snuggled up in her buggy. Poppy did not look happy. The marriage proposal had not been a winner. But then he had not promoted his own cause by depriving her of her employment, had he? However, an ever-recurring image of Poppy sailing away in a Brewett limo the following day never to return had driven him to a desperate act. He had known exactly what he'd been doing, he acknowledged grimly. He had cut the ground from beneath her feet in a manoeuvre calculated to make her more vulnerable to his arguments.

Glancing up and seeing him, Poppy froze. Dressed in tan chinos and a beige padded jacket that accentuated his black hair and olive skin, Santino looked stunning. Her mouth ran dry. Should she admit that she'd been a bit too hasty in turning him down?

'Won't your guests miss you?' she asked as he dropped down into an athletic crouch to look at Florenza.

'Country house guests entertain themselves and most of them are still in bed. As long as I show up for dinner, nobody's offended,' Santino told her, resting appreciative eyes on his baby daughter. 'She's something special, isn't she?'

In a sudden decision, Poppy reached into the buggy and lifted Florenza free of the covers. Santino vaulted upright, looking ever so slightly unnerved. 'I've never held a baby before. It might upset her.'

'She's a very easy-going baby. Just support her head so that she feels secure.'

Santino cradled Florenza in careful arms. He looked down into his daughter's big, trusting blue eyes and then he smiled, a proud, tender, almost shy smile that made Poppy's eyes glisten. 'She's not crying. Do you think she sort of knows who I am?'

'Maybe…' Her throat was thick.

'And maybe not, but she can learn.' Santino studied Poppy with sudden, unexpected seriousness. 'Let's hope that Florenza never does to me what I did to my own mother. I'm in your debt for what you said the night of the party about me having taken my father's side when my parents divorced.'

Poppy blinked. 'How in my debt?'

'I went over to Italy to see Mama and found out what a pious little jerk I'd been,' Santino admitted with a rueful grimace. 'I blamed her for the divorce and she didn't want to ruin my relationship with my father by telling me that throughout their marriage he'd had a whole string of casual affairs. I just wish he'd been man enough to admit that to me, instead of going for the sympathy vote to ensure that I chose to live with him when they broke up.'

Knowing how close he had been to his father, Maximo, Poppy muttered, 'I'm sorry…'

'No. Don't be.' Santino smiled. 'Thanks to what you said, my mother and I are getting to know each other again.'

Poppy was delighted at that news. 'That's brilliant!'

'I would never be unfaithful to you,' Santino informed her in steady continuation, and then his wide sensual mouth curved in self-mocking acknowledgement. 'I'm even working on my narrow-minded response to pink graphs…'

Poppy froze at that teasing conclusion. 'That was *you*…that emailed me the day of the party?'

'Who did you think it was?' Santino glanced at her in surprise before hunkering down to settle their sleeping daughter back into her buggy with gentle hands.

It meant so much to Poppy to know that that teasing exchange had been with him. Her heart just overflowed, and when Santino sprang back up again he was a little taken aback but in no mood to complain when Poppy flung her arms round him and hugged him. 'I think I might just want to marry you, after all,' she confided. 'Is the offer still open?'

'Very much,' Santino breathed not quite levelly, unable to drag his gaze from her happy, smiling face and absolutely terrified that she might change her mind. 'How do you feel about getting married next week in Italy?'

Her lashes fluttered up on shaken blue eyes. '*That*…soon?'

'I'm really not a fan of long engagements,' Santino swore with honest fervour.

'Neither am I,' Poppy agreed with equal conviction, her heart singing, for there was something very reassuring about a guy who just couldn't wait to get her to the altar.

CHAPTER NINE

WALKING back towards the priory, Santino said with smooth satisfaction, 'I'll feel a lot more comfortable when you sit down to dinner with my guests this evening.'

At that prospect, Poppy's eyes widened in dismay. 'But I can't do that. I came here as the Brewetts' nanny and what are people going to *think* if I suddenly—?'

'That you're my future wife with more right than most to grace the dining table.' Impervious, it seemed, to the finer points of the situation, Santino exuded galling masculine amusement.

'Well, it can't be done. I didn't bring any dressy clothes. I've got nothing but jeans!' Poppy exclaimed.

'If that's the only problem…we'll go out and get you something to wear right now, *cara mia.*'

Nothing pleased Santino so much as solving problems with decisive activity. The village a few miles away rejoiced in a very up-market boutique. It took him only twenty minutes to run Poppy there, stride in, select a short, strappy, soft blue dress off the rail, which struck him as absolutely Poppy, and herd her into the changing room, paying not the slightest attention to her breathless and shaken protests.

Inside the cubicle, Poppy stared at her reflection dreamily in the mirror and wondered how Santino had managed to pick the right size and a shade of blue that looked marvellous with her hair. Then she looked at the price tag and almost had a heart attack.

'Poppy...?' Santino prompted from the shop floor.

Poppy emerged. Santino had Florenza draped over one shoulder and looked for all the world like a male who had been dandling babies from childhood. Impervious to the sales woman oozing appreciation over him, he studied Poppy with shimmering dark golden eyes that made her cheeks fire with colour and her heart pound like a manic road drill.

'We'll take the dress,' Santino pronounced without hesitation. 'What about shoes?'

Before Poppy could part her lips Santino was requesting her opinion on the display, and within minutes she was trying a pair on. When she reappeared in her jeans, two women were clustered round Santino admiring Florenza and his deft touch with her. By the sound of the dialogue she could hear, he was showing off like mad. Both shoes and dress were removed from her grasp and paid for with Santino's credit card without her having any opportunity to speak to him in private.

'Do you have any idea how much that little lot cost?' Poppy whispered in total shock as they settled back into the limo.

Santino gave her an enquiring glance. 'No.'

Poppy told him.

Santino looked surprised. 'A real steal...'

'It's a fortune!' Poppy gasped.

'Allow me to let you into a secret,' Santino teased in the best of good humour. 'I'm not a poor man.'

Back at the priory, it was a further shock to discover that her possessions and Florenza's had been moved from the nursery wing to a magnificent guest suite on the first floor. 'Are you sure I'm supposed to be here?' she asked the butler, Jenkins.

'Of course,' he wheezed.

Poppy urged him to sit down. He looked shifty and muttered, 'You won't mention this to Mr Santino, will you?'

'Well, I...' Poppy felt the old man really ought not to be working in such a condition.

And then Jenkins explained. He lived alone and he had been

in retirement for five years, but he'd missed the priory and his old profession terribly. At his own request, Santino had allowed the old man to come back to the priory and relive what he termed the good old days on occasional weekends and he very much enjoyed that break. Touched by that explanation and by Santino's understanding, Poppy said no more.

Dinner was not at all the ordeal she had imagined it might be. But then she had always enjoyed meeting new people, and from the instant she entered the drawing room and Santino's dark and appreciative gaze fell on her she also felt confident that she looked her best. Late evening, Santino came upstairs with her and went into the dressing room off her bedroom to look in on his sleeping baby daughter. His lean, dark face softened, his sensual mouth curving. 'It's extraordinary how much I feel for her already,' he confided.

A discomfiting little pang assailed Poppy and she rammed it down fast. How could she possibly be envious of the hold Florenza already had on her father's heart? After all, he was marrying her for their daughter's sake. Keen not to dwell on that painful truth, she said awkwardly, 'You know, I really can't see how we can possibly get married this coming week. It takes ages to organise even the smallest wedding.'

'The arrangements are already well in hand, *cara*,' Santino delivered with a slashing grin that made her mouth run dry. 'Early Monday morning we fly over to Venice where a selection of wedding dresses will await your choice. There is nothing that you need do or worry about. I just want you to relax and enjoy yourself.'

'It sounds like total bliss,' Poppy admitted, thinking of the weighty responsibilities and decisions that had burdened her throughout the previous year when she had had nobody to rely on but herself.

'I have a question I meant to ask you earlier,' Santino declared then. 'Exactly when last year did you write to me to tell me that you had conceived our child?'

Her brow furrowing in puzzlement, Poppy told him. His eyes flared gold and then veiled.

'What?' she prodded, unable to see the relevance of that information so long after the event.

Santino shrugged, lean, strong face uninformative. 'It's not important.'

Ultra-sensitive on that issue, Poppy was taut, and in receipt of that casual dismissal she flushed. She was convinced that he had to believe that there had never been a letter in the first place and that she was merely trying to ease her conscience and fend off his annoyance by lying and pretending that there had been. And how could she prove otherwise?

'I'm tired,' she muttered, turning away.

Lost in his own suspicions of what might have happened to that letter and determined to check out that angle as soon as he could, Santino frowned. He could not imagine what he had said to provoke the distinct chill in the air, but caution prevented him probing deeper. Once they were married, caution could take a hike, but he was determined not to risk a misstep in advance of the wedding. Saying goodnight, much as if he had only been seeing an elderly grandparent up to bed, he departed.

Disconcerted, Poppy surveyed the space where he had been and her dismayed and hurt eyes stung with hot tears. The very passionate male, who had sworn she was an irresistible temptation earlier in the day, had not even kissed her. Had that plea just been a judicious piece of flattery aimed at persuading her to marry him so that he could gain total access to Florenza? Or was he just annoyed at the idea that she might be fibbing about that wretched letter? And if that was the problem, how was she ever to convince him that she *had* written to him?

Made restive by her anxious thoughts, Poppy got little sleep and, after feeding Florenza first thing the following morning, fell back into bed and slept late. Finally awakening again, she went downstairs to find Santino surrounded by his guests. A convivial lunch followed and then the visitors began to make

their departures. Only then appreciating that she still had to
pack up her possessions at the Brewetts' home, Poppy slipped
away to speak to her former employer and decided that it would
be simplest for her to return home with them and see to the
matter for herself.

'I'm catching a lift with the Brewetts to go and collect my
stuff,' Poppy informed Santino at the last minute.

'I can drive you over there,' Santino offered in surprise.

'No, I thought it would be easier if I left Florenza here with
you,' Poppy confided with a challenging sparkle in her gaze,
although she rather suspected the female domestic staff would
soon help him out with the task.

Santino was merely delighted that he would retain a hostage
as it were to Poppy returning again and proud that she felt that
he could be trusted. In fact, his keen mind returning to a concern
that had been nagging at him all morning since he had called
his secretary at her home and spoken to her, he knew exactly
what he intended to do during Poppy's absence.

Three hours later, in a triumphal mode, Santino hauled his
office drinks cabinet out from the wall and swept up the still-
sealed and dusty envelope that lay on the carpet. He resisted
the temptation to tear Poppy's lost letter open then and there.
He would surprise her with it. They would open it together.
Maybe that way, he would feel less bitter at the high cost of
Craig Belston's mean and petty act of malice.

'If it hadn't been for you being there, I'd have hammered
that little jerk,' Santino informed Florenza, where she sat
strapped in her baby carrier watching him with bright, uncritical eyes. 'Then maybe not,' he acknowledged for himself in re-
flective continuance. 'He was so scared he *was*... I suppose I
have to watch my language around you. But then you don't
know any Italian curse words, do you?'

Florenza was asleep by the time he got her slotted back into
the limo. Santino was really pleased with himself. He was naturally good father material, he was convinced of it. She hadn't

cried once, not even when it had taken four attempts to change her and his chauffeur, a long-time parent, had mercifully intervened with a little man-to-man advice on the most effective method. They had tea at the Ritz where she was very much admired. She glugged down her bottle of milk like a trooper and concluded with a very small ladylike burp that he didn't think anyone but him heard.

'We're a real team,' Santino told Florenza on the drive home, and around then it occurred to him to wonder how Poppy planned to get herself back to the priory. With a muttered curse, he rang the Brewetts only to discover that she had already gone.

Right up until Poppy had left the Brewetts' with her cases in a taxi, she had expected Santino to call and say that he would come and pick her up. Instead she'd had to catch the train. But when she saw him waiting on the station platform to greet her at the other end of her journey, a bright, forgiving smile formed on her lips.

'I ought to grovel, *amore*,' Santino groaned in apology, looking so gorgeous that there was little that she would not have forgiven. 'It didn't even cross my mind that you don't have your own transport.'

'I expect you were too taken up with Florenza.'

'We did have quite a busy afternoon,' Santino admitted with masculine understatement. 'And when we get back to the priory, I have a surprise for you.'

The very last thing, Poppy expected was to have her own letter set before her like a prize. She was gobsmacked. 'Where on *earth* did that come from?'

'I phoned my secretary this morning. She actually remembered your letter arriving the day before she went off on holiday last year because she noticed your name on the back of the envelope. That week, *I* was in Italy mending fences with my mother.' Santino's strong jawline hardened. 'And Belston was working his last day at Aragone Systems—'

'Craig?' Poppy was still transfixed by the sight of that dusty, *unopened* letter, and her fingers were twitching to snatch it up and bury it deep somewhere Santino could never find it. At one level, she was at a total loss as to what Craig Belston could have to do with the miraculous recovery of a letter that had gone missing almost a year earlier, but on another level she was already recalling with shrinking, squeamish regret the horribly emotional outpourings of her own heart within that letter. It was wonderful how what could seem right and appropriate in the heat of the moment could then threaten utter humiliation eleven months on…

'Yes, Belston. The minute I worked out that time frame, I was suspicious. So, I called at his apartment this afternoon and was fortunate enough to find him home—'

Poppy blinked in growing disconcertion, but Santino was far too caught up in his recital to notice her taut pallor. She was cringing at that very idea of him reading that letter while she still lived and breathed. Here they were on the brink of a marriage of very practical and unemotional convenience and pride demanded that she strive to match that challenge. But he would undoubtedly die of embarrassment *for* her if he was now confronted by those impassioned pages that declared how instantly, utterly and irrevocably she had once fallen in love with him.

'I really don't know why you would've thought Craig might remember anything about one stupid letter,' Poppy muttered abstractedly, regarding the item with all the aghast intensity of a woman faced with a man-eating shark.

'He had a grudge against you and he's a coward,' Santino informed her with expressive disgust. 'I had the advantage of surprise today. He was so taken aback by the sight of Florenza and I—'

'You took Florenza with you to call on Craig?' Poppy squeaked, her expectations of Santino taking yet another beating.

'I wasn't going to leave her behind when I'd promised to take care of her,' Santino pointed out with paternal piety. 'The minute I mentioned the letter and got tough, Belston spilled the beans about what he had done with it. He threw it behind a piece of office furniture where it's been ever since. Mind you, it shows you how the cleaners cut corners.'

Poppy winced. 'What a nasty, low thing to do…oh, well, all's well that ends well and all that,' she added breathlessly, snatching up the envelope and endeavouring to scrunch its fat proportions in one hand. 'I'm glad the mystery's been solved but time has kind of made this letter redundant.'

'I still want to read it…' Questioning dark golden eyes pinned to her, Santino extended an expectant hand.

Poppy turned very pale and bit her lip and closed her other hand round the crumpled envelope as well. 'I really don't want you reading it now…'

'Why?'

As the taut silence stretched Poppy chewed at her lower lip in desperation. Santino tensed, a cool, shuttered look locking his darkly handsome features. What the hell had she written? A total character assassination directed at him? The news that she hated him for taking advantage of her naive trust and over-looking contraception and never, ever wanted to lay eyes on him again? His taut mouth set hard. Self-evidently, the letter she had penned was of the poisonous and destructive ilk.

'So I won't open it, but it's still mine,' Santino heard himself counter with harsh clarity, and no sooner had that foolish offer left his lips than he regretted it.

Intimidated by the tone of that announcement, Poppy handed over the envelope with a reluctance that he could feel. Santino smoothed it out between long, lean fingers. 'I believed that we could read this together, that you'd be pleased I had the faith to believe that you'd sent it,' he continued in angry bewilder-ment. 'For the first time in my life, I feel pretty damned naive!'

Most unhappy to see him in possession of what was indis-putably *his* letter, Poppy lowered her head. 'It's not the sort of thing we'd want to read together,' she mumbled in considerable mortification. 'What did you say to Craig?'

'Nothing repeatable but I didn't hit him.' Santino's dark

drawl was rough-edged. 'I wanted to kill him…only not in front of Florenza.'

'Oh…' Poppy was shattered by that blunt admission.

'You see, I thought he'd cost us our chance of happiness.' Santino welded his teeth back together on the rest of what he had almost said, which was that, in his volatile opinion at that instant, *she* had just done that most conclusively. There was so much he had longed to ask and learn about those months they had spent apart, and that she could not be honest about her feelings then angered him and made him feel shut out.

'We have some forms to fill out to satisfy the wedding legalities,' Santino continued grittily. 'Then I've got some calls to make.'

He didn't even laugh when she confided that her middle name was Hyacinth. Before he went off to make those phone calls, Poppy shot a glance at his grim profile and gathered all her strength to ask, 'Are you still sure about this…sure you want to go ahead and marry me?'

'Of course, I am sure.' Having fallen still at that sudden question, Santino shook her by tossing the letter back on the table in front of her. 'Keep it. As you said, the passage of time has made it redundant.'

Poppy went up to her imposing bed and cried. What had gone wrong? Where had the wonderful warmth and intimacy gone? Surely a silly, outdated letter should not create such tension between them? And she knew that she had said and done the wrong thing. Even though it would have mortified them both beyond bearing, she should have let him have that letter…

CHAPTER TEN

AT FIVE the following afternoon after an incredibly busy day, Poppy stood out on a Venetian hotel balcony entranced by the magical scenes taking place on the quays and the canal below.

A group of masked men and women in superb medieval costumes were boarding a launch outside the imposing *palazzo* opposite. A Harlequin and a Pierrot passed by in a gliding gondola, their outfits blessing them with total anonymity. On the quay, a trio of children, dressed up as a clown, a milkmaid and a comic spotty dog were whooping with delight over the firework display streaking through the heavens above the rooftops. Venice at carnival time: noisy, colourful and so full of bustling, vivid life that the very air seemed to pulse with mystery and the promise of excitement.

'You are pleased to be here with us?' A designer-clad little dynamo of a lady of around sixty, Santino's mother, Dulcetta Caramanico, emanated vivacity and natural warmth.

'I have had the most wonderful day…' Poppy admitted with sincerity. 'And I can't thank you enough for the fantastic welcome you have given us.'

Poppy had not expected to meet her future in-laws alone, but urgent business had forced Santino at the eleventh hour to accept the necessity of his coming out on a later flight. Greeted at the airport by Santino's mother and Arminio, his charming stepfather, Poppy and Florenza had been wafted on to their motor launch and across the lagoon into the city of Venice. They had brought her to their hotel but it had taken her most of the day to work out that the older couple indeed owned an entire chain of international hotels, famed for their opulence, legendary customer service and exclusivity.

From the instant Dulcetta and Arminio had laid eyes on them, Poppy and Florenza had been treated as though they were already a much-loved part of the family circle. Florenza had been the star of the party. The luxurious suite of rooms allotted to them would have been at home in a palace. That morning, the Caramanicos had taken them to St Mark's Square to see the Flight of the Little Doves that officially opened the carnival, and after lunch Dulcetta had escorted Poppy to a fantastic bridal salon where a huge array of glorious gowns and accessories had awaited her inspection.

Dulcetta was delighted by Poppy's freely expressed gratitude, and her fine dark eyes shone with happy tears. 'It is a joy to please you, Poppy. You brought my son home to me and now you are even making him smile again. When Santino first visited me last year, he didn't confide in me but I sensed how very unhappy he was at heart.'

Poppy hung her bright head, wondering how low she would sink in the popularity stakes when Santino arrived in Venice looking as grim and detached as he had the night before at the priory.

'Santino may have inherited Maximo's looks and business acumen,' his loving mother continued. 'But inside, Santino is much more emotional and caring than ever his father was. So will you wear the dress for me this evening and surprise my son?'

Poppy focused on the utterly over-the-top eighteenth-century-style silk, brocade and lace gown on the dress form that awaited her and a rueful grin tilted her generous mouth. 'Just you try and stop me getting into the carnival spirit!' She laughed in spite of her aching heart. 'It's such a fantastic outfit…'

Maybe, even if Santino believed that she looked ridiculous,

he would at least smile at the effort she was making, Poppy thought when Dulcetta had left her. Tears prickled her eyes as she removed her make-up and freshened up with a bath. Only a few days before her wedding, she ought to be the happiest woman alive. After all, she was about to marry the man she loved…but a man who would not be marrying her had it not been for their daughter's birth. Santino adored Florenza though, and he would make a wonderful father. It was just selfish of her to want the moon into the bargain.

Santino had already been alienated by her foolishness over the letter and it had finally occurred to her that he might even have got the impression that what she had written was unpleasant in some way. His unashamed anger with Craig, his belief that the other man had cost them the chance of happiness the previous year, had shaken Poppy when he'd voiced it, but at the time she had been too enervated to appreciate what Santino had *really* been telling her. Too busy conserving her pride and protecting herself from embarrassment, she had neglected to note that Santino had been making no such pretences. It shamed her that he should be so much more open and unafraid than she was. He had told her how attracted he was to her, shown her in his anger what he believed Craig Belston had stolen from them, for without his spiteful interference they might have been together much sooner…

And what had she done? Let Santino continue thinking that the valentine card had been a joke. She had saved face at every turn and given not an inch because the memory of her own adoring generosity the night of the party still mortified her. Yet it had been a wonderful night of love and sharing and wasn't it time that she acknowledged that? It didn't matter that he didn't love her. He cared, he certainly *cared*. From now on, she swore that would be enough for her.

While Poppy was anxiously owning up to her sins of omission, Santino, who had just arrived in his own suite next door, was confronting *his* as well. He needed to squash the conviction that he deserved a woman who saw him in terms of being the sun around which her world resolved. Poppy was not in love with him but that was only the beginning of the story, *not* the end. Ego might urge him to play it cool, but playing it cool was not advancing his own cause in any way, was it? For a start, he had been downright childish about that letter, he conceded with gritted teeth. Her determination to prevent him from accessing material that would damage their present relationship had been sensible. Just as Santino *still* recalled every word Poppy had affixed to that valentine card almost twelve months earlier, so he knew that he would have been haunted for ever more by the accusations he imagined had to be contained in that letter.

Anchoring the glorious feathered head-dress to her upswept Titian hair took Poppy some time. Dulcetta and Arminio had invited her to dine with them and a maid was to come upstairs to sit with Florenza. Poppy attached the glittering diamanté-studded mask to her eyes and surveyed herself. The emerald-green gown had theatrical splendour and the neat low-cut bodice flattered her lush curves in a way that made her blush. Yet she felt her own mother would not have recognised her, a stray thought that hurt just a little for she had decided not to tell her family about her wedding until after the event. At such short notice and with flights from Australia and accommodation in Venice during the carnival being so expensive, it would have been impossible for her parents to attend their daughter's special day. But in her heart of hearts, Poppy had also feared to put what she deemed to be already strained affections to the test.

When the knock on the door sounded, Poppy hurried to answer it before Florenza, who had just gone to sleep, could awaken again.

Disconcerted that it was Santino, whom she had believed might not arrive much before midnight, she fell back an uncertain step. Intent golden eyes pinning to her, he murmured something in husky Italian and his heartbreaking smile slowly curved his handsome mouth. As ever, he looked devastatingly dark, vibrant and attractive.

Her breath caught in her throat, for she had truly wondered if Santino would ever smile at her again. Her heartbeat picked up tempo and a flock of butterflies flew free in her tummy, but she held her head high, firmly convinced he would not recognise her at first glance.

'Poppy…' Santino said without a second of hesitation.

'I thought you wouldn't know it was me!' Poppy wailed in helpless disappointment.

As he closed the door his wonderful smile deepened. 'I would know you anywhere. In any light and any disguise.'

'You'll be able to dine with your mother and stepfather, after all.' Feeling foolish, Poppy reached up and unfastened the diamanté mask to set it aside.

'No. I called them from the airport and expressed our mutual regrets.' Santino's expression was now very serious. 'We need to be alone so that we can talk.'

Poppy tensed in sudden apprehension. It was as if he had pushed a panic button. Suddenly she feared he was as keen to cancel the wedding as he had been to cancel the family dinner. 'Santino…'

'No, let me have the floor first…' Santino dealt her a taut look from his beautiful eyes, his raw tension palpable. 'I haven't been straight with you. I haven't been fair either—'

'You're stealing my lines…' Poppy sped past him to snatch up her handbag and withdraw the much-abused letter, which she thrust at him in near desperation. 'I didn't think how it must've looked when I wouldn't let you read it, but it is *your* letter—'

'Stuff the letter,' Santino groaned, not best pleased to have been interrupted just when he had got into his verbal stride and setting it straight back into her unwilling hand. 'It's unimportant. What matters is that I tell you how I feel…but you're not likely to be impressed by the news that you had blown me away in Wales before it dawned on me that I was in love with you.'

In the act of ripping in frustration into the envelope for herself to produce a thick wad of notepaper, Poppy stopped dead and viewed Santino with huge, incredulous blue eyes. She couldn't possibly have heard *that*, she told herself. In fact she must have been dreaming…

'*Porca miseria*…in advance of that day, strange as it may seem,' Santino disclaimed with touching discomfiture and a look that was a positive plea for understanding in his strained dark eyes. 'I just had no idea why I was always coming down personally to the marketing department, why the day seemed a little brighter when I saw you, why I just *liked* you, why I started finding fault with every other woman I met…have you anything to say?'

In shock, Poppy shook her head.

'Your very first day when I took you to hospital after you hurt your finger,' Santino reminded her doggedly, lean, strong features taut, 'I demonstrated how macho I was by passing out at the sight of the needle coming your way. Yet even though you were a real chatterbox and all my staff would have fallen about in stitches had you told them about that episode, you kept quiet. That was remarkably restrained of you…'

'I wouldn't have d-dreamt of embarrassing you at work.' A great rush of answering love was surging up inside Poppy and playing havoc with her speech.

'I know, *amore*…' But his shapely mouth only semi-curved. 'I was furious when my marketing head overreacted to that stupid cup of coffee. I was so protective of you, and then at the party, when Belston was scoring points off you, I could've ripped him apart! And when we were together in my office and I finally had you all to myself, it was more temptation than I was capable of withstanding—'

'I felt like I'd thrown myself at you…' Poppy shared painfully.

'Who stopped you from leaving? Who kissed you? Who made all the *real* moves?'

Only then did Poppy appreciate that the prime mover had been him. 'But you had been drinking—'

Santino groaned out loud. 'I was just making excuses for myself. That night nothing had ever felt so right to me and I knew exactly what I was doing, but the next day I felt appallingly guilty for seducing you—'

'I sneaked off because I thought it was all my fault—'

'And I was furious about that. I called round at your bedsit that afternoon—'

Poppy winced. 'Oh, no…you just missed me…'

'I suspected you were home and just not answering the door because you didn't want to see me—'

'I wouldn't have done that.'

'Then I had to phone round half of Australia to track down your sister-in-law, Karrie, to find out where you were. Didn't she tell you about my call?'

Even though her heart was singing, Poppy had paled. 'Yes, but I just assumed it was because you were really worried I might be pregnant 'cos at that stage I still believed you were engaged to Jenna. Santino…I think you ought to take a look at this letter of mine before I get so mad with myself that I scream!'

But Santino had other ideas. She was still listening and her lovely eyes were soft and warm and it had been a day and a half since he had last touched her. Tugging her into connection with his lean, powerful length, he brought his mouth swooping down with unashamed hunger and urgency on hers, and for timeless minutes she clung, every fibre of her being alive with joyful excitement and the wondrous relief of knowing herself loved.

Pausing to snatch in a ragged breath, gazing down into her shining eyes, Santino muttered, 'Sooner or later, I'll find the magic combination of making you love me back…if only you hadn't hated me when you were in Wales—'

'I didn't—'

'I was devastated for weeks after that. I tore up the belated valentine card I had searched high and low for—'

'You bought me a card?' Poppy was touched to the brink of tears.

'Signed it with an unadventurous question mark…the guy with few words. All I could think about was getting you back to London. I didn't understand I loved you until that day…'

Her throat thickened. Stepping back, she handed him the letter. 'Well, I always knew how I felt about you, but I'll forgive you for that.'

With perceptible reluctance he accepted the letter, and then as he scanned the first few lines with a frown such a stunned look began to form on his lean, strong face that she had to suppress a giggle. Suddenly he was glued to every page with total, focused concentration.

'It's a…it's a love letter…a wonderful, fantastic love letter,' Santino finally vocalised with a roughened edge to his deep voice.

'It wasn't meant to be, but when I learned I was expecting your child I wanted you to know that my card hadn't been a cheap joke—'

'I should skin you alive for having lied to me, *amore*.' But as at that point Santino was looking at her with wondering, loving intensity, she was in no danger of taking offence. 'I *still* have that card you sent me locked in my office safe. I pretended it wasn't there so that I didn't have to dump it!'

He followed that confession up with a beautiful sapphire engagement ring that took her breath away. Then he looked in on their infant daughter and smiled at her peaceful little face before he strode into his own suite next door to don the very rakish matching eighteenth-century outfit his romantic mother had laid on for his use that evening. The burgundy velvet surcoat, lace cravat and tight-fitting breeches and boots gave him an exotic and dangerous appeal that thrilled Poppy no end. For a while, all he wanted to talk about was what it had been like for her to carry their daughter during those months apart from him. Then they ended up in each other's arms again and Santino pulled back and announced that they were dining out.

'Oh…' Poppy mumbled in surprise.

'We're not going to share a bedroom until we're married,

amore mio,' Santino swore. 'It's the only way I can *ever* hope to live down that sofa.'

So he took her out into the city where he had been born and they dined in an intimate restaurant by candlelight, both of them so busy talking, both of them so incredibly happy that they had a glow about them that drew understanding and envious eyes.

On Poppy's wedding day, the early morning mist was lifted by sunlight.

She had actually forgotten that it was Valentine's Day, but then a giant basket of beautiful flowers and a glorious card covered with roses and containing a tender verse arrived. Inside, Santino had written those three little words that meant so much to her, 'I love you', and even *signed* it. So, it started out a fantastic day that just went on getting better and better.

She had only just finished her breakfast and was feeding Florenza when someone knocked on the door and her whole family—her mother and father and Peter and Karrie and her little nephew, Sam—trooped in. She couldn't believe her eyes. Santino had flown them out at his expense and they were staying in the same hotel. He had arranged that in secrecy for her benefit and she loved him even more for that sensitivity. All the awkwardness she might have felt in other circumstances with her family evaporated straight away and, watching her mother's eyes glisten over Florenza and enveloped in a hug by her father and her brother, Poppy was content.

Her mother and her sister-in-law helped her dress, enthusing over her exquisite ivory gown with its hand-painted hem of delicate pastel roses. A magnificent tiara and drop earrings arrived with a card signed by Santino. Tucked into a velvet-lined gondola for her passage to her wedding, Poppy felt like a princess. But when she saw Santino turn from the altar in the wonderful old church, that was when her heart truly overflowed with happiness.

The reception was staged in a superb ballroom and there

were masses of guests. The bridegroom and the bride were so absorbed in each other that their guests smiled and shook their heads in wonderment. They watched them dance every dance in a world of their own and then depart for their honeymoon.

Late that night in Santino's hideaway home in the wooded hills of Tuscany, Poppy lay in their incredible medieval bed draped with crewelwork drapes and surveyed her new husband with an excusable degree of satisfaction.

'Just to think you were falling in love with me all those weeks I worked for you…and I hadn't the foggiest idea.' Poppy sighed blissfully and reckoned that low self-esteem was likely to be a very rare sensation in her future.

'Neither had I,' Santino quipped, dark golden eyes resting on her with adoring intensity as he gathered her close again. 'But I missed you so much when you weren't there. I love you, *amore.*'

'I love you, too. But just to think of *me* almost breaking *your* heart, it's heady stuff—'

'You are revelling in your power,' Santino groaned in teasing reproach.

Wearing an ear-to-ear grin, Poppy nodded in agreement, for finding out that he had never, ever been in love before, no, not once, made her feel that providence had kept him safe for her. They chatted about whether or not they would return to Venice for a night or two, checked on Florenza and congratulated each other on having created such a truly wonderful baby. All too soon they melted back into each other's arms and kissed and hugged, both of them feeling as though they were the very first couple ever to discover that amount of love and revelling in their happiness.